COACHING FOOTBALL'S 40 NICKEL DEFENSE

Jeff Walker

COACHES CHOICE

ISBN: 1-57167-193-5
Library of Congress Catalog Card Number: 97-69615

Book Design: Michelle Summers
Cover Design: Deborah M. Bellaire
Cover Photo: Courtesy of *Dallas Cowboys Weekly*

Coaches Choice Books is a division of: Sagamore Publishing, Inc.
P.O. Box 647
Champaign, IL 61824-0647
Web Site: http//www.sagamorepub.com

DEDICATION

This book is dedicated to my two best friends, Paula and Gabe. Both were sent to me by God's grace. Their love and the joy of working for athletes such as Brad Abraham, Jean Paul Duhon, Larson Langston, Jeremy Pearcy, John Perryman, Brent Saltzman, and Andrew Tennies have enabled me to persevere when perseverance seemed impossible. To those boys I have not named—my love for you is not less; you will continue to play in the fields of my memory. My life, my career, my mission, will continue to be a living tribute to your commitment and loyalty. And finally—to Lisa who gave our family the greatest gift of all. This one is for all of you.

ACKNOWLEDGMENTS

Thankfully, I have had the fortune of studying the game with some of the best coaches in high school football. Many of the techniques described in this book were taught to me by Brownie Parmley, the highly respected 25-year veteran head coach of Bolton High School in Alexandria, Louisiana. I doubt that I would have obtained the ability to write a book on defensive football without experiencing his wisdom.

Further acknowledgment goes to the following people: Greg Miller of Kerrville for his time spent helping me in the finishing stage of this project; Steve Fry of Kerrville for his help in developing our game-plan format; and Stuart Cunyus of Kerrville's *Mountain Sun* for his photograph of the author.

I also offer thanks to the following brothers in coaching; to Phillip Mattingly of Port Arthur, Texas for the companionship and support all through my career; to Tommy Thomason of Sulphur, Louisiana for his demonstration of the ideal coaching spirit; to Bobby Dye of Red Level, Alabama for his friendship and never-ending belief; and to Lonnie Sewell of Cleveland, Texas for allowing me to experience the true essence of brotherhood and love.

CONTENTS

TENETS OF TEACHING DEFENSIVE FOOTBALL

To paraphrase the military strategist, Sun Tzu, with more sophistication comes more control. With sophistication comes also a visualization beyond common concepts and progress toward the path of perfection.

Too often the art of coaching is lost through individuals attempting to understate the depth to which the game is to be taught. A few football coaches fail to educate their athletes to the highest levels, choosing rather to adhere to the credo of coaching ignorance, the *KISS* formula—*K*eep *I*t *S*imple *S*tupid. The word, the thought of the word, "stupid" has no place in the fields of education, from the field of football to the field of science. Should the high school mathematics educator limit his own knowledge to that of the twelfth grade advanced mathematics course? Does the senior English teacher limit her knowledge to what she believes only can be taught to the high school senior? Obviously, these are ridiculous questions. But why is it some coaches choose not to examine the dynamics of their sport as a master educator? It is the obligation of the coach to learn all that he or she can learn, then set forth to teach all that he or she can teach. It is the responsibility of the coach to be talented enough to express all the sophistication and "complexity" in a manner that all can learn to the limit of their capacity.

> "Those known as sophisticated at strategy vanquish those who are easily vanquished...those sophisticated at strategy cultivate leadership and sustain rules so they can be the controllers of victory and of defeat."

> Sun Tzu
> *The Art of War*

CHAPTER 1

Characteristics of the Forty Nickel

1. Based around a two-linebacker system, taught either identically or specific to strength declaration.

    The defense is built around the fact that it is a two-linebacker system, thus eliminating the need for a bevy of athletes in your football stable to play linebacker. This fact affords all levels of programs the opportunity to succeed with the Forty Nickel. The teaching of each linebacker is principally a mirror image, but the coach may specialize each linebacker in alignment, assignment and technique responsibilities on the basis of the strength declaration. One linebacker may be principally taught the strongside while the other linebacker candidate may be taught the weakside nuances. Teaching the inside linebackers in relationship to the strength declaration brings the linebacker play of the Forty Nickel to its highest level. Weakside linebackers learn to deal primarily with open and closed doors, dragging the anchor, and squirming to cover the number two receiver from inside-out. Strongside linebackers focus on scrape angles, shuffling to stack and captaining the defensive front. Generic to both positions include fine points such as flashing colors, bright and dim light focusing, and attack angles.

2. Can meld the best characteristics of the seven-man front philosophy and eight-man front philosophy.

    The Forty Nickel cannot be identified as a member of either the seven-man front or eight-man front family. Its ability to transform through its inherent flexibility does not allow the offensive coach to singularly classify the Forty Nickel. Due to the simplicity of the Forty Nickel terminology and alignment rules, the front may change easily from a reading "bend but not break" seven-man front to an attacking, forcing, eight-man front.

3. Allows for a five-man secondary scheme.

    By allowing for a five-man secondary scheme, the Forty Nickel does not cause the usual defensive gnashing of teeth during the week of the big game with the lone run and shoot team in your area.

With the availability of the five-man (Nickel) secondary scheme, the defense is not susceptible to the one-back set that tries to get a numerical advantage through wide unbalanced formations. Due to the fifth man, the secondary is able to use the much-favored Cover Two (a coverage with hard corner support and twin safeties), and not be vulnerable to the vertical route of the inside receiver aligned on the strongside.

4. Allows for multiple eight-man pressure front alignments.

The two hybrid outside linebacker and strong safety perimeter players give the Forty Nickel its unique characteristic of being able to go from a zone-smothering pass defense to a smash-mouth eight-man front. While the five-man secondary scheme gives the coordinator a smorgasbord of coverages from which to choose against the passing attacks, the capacity of the Nickel Forty to defend as a 4-4 defense allows for a matchup with the power running attack. The two outside linebackers are trained daily on close alignment over the tight end or tight slotback. This training allows the defense to transform into an old-fashioned eight-man front which attacks the line of scrimmage. In no way is the Forty Nickel a "soft" defense. The front four is practiced daily on multiple outside shades and inside gap stunts. Even in the base defense at least one tackle in the front four is stunting inside on every snap of the ball. The teaching of the multiple alignments coupled with the ferocity of the personnel selected as outside linebackers makes executing a successful running attack against the Forty Nickel problematic, to say the least. The Forty Nickel front package can present multiple eight-man front alignments to the power running attack.

5. Dictates offensive adjustment, not defensive reaction.

The Forty Nickel allows the defensive coach to dictate offensive adjustments. The defensive coach can dictate the flow of the game by forcing the offensive coach to adjust to the Nickel Forty tactics. Dictating the flow can be accomplished because of the Forty Nickel terminology.

The precise terminology allows a coach the ability to overload an offense at its point of strength, thus dictating that the offense try a counterstroke to the defense. By making the offense counter the defense and not vice-versa, the defense controls the flow of the game.

CHAPTER 2

Forty Nickel Basics

The Forty Nickel is characterized by four defensive linemen, four linebackers, and three defensive backs. The base front alignment has two inside backers and two outside backers; the base coverage is a 3-deep zone. The basis of the Forty Nickel defensive philosophy is an attacking eight-man front with the availability of a five defensive back scheme.

Chart 2a: Position terminology.

ANTLER	The outside linebacker who aligns on the defensive left, or the three-man blocking side or other specified declaration.
BRAVE	The outside linebacker who aligns opposite the **ANTLER**.
CORNERBACK	One of two mirrored positions who plays a S3 technique in Cover 3; primarily responsible for deep zone coverage.
END	One of two defensive ends with TE side technique or open side technique.
FREE SAFETY	The hub of the secondary; has multiple responsibilities, including a S6 technique in Cover 3; the surest tackler in the secondary.
SAM	The linebacker who declares the defensive strength call and aligns to the declared side.
WILL	The linebacker who aligns opposite the **SAM**.
TACKLES	Align in shades designated by 1st and 2nd digits of call (e.g., "31" = Tackle to strength in a 3 technique; Tackle away from strength in a 1 technique).

Chart 2b: Huddle

DEFENSIVE HUDDLE	

ball

W - S

E - T - T - E

LC - A - FS - B - RC

HUDDLE RESPONSIBILITIES

SAM	• Looks to get signal for next play immediately after play is whistled dead. • Walks away from huddle to get clear view of signal-caller. • Alerts front that call is to be made by saying, "Defense." • Calls defensive front alignment and stunts. • Alerts Free Safety that secondary call is to be made by saying "Cover." • Breaks huddle with "Ready, Hit."
WILL	• Sets huddle. • Looks to get down and distance of next play immediately after huddle is set. • Steps to front to announce down and distance to huddle. • Alerts defense to possession down.
ENDS	• Stand tall and watch offensive huddle for scamble call.
TACKLES	• Rest with hands on knees.
FREE SAFETY	• Steps out to receive secondary call as huddle is formed. • Steps in huddle to give secondary call and secondary stunts. • Calls secondary coverage and secondary stunts when SAM says "Cover." • Relays coverage to CB's with hand signal after huddle is broken.
CORNERBACKS	• Stay alert for wide receivers breaking away from the offensive huddle while noting their location to help identify formation or sets.

Chart 2c: Defensive front techniques.

DEFENSIVE FRONT TECHNIQUES							
E	T	G	C	G	T	E
9 6 7	5 4	3 2	1　0 N 0　1	2 3	4 5	7 6 9

0, 3, 5 and **9** are outside leverage techniques (outside arm and leg free).

N and **6** are headup techniques with 2 gap responsibility (toe to toe).

2, 4 and **7** are inside leverage techniques (inside arm and leg free).

1 is a gap charge technique.

Chart 2d: Defensive gaps.

GAPS							
E	T	G	C	G	T	E
D　*C*	*B*	*A*	*A*	*B*	*C*	*D*

TECHNIQUE SPECIFICATIONS

The technique alignment will either be specifed as a crotch, shade, shadow or head-up; however, odd techniques are never head-up. The interpretation of the exact alignment of defensive front players can be confusing when players use the offensive lineman's head as a frame of reference. The concept and execution of alignment is achieved by using the offensive lineman's stance (area between his feet) as a frame of reference.

Terminology for the purpose of explanation of this concept includes the "anchor" foot and "leverage" foot. The "leverage" foot is the foot the defender must keep free in his gap responsibility. A defender must keep "leverage" in his gap; consequently, the gap-side foot is the "leverage" foot. Conversely, the other foot is the "anchor" foot. The "anchor" foot is the foot used for alignment specifications such as crotch, shade, or shadow.

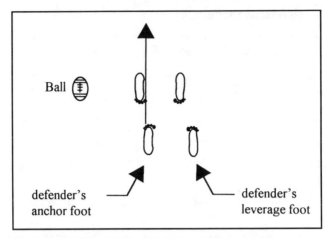

Diagram 2a: The shade alignment of the outside technique (e.g., 3, 5, and 9 technique).

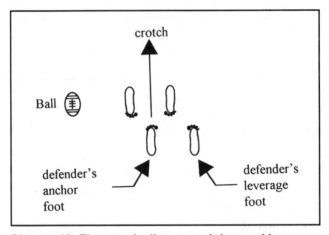

Diagram 2b: The crotch alignment of the outside technique (e.g., 3, 5, and 9 technique).

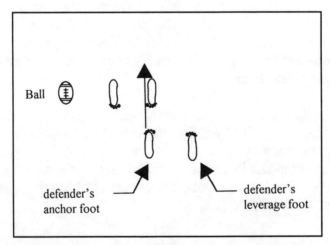

Diagram 2c: The shadow alignment of an outside shaded cut (e.g., 3, 5, and 9 technique).

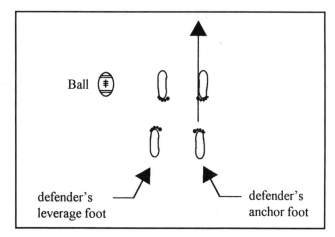

Diagram 2d: The shade alignment of the inside technique (e.g., 2, 4, and 7 technique).

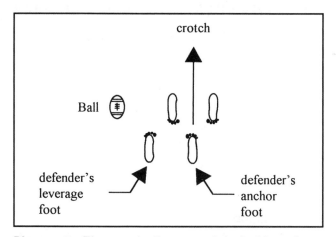

Diagram 2e: The crotch alignment of the inside technique (e.g., 2, 4, and 7 technique).

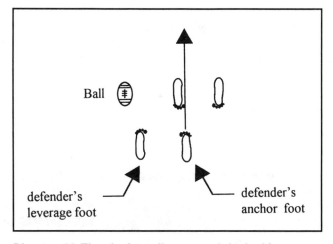

Diagram 2f: The shadow alignment of the inside technique (e.g., 2, 4, and 7 technique).

MORE ON ANCHOR AND LEVERAGE FOOT TERMINOLOGY

Examples of Use Anchor and Leverage Foot Terminology

A 3 technique aligns on the guard and has "B" gap responsibility. His anchor foot is his foot closest to the ball and his leverage foot is the foot closest to the "B" gap. Thus, a 3 technique's anchor foot is his inside foot while his leverage foot is his outside foot.

A 4 technique aligns on the tackle and has "B" gap responsibility. His anchor foot is his foot farthest from the ball. His leverage foot is the foot closest to the "B" gap, in this case also the foot closest to the ball. Thus, a 4 technique's anchor foot is his outside foot while his leverage foot is his inside foot.

- 2, 4 and 7 techniques use the foot *farthest* from the ball as the anchor foot.

- 0, 3, 5 and 9 techniques use the foot *closest* to the ball as the anchor foot.

- A 1 technique aligns in the gap and has no designated anchor foot.

SHADE

A shade technique puts his anchor foot just inside the stance of the offensive lineman. The shade technique will have a toe-to-inside track relationship on the offensive lineman, all the time keeping the leverage foot in a postion to be free in the responsible gap. A shade technique is what is commonly called a "tight eye" technique, whether tight inside eye or outside eye.

Outside leverage foot shade
- A shade 0 technique puts his *inside foot* just inside the *offside foot* of the center.

- A shade 3 technique puts his *inside foot* just inside the *inside foot* of the guard.

- A shade 5 technique puts his *inside foot* just inside the *inside foot* of the tackle.

- A shade 9 technique puts his *inside foot* just inside the *inside foot* of the end or 3rd man.

Inside leverage foot shade
- A shade 2 technique puts his *outside foot* just inside the *outside foot* of the guard.

- A shade 4 technique puts his *outside foot* just inside the *outside foot* of the tackle.

- A shade 7 technique puts his *outside foot* just inside the *outside foot* of the end or 3rd man.

CROTCH

The base alignment is a crotch technique. A crotch alignment puts his anchor foot on the midline of the offensive stance. His foot is pointed directly at the crotch of the blocker. A crotch technique is sometimes referred to as a "loose eye" technique, whether loose inside eye or outside eye.

Outside leverage foot crotch
- A crotch 0 technique puts his *inside foot* on the *crotch* of the center.
- A crotch 3 technique puts his *inside foot* on the *crotch* of the guard.
- A crotch 5 technique puts his *inside foot* on the *crotch* of the tackle.
- A crotch 9 technique puts his *inside foot* on the *crotch* of the end or 3rd man.

Inside leverage foot crotch
- A shade 2 technique puts his *outside foot* on the *crotch* of the guard.
- A shade 4 technique puts his *outside foot* on the *crotch* of the tackle.
- A shade 7 technique puts his *outside foot* on the *crotch* of the end or 3rd man.

SHADOW

Shadow is not used on 2 and 4 techniques except in adjusting to unusually large offensive line splits. Shadow is principally an outside eye alignment used as an adjustment to unusually tight splits or to guarantee outside leverage.

Outside leverage foot shadow
- A shadow 0 technique puts his *inside foot* just inside the *near foot* of the center.
- A shadow 3 technique puts his *inside foot* just inside the *outside foot* of the guard.
- A shadow 5 technique puts his *inside foot* just inside the *outside foot* of the tackle.
- A shadow 9 technique puts his *inside foot* just inside the *outside foot* of the end or 3rd man.

Inside leverage foot shadow
- A shade 2 technique puts his *outside foot* just inside the *inside foot* of the guard.
- A shade 4 technique puts his *outside foot* just inside the *inside foot* of the tackle.
- A shade 7 technique puts his *outside foot* just inside the *inside foot* of the end or 3rd man.

CHAPTER 3

Available Forty Nickel Fronts

This chapter illustrates many of the 73 fronts that can be run from the Forty Nickel package with standard terminology. Included within the individual front description are the alignment of each front player and the key coaching points of the respective positions. A diagram of each front accompanies the front description. Each front is diagrammed as it would appear with a "Lou" declaration by the Sam linebacker. When integral to the front, the outside linebackers are included in the front diagram. When not considered to be an integral part of the front, the outside linebackers are not included in the front diagram. When not shown in the diagram, the outside linebackers are assumed to be fulfilling their role as an S1, S2, or 8 technique in the secondary.

The Forty Nickel fronts are categorized by series. Each series is identified by the two tackles' techniques. For example, if the strongside tackle plays a 3 technique and the weakside technique plays a 0 technique, the series is a 30 series. The Forty Nickel coach has 13 basic series of fronts available.

Chart 3-A: Forty Nickel defensive front series.

10 Series	11 Series	12 Series	13 Series	
10	11	12	13	
10 Squeeze	11 Squeeze	12 Squeeze	13 Squeeze	
10 Weak Squeeze	11 Weak Squeeze	12 Weak Squeeze	13 Weak Squeeze	
10 Double Squeeze	11 Double Squeeze	12 Double Squeeze	13 Double Squeeze	
20 Series	**21 Series**	**23 Series**	**30 Series**	
20	21	23	30	
20 Squeeze	21 Squeeze	23 Squeeze	30 Squeeze	
20 Weak Squeeze	21 Weak Squeeze	23 Weak Squeeze	30 Weak Squeeze	
20 Double Squeeze	21 Double Squeeze	23 Double Squeeze	30 Double Squeeze	
20 Stack	21 Stack	23 Stack	30 Stack	
20 Weak Stack	21 Weak Stack	23 Weak Stack	30 Weak Stack	
20 Double Stack	21 Double Stack	23 Double Stack	30 Double Stack	
31 Series	**32 Series**	**33 Series**	**40 Series**	**50 Series**
31	32	33	40	50 Base
31 Squeeze	32 Squeeze	33 Squeeze		50 Base Weak Squeeze
31 Weak Squeeze	32 Weak Squeeze	33 Weak Squeeze	40 Weak Squeeze	50 Base Stack
31 Double Squeeze	32 Double Squeeze	33 Double Squeeze		50 Base Weak Stack
31 Stack	32 Stack		40 Stack	50 Nose Weak Blitz
31 Weak Stack	32 Weak Stack		40 Weak Stack	50 Nose Weak Squeeze Blitz
31 Double Stack	32 Double Stack	33 Double Stack		

12

STRENGTH DECLARATION: LOU

POSITION	ALIGNMENT	COACHING POINTS
SAM	Crotch 40 tech 4 yards deep	Key progression: Fullback, Nearback, Crosskey Read open-closed door
WILL	Crotch 30 tech 4 yards deep	Key progression: Nearback, Crosskey, Fullback Read open-closed door
LE	Crotch 7 tech	Attack inside "V," anchor "C" gap
LT	Gap 1 tech	Attack "A" gap, read feet of fullback
RT	Shade 2 tech	2 tech runs an automatic TIM
RE	Shade 7 tech	Attack inside "V," keep inside leverage Play shadow 5 if no tight end or slot

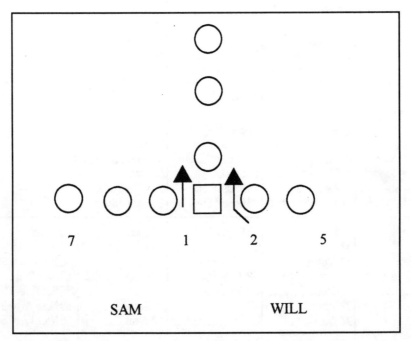

Diagram 3-1: 12.

12 SQUEEZE

STRENGTH DECLARATION: LOU

POSITION	ALIGNMENT	COACHING POINTS
SAM	Crotch 40 tech 4 yards deep	Key progression: Fullback, Nearback, Crosskey Read open-closed door
WILL	Crotch 30 tech 4 yards deep	Key progression: Nearback, Crosskey, Fullback Read open-closed door
ANTLER	Shadow 9 tech	Attack outside "V," keep outside leverage
LE	Crotch 7 tech	Attack inside "V," anchor "C" gap
LT	Gap 1 tech	Attack "A" gap, read feet of fullback
RT	Shade 2 tech	2 tech runs an automatic TIM
RE	Shade 7 tech	Attack inside "V," keep inside leverage Play shadow 5 if no tight end or slot

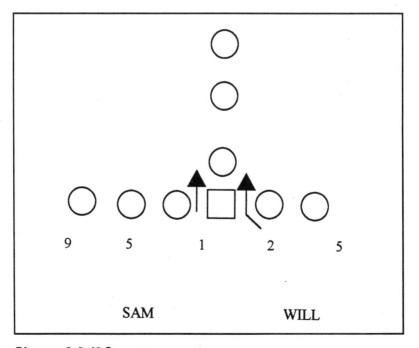

Diagram 3-2: 12 Squeeze.

12 WEAK SQUEEZE

STRENGTH DECLARATION: LOU

POSITION	ALIGNMENT	COACHING POINTS
SAM	Crotch 40 tech 4 yards deep	Key progression : Fullback, Nearback, Crosskey Read open-closed door
WILL	Crotch 30 tech 4 yards deep	Key progression : Nearback, Crosskey, Fullback Read open-closed door
LE	Crotch 7 tech	Attack inside "V," anchor "C" gap
LT	Gap 1 tech	Attack "A" gap, read feet of fullback
RT	Shade 2 tech	2 tech runs an automatic TIM
RE	Crotch 5 tech	Attack outside "V," anchor "C" gap
BRAVE	Shadow 9 tech	Play a ghost 9 if no tight end or slot Play a shadow 9 if tight end or slot is present

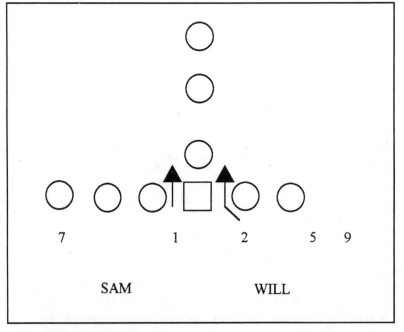

Diagram 3-3: 12 Weak Squeeze.

12 DOUBLE SQUEEZE

STRENGTH DECLARATION: LOU

POSITION	ALIGNMENT	COACHING POINTS
SAM	Crotch 40 tech 4 yards deep	Fey progression: Fullback, Nearback, Crosskey Read open-closed door
WILL	Crotch 30 tech 4 yards deep	Key progression: Nearback, Crosskey, Fullback Read open-closed door
ANTLER	Shadow 9 tech	Attack outside "V," keep outside leverage
LE	Crotch 5 tech	Attack outside "V," anchor "C" gap
LT	Gap 1 tech	Attack "A" gap, read feet of fullback
RT	Shade 2 tech	2 tech runs an automatic TIM
RE	Crotch 5 tech	Attack outside "V," anchor "C" gap
BRAVE	Shadow 9 tech	Play a ghost 9 if no tight end or slot Play a shadow 9 if tight end or slot is present

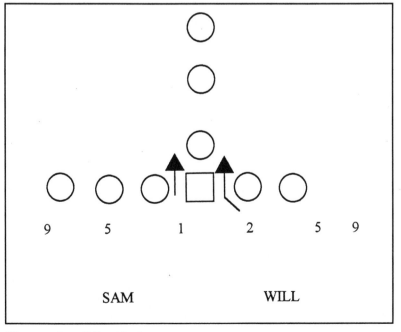

Diagram 3-4: 12 Double Squeeze.

STRENGTH DECLARATION: LOU

POSITION	ALIGNMENT	COACHING POINTS
SAM	Crotch 30 tech 3 1/2 yards deep	Key progression: Fullback, Nearback, Crosskey Read open-closed door
WILL	Crotch 20 tech 3 1/2 yards deep	Key progression: Nearback, Crosskey, Fullback Attack the "in," scrape to stack, shuffle to stack
LE	Shade 7 tech	Attack inside "V," anchor "C" gap
LT	Shade 2 tech	2 tech runs an automatic TIM
RT	Crotch 3 tech	Attack outside "V," anchor "B" gap
RE	6 tech toe-to-toe	Attack chin of TE, anchor "C" gap Play a ghost 6 tech if no tight end or slot

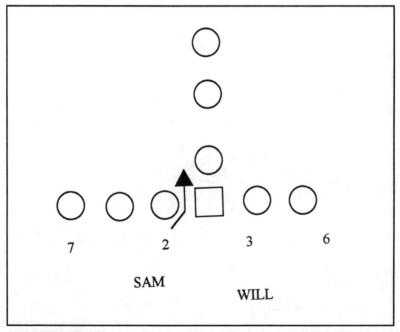

Diagram 3-5: 23.

23 SQUEEZE

STRENGTH DECLARATION: LOU

POSITION	ALIGNMENT	COACHING POINTS
SAM	Crotch 30 tech 3¹/₂ yards deep	Key progression: Fullback, Nearback, Crosskey Attack the "in," scrape to "B," shuffle to stack
WILL	Crotch 30 tech 3¹/₂ yards deep	Key progression: Nearback, Crosskey, Fullback Attack the "in," scrape to "B," shuffle to stack
ANTLER	Shadow 9 tech	Attack outside "V," keep outside leverage
.LE	Crotch 5 tech	Attack inside "V," anchor "C" gap
LT	Shade 2 tech	2 tech runs an automatic TIM
RT	Crotch 3 tech	Attack outside "V," anchor "B" gap
RE	6 tech toe-to-toe	Attack chin of TE, anchor "C" gap

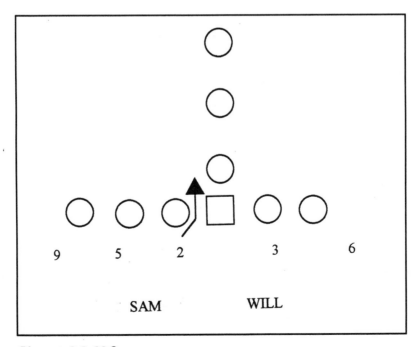

Diagram 3-6: 23 Squeeze.

23 WEAK SQUEEZE

STRENGTH DECLARATION: LOU

POSITION	ALIGNMENT	COACHING POINTS
SAM	Crotch 30 tech 3½ yards deep	Key progression: Fullback, Nearback, Crosskey Attack the "in," scrape to "B," shuffle to stack
WILL	Crotch 30 tech 3½ yards deep	Key progression: Nearback, Crosskey, Fullback Attack the "in," scrape to "B," shuffle to stack
LE	Shade 7 tech	Attack inside "V," anchor "C" gap
LT	Shade 2 tech	2 tech runs an automatic TIM
RT	Crotch 3 tech	Attack outside "V," anchor "B" gap
RE	Crotch 5 tech	Attack inside "V," anchor "C" gap
BRAVE	Shadow 9 tech	Play a ghost 9 if no tight end or slot Play a shadow 9 if tight end or slot is present

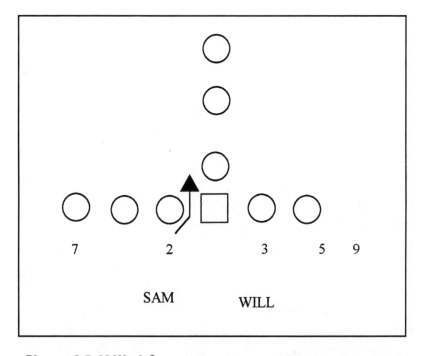

Diagram 3-7: 23 Weak Squeeze.

23 DOUBLE SQUEEZE

STRENGTH DECLARATION: LOU

POSITION	ALIGNMENT	COACHING POINTS
SAM	Crotch 30 tech 3¹/₂ yards deep	Key progression: Fullback, Nearback, Crosskey Attack the "in," scrape to "B," shuffle to stack
WILL	Crotch 30 tech 3¹/₂ yards deep	Key progression: Nearback, Crosskey, Fullback Attack the "in," scrape to "B," shuffle to stack
ANTLER	Shadow 9 tech	Attack outside "V," keep outside leverage
LE	Shade 7 tech	Attack inside "V," anchor "C" gap
LT	Shade 2 tech	2 tech runs an automatic TIM
RT	Crotch 3 tech	Attack outside "V," anchor "B" gap
RE	Crotch 5 tech	Attack inside "V," anchor "C" gap
BRAVE	Shadow 9 tech	Play a ghost 9 if no tight end or slot Play a shadow 9 if tight end or slot is present

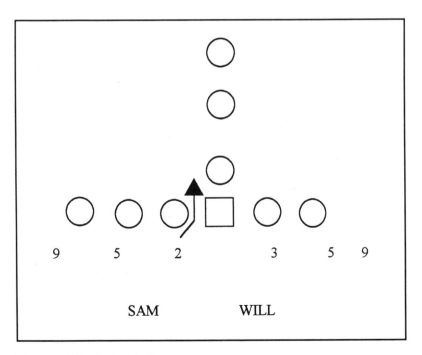

Diagram 3-8: 23 Double Squeeze.

23 STACK

STRENGTH DECLARATION: LOU

POSITION	ALIGNMENT	COACHING POINTS
ANTLER	Gap 50 tech	Key progression: Nearback, Crosskey, Fullback
	4 yards deep	Ignore the "in," play "at" with outside leverage Attack the "out," shuffle to stack with 7 tech
SAM	00 tech toe-to-toe 4 yards deep	Key progression: Nearback, Crosskey, Fullback Attack the "in," scrape to "B," shuffle to stack
WILL	Gap 50 tech 4 yards deep	Key progression: Nearback, Crosskey, Fullback Ignore the "in," play "at" with outside leverage Attack the "out," shuffle to stack with 6 tech
LE	Shade 7 tech	Attack inside "V," anchor "C" gap
LT	Shade 2 tech	2 tech runs an automatic TIM
RT	Crotch 3 tech	Attack outside "V," anchor "B" gap
RE	6 tech toe-to-toe	Attack chin of TE, anchor "C" gap Play ghost 6 tech if no tight end or slot

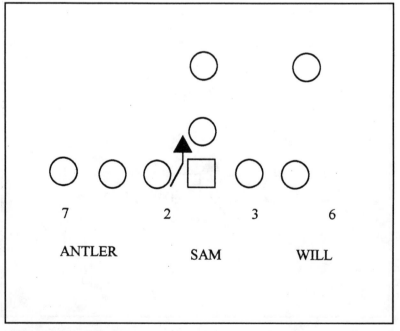

Diagram 3-9: 23 Stack.

23 WEAK STACK

POSITION	ALIGNMENT	COACHING POINTS
SAM	Gap 50 tech 4 yards deep	Key progression: Fullback, Nearback, Crosskey Ignore the "in," play "at" with outside leverage Attack the "out," shuffle to stack with 7 tech
WILL	00 tech toe-to-toe 3½ yards	Key Fullback Attack the "in," scrape to "B," shuffle to stack
BRAVE	Gap 50 tech 4 yards deep	Key progression: Fullback, Nearback, Crosskey Ignore the "in," play "at" with outside leverage Attack the "out," shuffle to stack with 6 tech
LE	Shade 7 tech	Attack inside "V," anchor "C" gap
LT	Shade 2 tech	2 tech runs an automatic TIM
RT	Crotch 3 tech	Attack outside "V," anchor "B" gap
RE	6 tech toe-to-toe	Attack chin of TE, anchor "C" gap Play ghost 6 tech if no tight end or slot

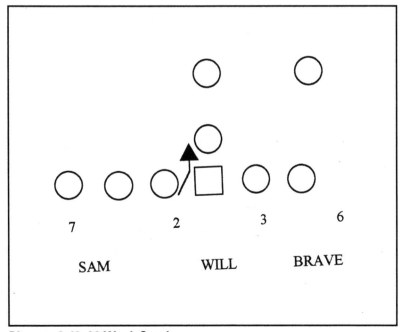

Diagram 3-10: 23 Weak Stack.

23 DOUBLE STACK

STRENGTH DECLARATION: LOU

POSITION	ALIGNMENT	COACHING POINTS
ANTLER	Gap 50 tech 4 yards deep	Key progression: Nearback, Crosskey, Fullback Ignore the "in," play "at" with outside leverage Attack the "out," shuffle to stack with 7 tech
SAM	20 tech toe-to-toe 3½ yards deep	Key progression: Fullback, Nearback, Crosskey Attack the "in," scrape to "B," shuffle to stack
WILL	20 tech toe-to-toe 3½ yards deep	Key progression: Nearback, Crosskey, Fullback Attack the "in," scrape to "B," shuffle to stack
BRAVE	Gap 50 technique 4 yards deep	Key progression: Nearback, Crosskey, Fullback Ignore the "in," play "at" with outside leverage Attack the "out," shuffle to stack with 6 tech
LE	Shade 7 tech	Attack inside "V," anchor "C" gap
LT	Shade 2 tech	2 tech runs an automatic TIM
RT	Crotch 3 tech	Attack outside "V," anchor "B" gap
RE	6 tech toe-to-toe	Attack chin of TE, anchor "C" gap Play ghost 6 tech if no tight end or slot

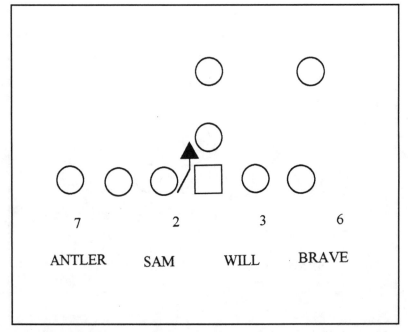

Diagram 3-11: 23 Double Stack.

30

STRENGTH DECLARATION: LOU

POSITION	ALIGNMENT	COACHING POINTS
SAM	20 tech toe-to-toe 3½ yards deep	Key progression: Fullback, Nearback, Crosskey Attack the "in," scrape to stack, shuffle to stack
WILL	Crotch 30 tech 4 yards deep	Key progression: Nearback, Crosskey, Fullback Read open-closed door
LE	6 tech toe-to-toe	Attack chin of tight end, anchor "C" gap
LT	Crotch 3 tech	Attack outside "V," anchor "B" gap
RT	Crotch 0 tech	Anchor weakside "A" gap, keep center off WILL
RE	Crotch 5 tech	Attack outside "V," keep outside leverage

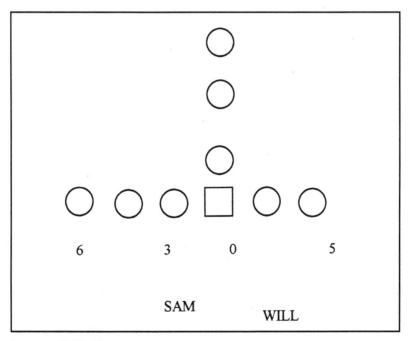

Diagram 3-12: 30.

30 SQUEEZE

STRENGTH DECLARATION: LOU

POSITION	ALIGNMENT	COACHING POINTS
SAM	20 tech toe-to-toe 3½ yards deep	Key progression: Fullback, Nearback, Crosskey Attack the "in," scrape to stack, shuffle to stack
WILL	Crotch 30 tech 4 yards deep	Key progression: Nearback, Crosskey, Fullback Read open-closed door
ANTLER	Shadow 9 tech	Attack outside "V," keep outside leverage
LE	Crotch 5 tech	Attack outside "V," anchor "C" gap
LT	Crotch 3 tech	Attack outside "V," anchor "B" gap
RT	Crotch 0 tech	Anchor weakside "A" gap, keep center off WILL
RE	Crotch 5 tech	Attack outside "V," keep outside leverage

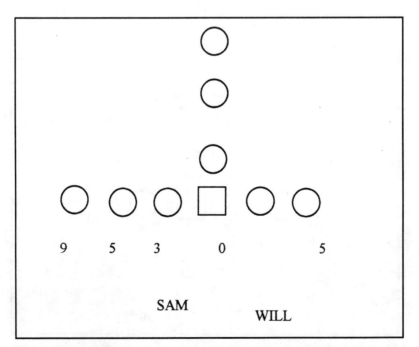

Diagram 3-13: 30 Squeeze.

30 WEAK SQUEEZE

STRENGTH DECLARATION: LOU

POSITION	ALIGNMENT	COACHING POINTS
SAM	20 tech toe-to-toe $3^{1}/_{2}$ yards deep	Key progression: Fullback, Nearback, Crosskey Attack the "in," scrape to stack, shuffle to stack
WILL	Crotch 30 tech 4 yards deep	Key progression: Nearback, Crosskey, Fullback Read open-closed door
LE	6 tech toe-to-toe	Attack chin of tight end, anchor "C" gap
LT	Crotch 3 tech	Attack outside "V," anchor "B" gap
RT	Crotch 0 tech	Anchor weakside "A" gap, keep center off WILL
RE	Crotch 5 tech	Attack outside "V," anchor "C" gap
BRAVE	Shadow 9 tech	Play a ghost 9 if no tight end or slot Play a shadow 9 if tight end or slot is present

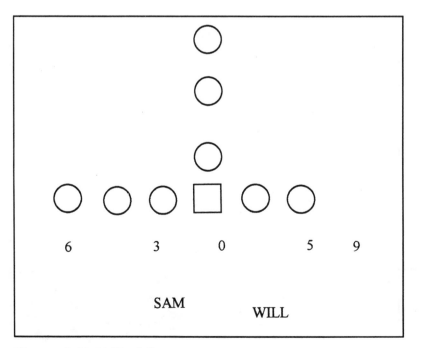

Diagram 3-14: 30 Weak Squeeze.

30 DOUBLE SQUEEZE

STRENGTH DECLARATION: LOU

POSITION	ALIGNMENT	COACHING POINTS
SAM	20 tech toe-to-toe 3 1/2 yards deep	Key progression: Fullback, Nearback, Crosskey Attack the "in," scrape to stack, shuffle to stack
WILL	Crotch 30 tech 4 yards deep	Key progression: Nearback, Crosskey, Fullback Read open-closed door
ANTLER	Shadow 9 tech	Attack outside "V," keep outside leverage
LE	Crotch 5 tech	Attack outside "V," anchor "C" gap
LT	Crotch 3 tech	Attack outside "V," anchor "B" gap
RT	Crotch 0 tech	Anchor weakside "A" gap, keep center off WILL
RE	Crotch 5 tech	Attack outside "V," anchor "C" gap
BRAVE	Shadow 9 tech	Play a ghost 9 if no tight end or slot Play a shadow 9 if tight end or slot is present

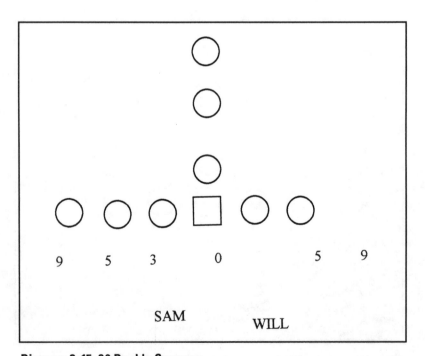

Diagram 3-15: 30 Double Squeeze.

30 STACK

STRENGTH DECLARATION: LOU

POSITION	ALIGNMENT	COACHING POINTS
ANTLER	Gap 50 tech 4 yards deep	Key progression: Nearback, Crosskey, Fullback Ignore the "in," play "at" with outside leverage Attack the "out," shuffle to stack with 6 tech
SAM	00 tech toe-to-toe 3½ yards deep	Key Fullback Attack the "in," scrape to "B," shuffle to stack
WILL	Gap 50 tech 4 yards deep	Key progression: Nearback, Crosskey, Fullback Ignore the "in," play "at" with outside leverage Attack the "out".
LE	6 tech toe-to-toe	Attack chin of TE, anchor "C" gap
LT	Crotch 3 tech	Attack outside "V," anchor "B" gap
RT	Crotch 0 tech	Anchor weakside "A" gap, keep center off SAM
RE	Crotch 5 tech	Attack outside "V," keep outside leverage

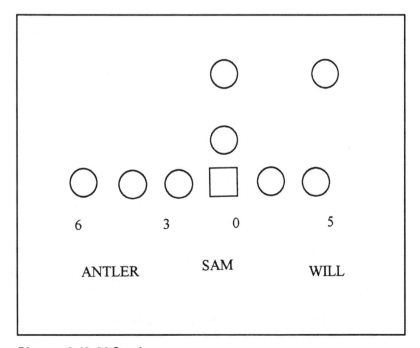

Diagram 3-16: 30 Stack.

30 WEAK STACK

STRENGTH DECLARATION: LOU

POSITION	ALIGNMENT	COACHING POINTS
SAM	Gap 50 tech 4 yards deep	Key progression: Fullback, Nearback, Crosskey Ignore the "in," play "at" with outside leverage Attack the "out," shuffle to stack with 6 tech
WILL	00 tech toe-to-toe 4 yards deep	Key Fullback Attack the "in," scrape to "B," shuffle to stack
BRAVE	Gap 50 tech 4 yards deep	Key progression: Nearback, Crosskey, Fullback Ignore the "in," play "at" with outside leverage Attack the "out".
LE	6 tech toe-to-toe	Attack chin of TE, anchor "C" gap
LT	Crotch 3 tech	Attack outside "V," anchor "B" gap
RT	Crotch 0 tech	Anchor weakside "A" gap, keep center off WILL
RE	Crotch 5 tech	Attack outside "V," keep outside leverage

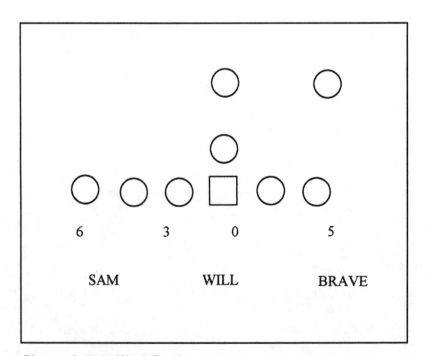

Diagram 3-17: 30 Weak Stack.

30 DOUBLE STACK

STRENGTH DECLARATION: LOU

POSITION	ALIGNMENT	COACHING POINTS
ANTLER	Gap 50 tech 4 yards deep	Key progression: Nearback, Crosskey, Fullback Ignore the "in," play "at" with outside leverage Attack the "out," shuffle to stack with 7 tech
SAM	20 tech toe-to-toe 3 ½ yards deep	Key progression: Fullback, Nearback, Crosskey Attack the "in," scrape to "B," shuffle to stack
WILL	20 tech toe-to-toe 3 ½ yards deep	Key progression: Nearback, Crosskey, Fullback Attack the "in," scrape to "B," shuffle to stack
BRAVE	Gap 50 technique 4 yards deep	Key progression: Nearback, Crosskey, Fullback Ignore the "in," play "at" with outside leverage Attack the "out"
LE	Shade 7 tech	Attack inside "V," anchor "C" gap
LT	Crotch 3 tech	Attack outside "V," anchor "B" gap
RT	Crotch 0 tech	Anchor weakside "A" gap
RE	Crotch 5 tech	Attack outside "V," keep outside leverage

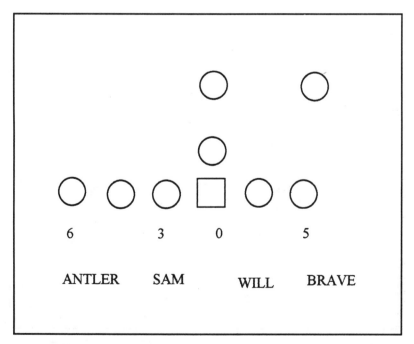

Diagram 3-18: 30 Double Stack.

33

STRENGTH DECLARATION: LOU

POSITION	ALIGNMENT	COACHING POINTS
SAM	Crotch 20 tech 3½ yards deep	Key progression: Fullback, Nearback, Crosskey Attack the "in," scrape to "B," shuffle to stack
WILL	Crotch 20 tech 3½ yards deep	Key progression: Nearback, Crosskey, Fullback Attack the "in," scrape to "B," shuffle to stack
LE	6 tech toe-to-toe	Attack chin of TE, anchor "C" gap
LT	Crotch 3 tech	Attack outside "V," anchor "B" gap
RT	Crotch 3 tech	Attack outside "V," anchor "B" gap
RE	6 tech toe-to-toe	Attack chin of TE, anchor "C" gap Play ghost 6 tech if no tight end or slot

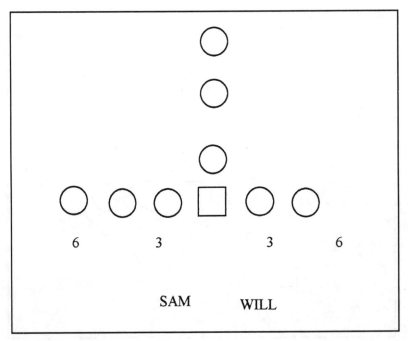

Diagram 3-19: 33.

33 SQUEEZE

STRENGTH DECLARATION: LOU

POSITION	ALIGNMENT	COACHING POINTS
SAM	Crotch 30 tech 3½ yards deep	Key progression: Fullback, Nearback, Crosskey Attack the "in," scrape to "B," shuffle to stack
WILL	Crotch 30 tech 3½ yards deep	Key progression: Nearback, Crosskey, Fullback Attack the "in," scrape to "B," shuffle to stack
ANTLER	Shadow 9 tech	Attack outside "V," keep outside leverage
LE	Crotch 5 tech	Attack outside "V," anchor "C" gap
LT	Crotch 3 tech	Attack outside "V," anchor "B" gap
RT	Crotch 3 tech	Attack outside "V," anchor "B" gap
RE	6 tech toe-to-toe	Attack chin of TE, anchor "C" gap Play ghost 6 tech if no tight end or slot

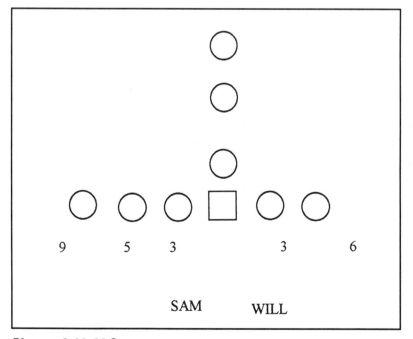

Diagram 3-20: 33 Squeeze.

33 WEAK SQUEEZE

STRENGTH DECLARATION: LOU

POSITION	ALIGNMENT	COACHING POINTS
SAM	Crotch 30 tech 3½ yards deep	Key progression: Fullback, Nearback, Crosskey Attack the "in," scrape to "B," shuffle to stack
WILL	Crotch 30 tech 3½ yards deep	Key progression: Nearback, Crosskey, Fullback Attack the "in," scrape to "B," shuffle to stack
LE	6 tech toe-to-toe	Attack chin of TE, anchor "C" gap
LT	Crotch 3 tech	Attack outside "V," anchor "B" gap
RT	Crotch 3 tech	Attack outside "V," anchor "B" gap
RE	Crotch 5 tech	Attack inside "V," anchor "C" gap
BRAVE	Shadow 9 tech	Play a ghost 9 if no tight end or slot Play a shadow 9 if tight end or slot is present

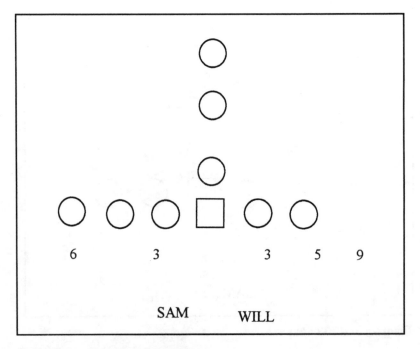

Diagram 3-21: 33 Weak Squeeze.

33 DOUBLE SQUEEZE

STRENGTH DECLARATION: LOU

POSITION	ALIGNMENT	COACHING POINTS
SAM	Crotch 20 tech 3½ yards deep	Key progression: Fullback, Nearback, Crosskey Attack the "in," scrape to "B," shuffle to stack
WILL	Crotch 20 tech 3½ yards deep	Key progression: Nearback, Crosskey, Fullback Attack the "in," scrape to "B," shuffle to stack
ANTLER	Shadow 9 tech	Attack outside "V," keep outside leverage
LE	Crotch 5 tech	Attack outside "V," anchor "C" gap
LT	Crotch 3 tech	Attack outside "V," anchor "B" gap
RT	Crotch 3 tech	Attack outside "V," anchor "B" gap
RE	Crotch 5 tech	Attack inside "V," anchor "C" gap
BRAVE	Shadow 9 tech	Play a ghost 9 if no tight end or slot Play a shadow 9 if tight end or slot is present

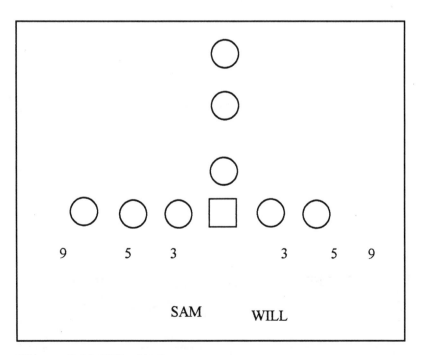

Diagram 3-22: 33 Double Squeeze.

33 DOUBLE STACK

STRENGTH DECLARATION: LOU

POSITION	ALIGNMENT	COACHING POINTS
ANTLER	Gap 50 tech 4 yards deep	Key progression: Nearback, Crosskey, Fullback Ignore the "in," play "at" with outside leverage Attack the "out," shuffle to stack with 6 tech
SAM	Crotch 20 tech 3½ yards deep	Key progression: Fullback, Nearback, Crosskey Attack the "in," scrape to "B," shuffle to stack
WILL	Crotch 20 tech 31/2 yards deep	Key progression: Nearback, Crosskey, Fullback Attack the "in," scrape to "B," shuffle to stack
BRAVE	Gap 50 technique 4 yards deep	Key progression: Nearback, Crosskey, Fullback Ignore the "in," play "at" with outside leverage Attack the "out," shuffle to stack with 6 tech
LE	6 tech toe-to-toe	Attack chin of TE, anchor "C" gap
LT	Crotch 3 tech	Attack outside "V," anchor "B" gap
RT	Crotch 3 tech	Attack outside "V," anchor "B" gap
RE	6 tech toe-to-toe	Attack chin of TE, anchor "C" gap Play ghost 6 tech if no tight end or slot

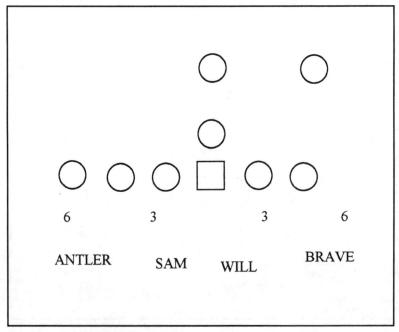

Diagram 3-23: 33 Double Stack.

40

STRENGTH DECLARATION: LOU

POSITION	ALIGNMENT	COACHING POINTS
SAM	20 tech toe-to-toe 3½ yards deep	Key progression: Fullback, Nearback, Crosskey Scrape to "B" gap or shuffle to stack
WILL	Crotch 30 tech 4 yards deep	Key progression: Nearback, Crosskey, Fullback Read open-closed door
LE	6 tech toe-to-toe	Attack chin of TE, anchor "C" gap
LT	Shade 4 tech	2 tech runs an automatic TIM
RT	Crotch 0 tech	Anchor weakside "A" gap, keep center off WILL
RE	Crotch 5 tech	Attack outside "V," keep outside leverage

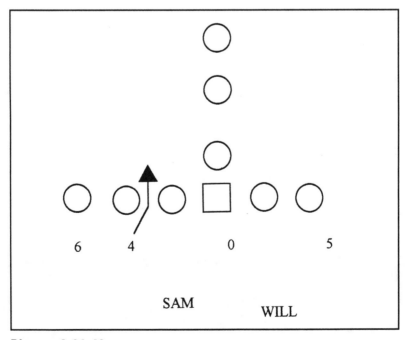

Diagram 3-24: 40.

40 WEAK SQUEEZE

STRENGTH DECLARATION: LOU

POSITION	ALIGNMENT	COACHING POINTS
SAM	20 tech toe-to-toe 3½ yards deep	Key progression: Fullback, Nearback, Crosskey Scrape to "B" gap or shuffle to stack
WILL	Crotch 30 tech 4 yards deep	Key progression: Nearback, Crosskey, Fullback Read open-closed door
LE	6 tech toe-to-toe	Attack chin of TE, anchor "C" gap
LT	Shade 4 tech	4 tech runs an automatic TIM
RT	Crotch 0 tech	Anchor weakside "A" gap, keep center off WILL
RE	Crotch 5 tech	Attack outside "V," anchor "C" gap
BRAVE	Shadow 9 tech	Play a ghost 9 if no tight end or slot Play a shadow 9 if tight end or slot is present

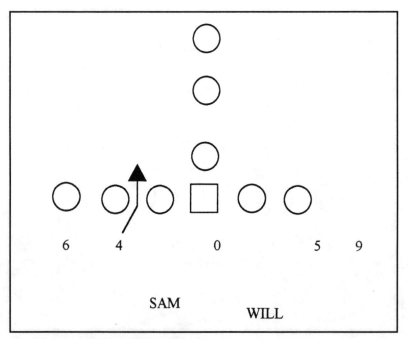

Diagram 3-25: 40 Weak Squeeze.

40 STACK

STRENGTH DECLARATION: LOU

POSITION	ALIGNMENT	COACHING POINTS
ANTLER	Gap 50 tech 4 yards deep	Key progression: Nearback, Crosskey, Fullback Ignore the "in," play "at" with outside leverage Attack the "out," shuffle to stack with 6 tech
SAM	00 tech toe-to-toe 3½ yards deep	Key Fullback Attack the "in," scrape to "B," shuffle to stack
WILL	Gap 50 tech 4 yards deep	Key progression: Nearback, Crosskey, Fullback Ignore the "in," play "at" with outside leverage Attack the "out"
LE	6 tech toe-to-toe	Attack chin of TE, anchor "C" gap
LT	Shade 4 tec	4 tech runs an automatic TIM
RT	Crotch 0 tech	Anchor weakside "A" gap, keep center off SAM
RE	Crotch 5 tech	Attack outside "V," keep outside leverage

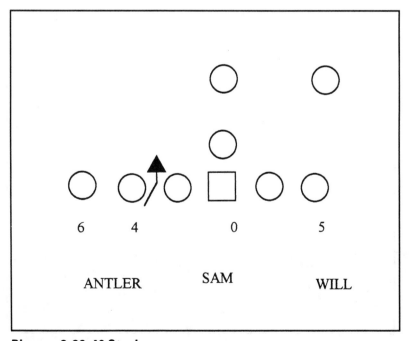

Diagram 3-26: 40 Stack.

40 WEAK STACK

STRENGTH DECLARATION: LOU

POSITION	ALIGNMENT	COACHING POINTS
SAM	Gap 50 tech 4 yards deep	Key progression: Fullback, Nearback, Crosskey Ignore the "in," play "at" with outside leverage Attack the "out," shuffle to stack with 6 tech
WILL	00 tech toe-to-toe 3½ yards deep	Key Fullback Attack the "in," scrape to "B," shuffle to stack
BRAVE	Gap 50 tech 4 yards deep	Key progression: Nearback, Crosskey, Fullback Ignore the "in," play "at" with outside leverage Attack the "out"
LE	6 tech toe-to-toe	Attack chin of TE, anchor "C" gap
LT	Shade 4 tech	4 tech runs an automatic TIM
RT	Crotch 0 tech	Anchor weakside "A" gap, keep center off WILL
RE	Crotch 5 tech	Attack outside "V," keep outside leverage

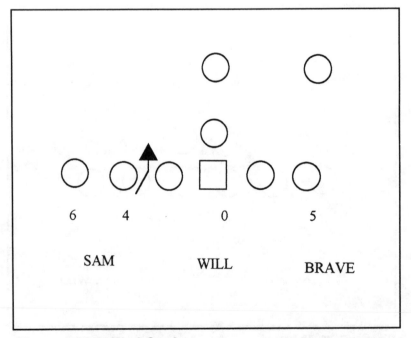

Diagram 3-27: 40 Weak Stack.

CHAPTER 4

Defensive Tackles

TACKLE CHARACTERISTICS

Strength is the primary feature of the tackle. Mobility is also important, and either feature may be exclusive as long as the coach restricts the roles. If a coach is faced with one tackle with strength and one with quickness, the defense is best served by placing the stronger, less mobile tackle on the defensive left and the quicker one on the right. It is important to place the defensive tackle who displays the characteristic ability of a nose tackle on the defensive right, because he will play nose against the common right-handed offenses.

An important characteristic of a nose tackle is the ability to play with a low center of gravity. Impressive upper body strength (e.g., a bench press near the 350-pound mark for the high school player) is also a mark of a prospective nose tackle. Speed is a characteristic which may be evaluated in lieu of the tremendous upper body strength. A good nose tackle is sometimes found in the backfield as a fullback. He possesses excellent speed, good body strength and an uncanny ability to keep on his feet when in contact with large-bodied offensive players. If the nose tackle candidate is a lineman prototype, he is exceptionally strong and able to play with a low center of gravity. The actual weight of the prospective nose tackle is not the primary criteria of selection. We have seen a 145-pound nose tackle unleash tremendous power when playing the "read" 0 technique.

TACKLE ALIGNMENT

The defensive front call will be a two-digit number (i.e., 33, 32, etc.) The first digit will determine the technique of the tackle on the side to which the strength is directed. The linebacker will say either "Ray" or "Lou" to direct the defensive strength right or left, respectively. The linebacker will yell this strength call two times.

If the linebacker yells "Ray" in a 32 front, then the *right* tackle will align in a *3 technique* and the *left tackle* will align in a *2 technique*.

If the linebacker yells "Lou" in a 32 front, then the *left* tackle will align in a *3 technique* and the *right tackle* will align in a *2 technique*.

Note: The tackle aligned in a 0 technique will align in a crotch technique away from the side of the "Ray-Lou" strength declaration and defend the nearest "A" gap.

TACKLE ECHOES

The tackles will echo the "Ray-Lou" strength call after hearing it the first time, so that the tackles are yelling the call in unison with the linebacker as the linebacker repeats his strength call. This tactic is critical in order to avoid miscommunication and other similar breakdowns.

TACKLE STANCE

Stance in the trenches is not an issue of major concern. The defensive tackle should work from the stance which best facilitates his movement. The tackle may be in a four-point stance with a balanced foot positioning. This stance will allow the tackle to push off either foot equally well. A stagger of up to four inches is permissible. The tackle may assume a three-point stance with a slight inside or outside foot stagger. If the feet are staggered, the stagger should be slight and consistent. Staggering the feet according to the assignment or technique is discouraged, but a change of stagger is allowed in order to get a jump on the ball on a passing down. The stagger is not a concern if the technique is a gap-alignment technique. The coach should encourage defensive linemen, particularly the player who often aligns at the nose tackle position (e.g., the right tackle), to use the balanced stance.

The bottom line in the base stance is comfort. The defensive player should align comfortably with the weight resting primarily in his hips. The heels should be slightly off the ground and the off-hand (if using a three-point stance) should be either cocked or hanging loosely at knee level.

GOAL-LINE STANCE

The goal-line stance is used to guarantee the tackle the opportunity to penetrate. The primary benefit of the goal-line stance is psychological. An offensive lineman who is not accustomed to facing a defensive lineman in a goal line will be affected by the sight. Many offensive linemen will simply allow the goal line charge to penetrate as the offensive lineman falls on the defensive linemen. The offensive linemen think they are blocking the defender, but they are only *stopping* him. The victory in the trenches is ours in this scenario. By simply falling on the gap-penetrating defender, instead of hooking and digging him out, the offensive lineman gets no movement. Instead of movement, the feet of the offensive lineman will actually kick out behind him as he falls, adding to our penetration and creating a further obstacle to the ballcarrier.

The goal line stance charging technique will do a push up as he continues churning his feet. The passive "fall-on-them" blocking technique is easily defeated and the defensive tackle gets off the ground and pursues to the ball. The goal-line stance guidelines are as follows:

- The hips are high, the chin is only inches from the ground.

- The arms are naturally bent.

- The feet are brought far under the body to provide explosive power.

- The eyes are up, looking through the gap to the heels of the offensive line.

BALL MOVEMENT KEY

The ball, not the blocker, is the primary movement key for the defensive line. The ball is a better key because moving on the ball allows the defensive tackle to use his quickness to gain an advantage over the offensive lineman. Coaches hope that their defensive linemen are somewhat quicker than the opponent's offensive linemen. Nevertheless, keying the ball movement is, at worst, an equalizer of the quickness off the ball factor.

TACKLE TECHNIQUE

Tackles may play a 0, 1, 2, 3, 4, or 5 technique. The tackle normally has no read responsibility when aligned in an inside leverage technique. He will slide stunt (TIM) by rule when in a 2 or 4 technique. If he is to read, then "base" is added to the call.

The tackle has limited read responsibility when in outside leverage technique (3 and 5 technique). His responsibility is to attack the "V," keeping the head in outside leverage to defeat the hook (reach) block. Gap responsibility is most important in an outside leverage technique, particularly the 3 technique.

The 0 technique reads more than others, keeping gapside leverage but being able to squeeze and control the center's ability to zone block the backside linebacker. The 0 technique can never be reached by the center and must be able to cross hat on check blocks by the center.

The 1 technique should align in a goal-line stance and charge to one foot behind the heels of the offensive linemen, then scramble to the ball.

RUSHING THE PASSER

The defensive tackle should rush the passer and push the middle, so that the quarterback will believe he should step outside. The defensive tackle should rush with at least one hand up. If a defensive tackle jumps to block a pass, he should leap upward so that he lands in the same spot from which he left the ground.

When engaging a pass blocker, the defensive tackle should use the rip technique. The rip technique is sometimes referred to as the speed rush—particularly when the technique is used by a defensive end. In the rip technique, the defensive tackle will dip his shoulder nearest the blocker as he powers past the blocker. The pass rusher drives his leverage arm (the arm closest to the blocker) upward in a manner similar to uppercut punch to the middle of the humerus bone. This uppercut punch will drive the pass protector's leverage arm upward and force him to turn, opening the gate to the quarterback. By dipping the leverage shoulder, the defender gives the pass protector less blocking surface for contact. The lateral arm (the arm farthest from the defenders' path) really has no available frontal surface to contact. The blocker has to try to "hip steer" the pass rusher with the lateral arm. The "hip steering" technique—a technique where the protector puts his off hand on the hip of the speed rusher—is an effective technique on the edge but not in the interior. The interior defensive lineman has the advantage of a direct line to the quarterback on level-three action. The defensive tackle pushes the middle with the offside arm up to distract the quarterback. Once the defensive tackle is free of contact with the pass protector, the defensive tackle should rush with both arms extended.

DRAPING THE QUARTERBACK

The quarterback should always be sacked with a draping technique. Draping entails bringing both arms down on the shoulders of the quarterback as contact is made. The defensive tackle should sack the quarterback with his arms above the plane of the quarterback's shoulders. The arm nearest the quarterback's throwing arm should reach to hook the elbow of the passing arm as the quarterback cocks his arm in the throwing movement.

The downward impetus of the draping technique also helps the pass rusher finish the sack on the agile quarterback who ducks under the pass rusher. By being under control and draping the quarterback, the defender is able to smother the "duck" move by the quarterback. The drape technique prevents the defender from continuing his forward momentum past the quarterback's duck move.

PASS RUSH TECHNIQUE CONSIDERATIONS

"Daily must" drills by the defensive tackle coach should include the rip technique pass rush and the draping technique. Players are often resistant to using the drape technique. They want to smash the quarterback. Additionally, running full speed with one or both arms extended into the air is not a natural movement, so players need drills to help this technique become an unconsciously exhibited technique.

An alternative to the rip technique is the "swim" technique. The swim is a move which is most effective when used by the taller defensive pass rusher. In order to swim effectively, the pass rusher cannot be shorter than the pass protector.

The swim is an excellent pass rushing move. However, to effectively swim, the pass rusher must have a hitch in his upfield push. The swim demands a fast push upfield and a momentary stop to snatch and grab the lateral portion of the blocker's upper body near the armpits and shoulders. This momentary stop is not a complete cessation of movement; rather, it is a setting point for the pull of the jersey in the swim move.

The arm to the side of the player's swim move will snatch the jersey of the blocker as the defender's hips sink. The pass rusher uses this arm to pull the pass protector's shoulder downward. The pass rusher attempts to pull the protector's shoulder toward the opposite knee of the pass protector, across the body of the protector.

As the shoulder is pulled downward by the snatch and grab arm, the opposite knee drives to a point behind the foot of the blocker. The swimming arm, in conjunction with the knee movement, is punched over the depressed shoulder of the protector in a swimming movement. The key to an effective move is the swing foot of the defender being placed immediately behind the pass protector's near foot (foot nearest defender). Thus, the arm opposite the pull punches over the top while the corresponding foot is swung behind the protector. Once the swing foot is planted in a heel-to-heel relationship with the protector's foot, the swim move is complete. The pass protector has no chance to recover.

The major flaw of a typical swim maneuver attempt occurs when the rusher pulls the protector's shoulder and punches the opposite arm over. The novice will not follow through with the foot corresponding to the arm swim. In other words, the defender may pull with his left arm to swim around to the defender's left, punch the right arm over correctly, but fail to swing the right foot to a position immediately behind the blocker's right foot. The protector may recover if the defender's right foot is not swung to a point behind the blocker's right foot.

Consider the following swim scenario. The left defensive tackle attacks the pass protector and uses both hands to grab the protector. The pass rusher then uses this two-arm grab to "feel" the balance or imbalance of the pass protector. Upon recognizing the opportune direction for the swim move through his feel of the protector, the pass rusher makes his move to the left. The rusher pulls with his left arm to depress the right shoulder of the pass blocker. When the shoulder is depressed the right hand releases the left shoulder of the pass protector. The right arm is punched over the depressed shoulder and head of the protector as the defender's right knee leads the right foot to a point immediately behind the right foot of the protector. The pass rusher's left hand releases the depressed right shoulder of the protector as the defender's right knee drives forward. Once the defender's right foot gets to a heel-to-heel relationship with the protector's right foot, the swim move is complete and the pass protector can not recover.

TACKLE STUNTS

T	Slant to direction called.
TIGER	Tackle in gap—charge gap from crotch alignment.
TIM	Tackle inside move—slant inside.
TOM	Tackle outside move—slide outside.
TWIST	Twist with low number going first, or strong side when both techniques are same.
2 or 4	Automatic inside slide when corresponding digit of front call is 2 or 4.
BASE	Play base 2 or 4 technique when "base" is called.
NOSE	Nose strong slide.
NOSE SLANT	Nose strong slant.
NOW	Nose weak slide.
NOW SLANT	Nose weak slant.

TACKLE COMBINATION STUNTS

DOG

Both tackles run a TIGER while inside linebackers rush their gaps.

NOSE SAM LOOP

Nose runs a NOSE, while SAM loops through weakside "A" gap.

NOW WILL LOOP

Nose runs a NOW, while WILL loops through strongside "A" gap.

TEXAS

Tackle and end X—run a wide looping slant to contain and watch for screen.

TOE

Tackle outside of end.

Dropstep and rush outside of end, looking for screen and keeping containment.

TACKLE ADJUSTMENTS

GREEN

When a "green" is called at the LOS, the nose tackle moves to a 1 technique.

ATTACKING THE "V"

The Forty Nickel defensive tackle usually plays base technique from the outside technique alignment. The tackle is asked to attack the outside "V" of the offensive lineman. The "V" is a defensive landmark which identifies three possible target points at which the defensive lineman may direct his facemask crossbar. The lowest point of the "V" of the offensive lineman is his chin. The lateral arms of the "V" signify the anatomical point on the body just two to three inches lateral of the point at which the sternum and clavicle meet.

One way to visualize the "V" is to imagine a giant letter "V" on the face of the blocker. The lowest point of the letter is the sternal notch located below the chin. The arms of the letter extend from that point of the body to the earlobes of the blocker. The earlobe closest to the ball would be relative to the inside "V," the earlobe farthest from the ball would be relative to the outside "V."

The landmarks are the outside "V," the point located near the pulse point in the neck that is farthest from the ball, the chin of the offensive lineman, and the outside "V," the point located near the pulse point in the neck that is closest to the ball. The outside "V" is technically the earlobe of the blocker.

The Forty Nickel defensive lineman attacks the "V," not the shoulder pad. We do not use the shoulder blow technique. Our linemen use the thumbs up, chest and shoulder leverage technique to control and separate from the blocker. The facemask crossbar is our targeting device, but his head isn't part of the blow delivery. By using the facemask as the targeting device, the head is kept back with the neck bowed. The face will strike the "V" target but only with the force needed to topple a toddler. We like to say that we could put an egg on his screws at the top of his facemask and it wouldn't get broken in a proper blow delivery. The upper portion of the facemask should not make contact with the "V" landmark.

SHOULDER BLOW DELIVERY

The shoulder blow technique is an effective technique, particularly at the lower levels of play. However, the emphasis of upper-body strength in the higher-level programs has led the thought of blow delivery to the tighter targets of the "V" landmarks. Shoulder blow delivery to a landmark tends to put the defensive player on the "corner" of the block, making the defender easy prey to position block. (A position block is a weak block in which the offensive player simply steps to a leverage point on the defensive player and swivels his buttocks into the hole, thus sealing the defensive player from the ball with minimal effort by the offensive player.)

Coaches at the lower levels are under a mandate to teach the shoulder blow technique. Younger players have skinny, undeveloped necks. They also want to please the coach and will put everything into a blow delivery. Developmentally, they are not ready for the technique of attacking the "V." Attempting to use this method at the lower level carries a high risk of a player injuring his neck due to improper technique. Younger players want to hit hard but sometimes have problems understanding the concept of keeping the head back and the neck bowed. Younger players tend to "duck" their head by tucking their chin as they deliver a blow or make a hit.

The "V" attack method is not introduced until the ninth-grade level. During the offseason between the ninth- and tenth-grade seasons, the players are instructed in the technique in noncontact drills; the average player usually begins to demonstrate the technique as a matter of habit during his tenth-grade year. It normally takes a year of offseason teaching the technique to a player before he really understands and can safely execute the technique.

In the Forty Nickel scheme, the defensive tackle may play five possible techniques. Of the five techniques, three techniques are lateral shades (i.e., outside shades). The other two techniques are inside shades; however, the two base inside shades are not part of the base reading package. They are included in the extended defensive package and are used by the more experienced and talented defensive tackles. The base inside shade alignment is used for stunting in the base package, not for reading. A breakdown of each possible defensive line technique follows.

ZERO TECHNIQUE

The 0 technique aligns on the center in a crotch alignment to the weakside. This is fundamental weakside tackle technique in the Forty Nickel package. His primary gap responsibility is the weakside "A" gap. His primary assignment is to anchor the weakside "A" gap and keep the center off the Will linebacker. The various blocks that the 0 technique will face along with the coaching points of the appropriate defensive reaction are detailed below.

- Check Block—The defensive tackle takes the easiest path in pursuit of the ballcarrier. The blocking landmark of the center as well as the skill of the defensive tackle dictate the path the defender takes. He has a choice of crossing the face of the blocker and pursuing flat down the line of scrimmage or dipping his playside shoulder and running around (i.e., behind) the blocker.

- Cutoff Block—The defensive tackle squeezes down the line of scrimmage, so that the backside guard cannot cutoff the tackle from the pursuit. The main objective of the tackle is to ride the center's block, thus keeping him from zone blocking the Will linebacker.

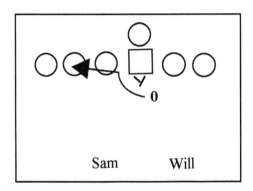 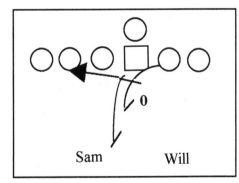

Diagram 4-1. **Diagram 4-2.**

- Double Team Block—The defensive tackle attacks the post blocker (i.e., center) and dips the shoulder closest to the lead blocker (i.e., guard). He hooks the lead blocker's inside leg with his outside arm. He makes a pile while churning his feet so that he may split the double team and rise to his feet to pursue the ballcarrier.

- Dropback Pass Block—The defensive tackle pushes the middle, using either the rip or swim technique to clear the blocker. He pressures the quarterback with at least one arm up, and tackles the quarterback using a drape technique.

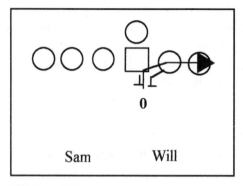

Diagram 4-3.

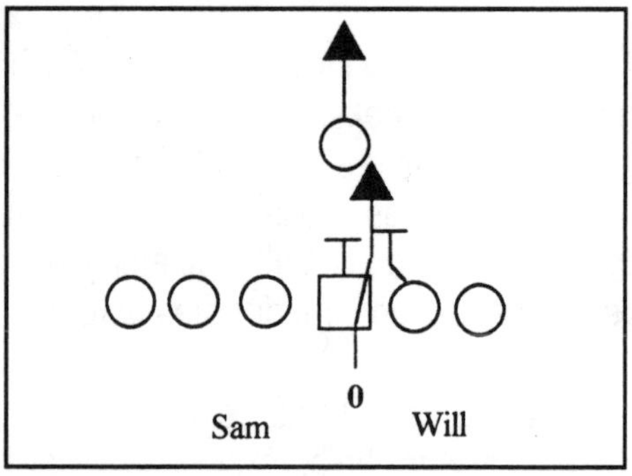

Diagram 4-4.

- Hinge Pass Block—The defensive tackle crosses the face of the center and charges through the strongside "A" gap. He attempts to drive upfield from that point to pressure the quarterback.

- Reach Block—The defensive tackle maintains outside leverage on the center and pursues laterally down the line of scrimmage.

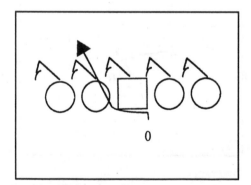

Diagram 4-5.

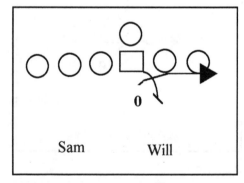

Diagram 4-6.

- Turnback Pass Block—The defensive tackle crosses the face of the playside guard and charges through the "B" gap to pressure the quarterback. He reacts to the flow of the quarterback and flattens his pursuit angle if the quarterback breaks outside the tackle box.

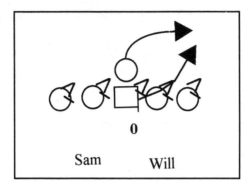

Diagram 4-7.

ONE TECHNIQUE

The 1 technique is a gap alignment technique of the defensive tackle. The 1 technique defensive tackle's primary assignment is to penetrate the weakside "A" gap. He reads the feet of the fullback for a key to the direction of the ball flow. If there is no fullback aligned behind the center, the 1 technique may key the feet of the nearback.

- Check Block—The defensive tackle penetrates and flattens his angle of pursuit behind the center's block. In the diagram below, the fullback dives to the onside, but the pulling guard is a "flashing color" to the 1 technique. The "flashing color" overrules the direction of a flow key. (See "flashing color" in the inside linebacker section of this text).

- Cutoff Block—The defensive tackle penetrates while keeping his playside shoulder free. He stays on his feet and pursues laterally.

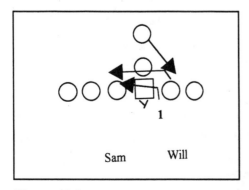

Diagram 4-8.

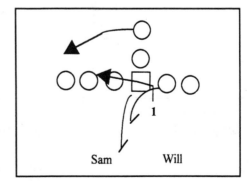

Diagram 4-9.

- Double Team Block—The defensive tackle attacks the gap and makes a pile. He keeps his feet moving, splits the double team, and gets up to pursue the ballcarrier.

- Down Block—The defensive tackle attacks the gap and flattens his angle of pursuit behind the guard's block. If the offense has a pulling guard, the 1 technique tackle will attempt to knock him down. In Diagram 4-11, the fullback dives to the offside, but the pulling guard is a "flashing color." The "flashing color" overrules the direction of a flow key. (See "flashing color" in the inside linebacker section of this text.)

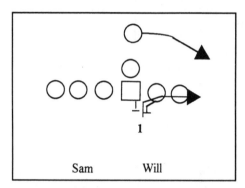

Diagram 4-10.

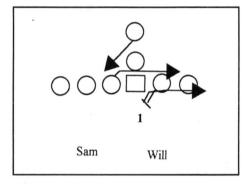

Diagram 4-11.

- Dropback Pass Block—The defensive tackle pushes the middle, using either the rip or swim technique to clear the blocker. He pressures the quarterback with at least one arm up, and tackles the quarterback using a drape technique.

- Hinge Pass Block—The defensive tackle charges the "A" gap and dips the playside shoulder to flatten his angle of pursuit to the quarterback.

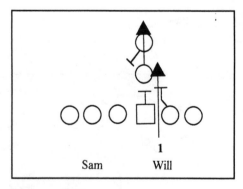

Diagram 4-12.

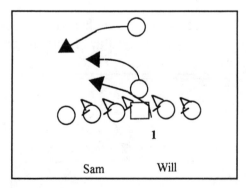

Diagram 4-13.

- Turnback Pass Block—The defensive tackle charges through the "A" gap to pressure the quarterback. He reacts to the flow of the quarterback and flattens his pursuit angle if the quarterback breaks outside the tackle box.

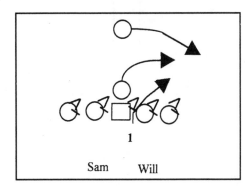

Diagram 4-14.

TWO TECHNIQUE

Normally, the defensive tackle does not play the reading 2 technique in the Forty Nickel defensive scheme. However, for the athlete who plays above the level of his competitors and demonstrates exceptional strength, the base reading 2 technique is included within the package. Inside shades such as the 2 and 4 technique are normally the shades from which the tackles slide stunt inside. Described below are the proper reactions to the various blocks that are attempted versus the base 2 technique.

- Base Block—The defensive tackle attacks the inside "V" of the guard. He attempts to control the blocker and separate from him while securing the "A" gap.

- Check Block—The defensive tackle takes the easiest path in pursuit of the ballcarrier. The blocking landmark of the center and the skill of the defensive tackle dictate the path the defender takes. He has a choice of crossing the face of the center and pursuing flat down the line of scrimmage or dipping his playside shoulder to get in the "hip pocket" of the pulling guard to pursue down the line of scrimmage.

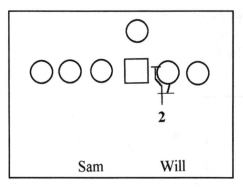

Diagram 4-15.

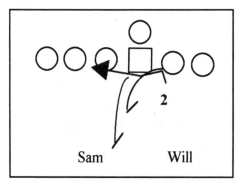

Diagram 4-16.

- Cutoff Block—The defensive tackle attacks the inside "V" of the guard while keeping his playside shoulder free. The tackle stays on his feet and pursues down the line of scrimmage.

- Double Team Block—The defensive tackle attacks the post blocker (i.e., guard) and dips the shoulder closest to the lead blocker (i.e., center). He hooks the lead blocker's outside leg with his inside arm. He makes a pile while churning his feet so that he can split the double team and rise to his feet to pursue the ballcarrier.

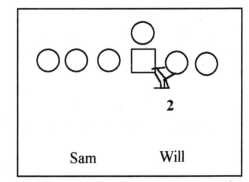

Diagram 4-17.

Diagram 4-18.

- Down Block—The defensive tackle takes the easiest path in pursuit of the ballcarrier. The blocking landmark of the guard and the skill of the defensive tackle dictate the path the defender takes. He has a choice of crossing the face of the guard and pursuing flat down the line of scrimmage or dipping his outside shoulder to run around the guard's down block. The run around technique is used when the guard overextends his landmark and loses his blocking surface on the 2 technique.

- Dropback Pass Block—The defensive tackle pushes the middle, using either the rip or swim technique to clear the blocker. He pressures the quarterback with at least one arm up, and tackles the quarterback using a drape technique.

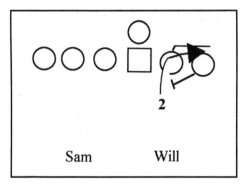

Diagram 4-19.

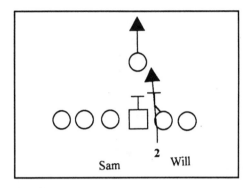

Diagram 4-20.

- Hinge Pass Block—The defensive tackle crosses the face of the center and charges through the strongside "A" gap. He attempts to drive upfield from that point to pressure the quarterback.

- Influence Block—The defensive tackle attacks the inside "V" of the guard. As the guard fakes the pass block (i.e., shows pass), the defensive tackle throws his eyes inside to check for a trap blocker. As he recognizes the trapper, the defensive tackle attacks the trapper. His objective is to place the outside shoulder to the inside knee of the blocker.

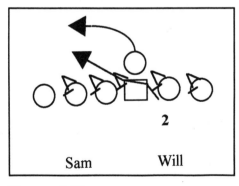

Diagram 4-21.

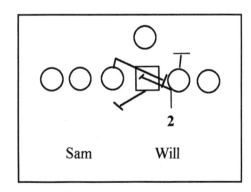

Diagram 4-22.

- Reach Block—The defensive tackle attacks the inside "V" of the guard. Upon feeling the outside pressure of the reach blocking guard, the defensive tackle dips his inside shoulder and crosses the face for the guard to pursue the ballcarrier.

- Turnback Pass Block—The defensive tackle crosses the face of the playside guard and charges through the "B" gap to pressure the quarterback. He reacts to the flow of the quarterback and flattens his pursuit angle if the quarterback breaks outside the tackle box.

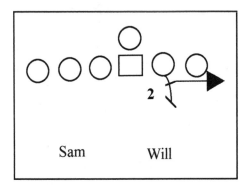

Diagram 4-23.

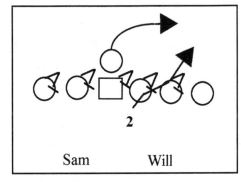

Diagram 4-24.

- Zone Block—The defensive tackle flattens the guard's block down the line of scrimmage. His objective is to ride the block of the guard and keep him from working to the second level. Ideally, the 2 technique crosses the face of the zone-blocking guard, preventing the guard from cutting off the linebacker. The defensive tackle pursues the ballcarrier by sliding down the line of scrimmage.

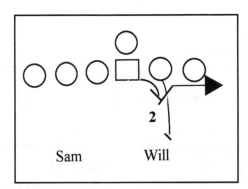

Diagram 4-25.

THREE TECHNIQUE

The 3-technique alignment of the defensive tackle is an outside alignment on the guard and may be specified as a shade, crotch, or shadow alignment. The base 3 technique is a crotch alignment on the guard. The primary responsibility of the guard is to anchor the "B" gap. He should never be reach blocked by the guard. If the offensive unit desires to run off-tackle, the 3 technique should force a double team at the point of attack.

- Base Block—The defensive tackle attacks the outside "V" of the guard. He uses his hands to separate from the guard and control the "B" gap. Against the base block, his objective is squeeze the block of the guard and narrow the "A" gap.

- Check Block—The defensive tackle defeats the check block by dipping his playside shoulder and running around the block of the center while staying in the "hip pocket" of the pulling guard. He pursues down the line of scrimmage over the top of the center's block.

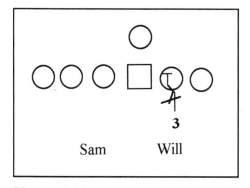

Diagram 4-26.   **Diagram 4-27.**

- Cutoff Block—The defensive tackle attacks the outside "V" of the guard while keeping his outside shoulder free. He keeps the tackle from gaining inside leverage by riding the guard's block inside and staying on his feet. He squeezes down the line of scrimmage to the pursue the ballcarrier.

- Double Team Block—The defensive tackle attacks the post blocker (i.e., guard) and dips the shoulder closest to the lead blocker (i.e., tackle). He hooks the lead blocker's inside leg with his outside arm. He makes a pile while churning his feet so that he can split the double team and rise to his feet to pursue the ballcarrier. A coaching point of the double team is to drop on the outside hip to reduce the blocking surface for the tackle.

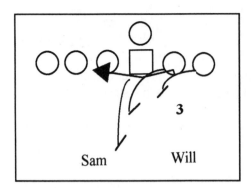

Diagram 4-28. **Diagram 4-29.**

- Down Block—The defensive tackle takes the easiest path in pursuit of the ballcarrier. The blocking landmark of the tackle and the skill of the defensive tackle dictate the path the defender takes. He has a choice of crossing the face of the tackle and pursuing down the line of scrimmage or dipping his outside shoulder to run around the tackle's down block. The run around technique is used when the tackle overextends his landmark and loses his blocking surface on the 2 technique. Ideally, the defensive tackle crosses the face of the tackle's down block and pursues outside to tackle the ballcarrier.

- Dropback Pass Block—The defensive tackle pushes the middle, attacking through the "B" gap while using either the rip or swim technique to clear the blocker. He pressures the quarterback with at least one arm up, and tackles the quarterback using a drape technique.

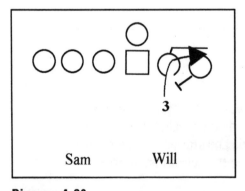

Diagram 4-30. **Diagram 4-31.**

- Hinge Pass Block—The defensive tackle crosses the face of the guard and charges through the weakside "A" gap. He attempts to drive upfield from that point to pressure the quarterback.

- Influence Block—The defensive tackle attacks the outside "V" of the guard. As the guard fakes the pass block (i.e., shows pass), the defensive tackle throws his eyes inside to check for a trap blocker. As he recognizes the trap, the defensive tackle attacks the trapping guard. His objective is to place the outside shoulder to the inside knee of the blocker.

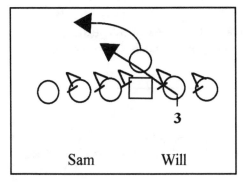

Diagram 4-32.

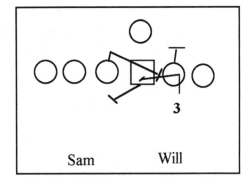

Diagram 4-33.

- Inside Block—The defensive tackle attacks the outside "V" of the guard and squeezes in response to the target moving inside. He uses his hands to keep the guard off the linebacker and attacks the trapper with his outside shoulder to the inside knee of the blocker.

- Reach Block—The defensive tackle attacks the outside "V" of the guard and stalemates his block. The defensive tackle attempts to maintain outside leverage and pursue laterally down the line of scrimmage.

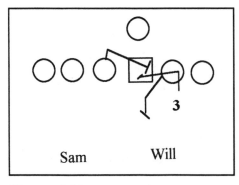

Diagram 4-34.

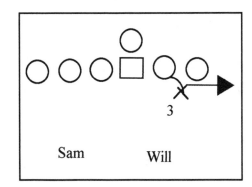

Diagram 4-35.

- Turnback Pass Block—The defensive tackle crosses the face of the playside tackle and charges through the "C" gap to pressure the quarterback. He reacts to the flow of the quarterback and flattens his pursuit angle if the quarterback breaks outside the tackle box.

- Zone Block—The defensive tackle's objective is to ride the block of the guard and keep him from working to the second level. The zone block is defeated in exactly the same manner as the reach block. The defensive tackle stalemates the guard and pursues the ballcarrier by sliding down the line of scrimmage.

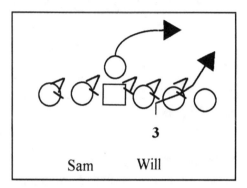

Diagram 4-36.

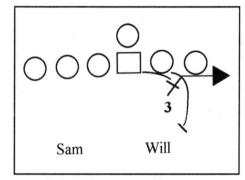

Diagram 4-37.

FOUR TECHNIQUE

Like the 2 technique, the defensive tackle normally does not play the reading 4 technique in the Forty Nickel defensive scheme. Of the two inside shades, however, the 4 technique is more likely to be used. For the athlete who plays above the level of his competitors and demonstrates exceptional strength, the base reading 4 technique is included within the package. Inside shades such as the 2 and 4 technique are normally the shades from which the tackles slide stunt inside. Described below are the proper reactions to the various blocks that are attempted versus the base 4 technique.

- Base Block—The defensive tackle attacks the inside "V" of the tackle. He attempts to control the blocker and separate from him while securing the "A" gap.

- Cutoff Block—The defensive tackle attacks the inside "V" of the tackle while keeping his playside shoulder free. The tackle stays on his feet and pursues down the line of scrimmage.

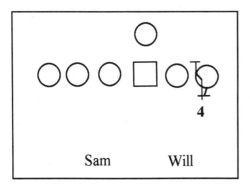

Diagram 4-38.

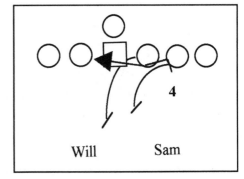

Diagram 4-39.

- Double Team Block—The defensive tackle attacks the post blocker (i.e., tackle) and dips the shoulder closest to the lead blocker (i.e., guard). He hooks the lead blocker's outside leg with his inside arm. He makes a pile while churning his feet so that he can split the double team and rise to his feet to pursue the ballcarrier.

- Dropback Pass Block—The defensive tackle pushes the middle, using either the rip or swim technique to clear the blocker. He pressures the quarterback with at least one arm up, and tackles the quarterback using a drape technique.

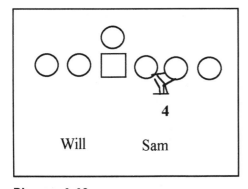

Diagram 4-40.

Diagram 4-41.

- Hinge Pass Block—The defensive tackle crosses the face of the guard and charges through the weakside "A" gap. He attempts to drive upfield from that point to pressure the quarterback.

- Influence Block—The defensive tackle attacks the inside "V" of the tackle. As the tackle sets and blocks out, the defensive tackle throws his eyes inside to check for a trap blocker. As he recognizes the trapper, the defensive tackle attacks the trapper. His objective is to place the outside shoulder to the inside knee of the blocker.

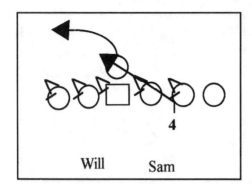

Diagram 4-42.

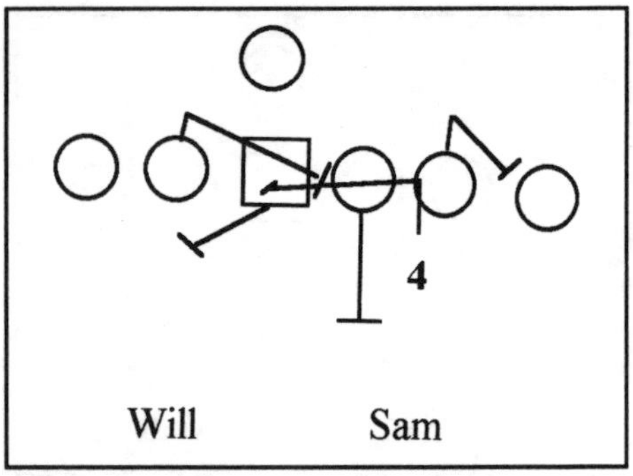

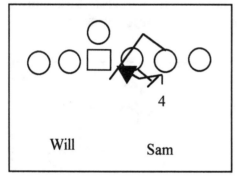

Diagram 4-43.

- Out Block—The defensive tackle attacks the inside "V" of the tackle and recognizes the loop block technique of the tackle and the out block of the guard. The defensive tackle crosses the face of the guard by dipping his outside shoulder and ripping his outside arm underneath the blocking surface of the guard. The technique is the same for any combination block of which the out block is an integral part.

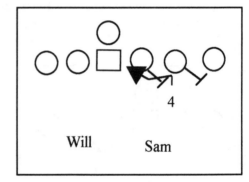

Diagram 4-44.

Diagram 4-45.

- Reach Block—The defensive tackle attacks the inside "V" of the tackle. Upon feeling the outside pressure of the reach blocking tackle, the defensive tackle dips his inside shoulder and crosses the face for the tackle to pursue the ballcarrier.

- Tackle Pulls Outside—The defensive tackle attacks the inside "V" of the tackle and pursues flat down the line of scrimmage to the outside.

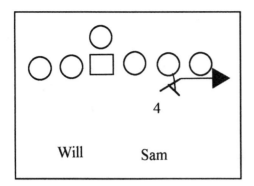

Diagram 4-46.

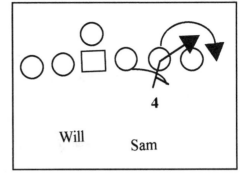

Diagram 4-47.

- Trey Block—The defensive tackle attacks the inside "V" of the tackle and attempts to disrupt the play by either getting into the legs of the pulling tackle to knock him down or trailing in the hip pocket of the tackle flat down the line of scrimmage to make the tackle.

- Turnback Pass Block—The defensive tackle crosses the face of the playside tackle and charges through the "C" gap to pressure the quarterback. He reacts to the flow of the quarterback and flattens his pursuit angle if the quarterback breaks outside the tackle box.

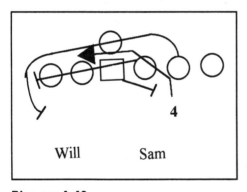

Diagram 4-48.

Diagram 4-49.

- Veer Block—The defensive tackle attacks the inside "V" and gets the eyes inside while throwing his hands into the tackle to widen his path. The defensive tackle attacks the mesh-point and tackles the diveback while keeping his outside arm free.

- Zone Block—The defensive tackle stretches the tackle's block down the line of scrimmage. His objective is to ride the block of the tackle and keep him from working to the second level. Ideally, the 4 technique prevents the guard from getting around to cut him off from the pursuit. The defensive tackle pursues the ballcarrier by sliding down the line of scrimmage.

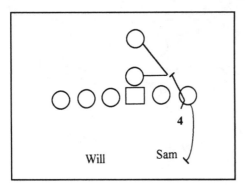

Diagram 4-50.

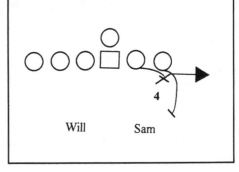

Diagram 4-51.

STUNTS

The defensive tackle automatically stunts if his technique is a 2 or a 4 technique. The lone exception to this rule is the "base" call. When the word "base" is used with a 2 and 4 technique, the tackle does not automatically run an inside slide stunt. The inside slide stunt is called a Tim stunt.

All tackle stunts begin with the letter "t." A tackle playing the nose technique will respond to stunt calls that begin with the letter "n." The peculiar nature of the stunt calls in the Forty Nickel system omit the word "strong" to denote which tackle is to perform the stunt. Most defensive systems call strongside stunts with the preface of "strong," (e.g., strong blitz, strong thunder, etc.). The Forty Nickel system does not specify the stunt as a strong stunt by using the word "strong" to identify the stunt. In the Forty Nickel system, all stunts are strongside stunts unless otherwise specified as "weak" or "double." For example, a Tim stunt is a strongside tackle stunt. A "weak" Tim stunt is a weakside tackle stunt. A "double" Tim is an inside move made by both strongside and weakside tackles.

Forty Nickel tackle stunts, tackle-end combination stunts, and tackle-linebacker combination stunts are illustrated and detailed below.

- "T" stunt—A "T" stunt is a slant by the 2-technique or 4-technique tackle toward the inside. The aiming point is the hip of the nearest inside offensive player. The stunting tackle penetrates to a point six inches behind the heels of the offensive lineman. The slanting tackle reacts to the angle of the inside blocker's movement. If the blocker moves away from the slanting tackle, the tackle flattens his slant angle. If the blocker pulls outside, the slanting tackle attempts to vertically redirect the slant and pursue the ballcarrier.

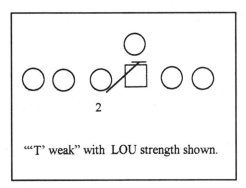

"'T' weak" with LOU strength shown.

Diagram 4-52: "T" stunt.

- Tiger stunt—The tackle takes a shadow alignment in his responsible gap and charges forward on the snap of the football. The stunt is used on passing situations in combination with linebacker stunts as a means for changing the momentum in the trench. The Tiger-stunting tackle charges to a depth of one to two feet behind the heels of the offensive linemen as he looks inside. The letters in the name Tiger have specific connotations—"T" for tackle, "in" for inside, "g" for gap. "Tiger" equals "tackle" "in" the "gap." A nose tackle can run a Tiger from the shadow alignment as shown in Diagram 4-54.

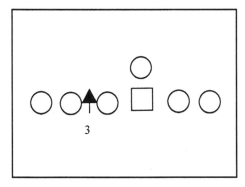

Diagram 4-53: Tiger.

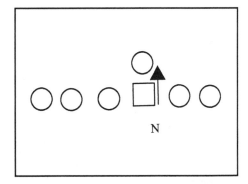

Diagram 4-54: Weak Tiger (from nose).

- Tim stunt—The Tim stunt is an inside slide. A tackle automatically runs a Tim stunt when in a 2 or 4 technique unless the word "base" is included in the call. The aiming point of the stunt is the hip of the inside man. He penetrates no deeper than six inches behind the heels of the defensive lineman before finding the football. The slide is significantly different from the slant as the sliding defensive tackle attempts to gain more vertical penetration and offers more resistance to the blocker who is attempting to pin him. The first step of the Tim-stunting tackle is made perpendicular to the line of scrimmage. When called in the huddle, the Tim stunt is applicable to any specified tackle regardless of his technique. A Tim call refers to the strong tackle; a Weak Tim refers to the weakside tackle, and a Double Tim refers to both tackles.

- Tom stunt—The Tom stunt is a slide stunt to the outside. The letters of the name "Tom" have a significance. "T" stands for "tackle," "o" stands for "outside," and "m" stands for "move"—"Tom" stands for "tackle outside move." The aiming point of the Tom stunting tackle is the near hip of the offensive player to his outside. As in the Tim stunt, the tackle attempts to achieve a vertical penetration no deeper than six inches behind the heels of the offensive lineman. His first step is made with the toe pointed toward the line of scrimmage. A Tom stunt may be run by any technique except a 1 technique.

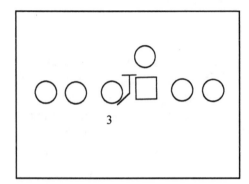

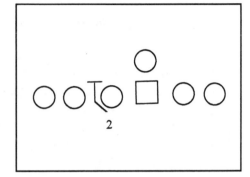

Diagram 4-55: Tim stunt.   **Diagram 4-56: Tom stunt.**

- Twist stunt—The Twist stunt is a stunt with both tackles. The low number technique has the right of way and goes first. When both techniques are the same, the strongside technique goes first. The Twist stunt is a passing situation stunt. The tackle who goes first runs a Tim stunt one gap farther over while the second tackle steps forward to bait the blocker. The second tackle quickly follows the bait step with an inside dropstep. He continues to loop underneath the Tim stunting tackle and rushes through the appropriate gap. His appropriate gap is the replacement of the first tackle's gap responsibility. For example, on a "32" call, the three technique tackle will loop through the weakside "A" gap— the primary responsibility of the 2-technique tackle.

- Two or Four stunt—Not a called stunt, the 2 technique and 4 technique automatically slides inside unless the word "base" is added to the defensive call. The nature of the attacking style of the Forty Nickel demands front movement. In order to avoid the redundancy of continually calling an inside slide on most of the scrimmage downs, the system provides for an automatic inside slide of the 2- or 4-technique tackle. The coaching points for this slide are covered in the section on the Tim stunt.

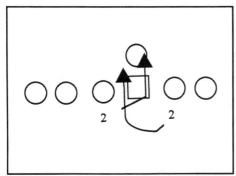

Diagram 4-57: Twist stunt.

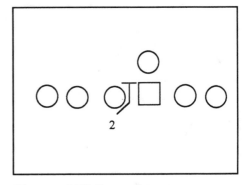

Diagram 4-58: Two or four stunt.

- Texas—A combination stunt with the defensive end. The defensive tackle slants outward as the defensive end dropsteps with his inside foot and dips his outside shoulder to go behind the defensive tackle. The letters in the name "Texas" have significance. "T" stands for tackle, "e" stands for end, and "x" for the crossing nature of the stunt. On a Texas stunt, the defensive tackle is responsible for containment. This stunt is an excellent stunt in pass situations. It may be called at the line of scrimmage during the offensive two-minute drill. A Texas is a strongside stunt; a Weak Texas is a weakside stunt; and a Double Texas involves both tackles and ends. A nose tackle may also run a Weak Texas as shown in Diagram 4-60.

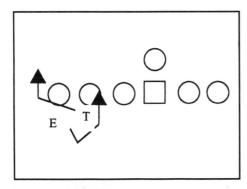

Diagram 4-59: Texas.

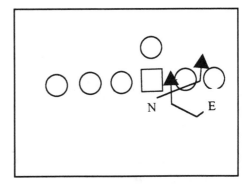

Diagram 4-60: Weak Texas (from nose).

- Toe—A combination tackle and end stunt. The defensive end runs a bingo stunt while the defensive tackle dropsteps with his outside foot and dips his inside shoulder to loop behind the defensive end. The letters of the name "Toe" have special significance. The "t" stands for "tackle," the "o" stands for "outside," and the "e" stands for "end"—"toe" equals "tackle outside end." The Toe stunt is a mirror of the Texas stunt. It is an excellent pass situation stunt. Like the Texas stunt, the Toe stunt may be called at the line of scrimmage during the two-minute drill. A nose tackle may also run a Weak Toe as shown in Diagram 4-62.

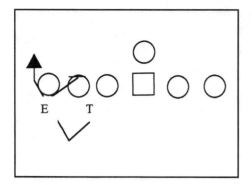

Diagram 4-61: Toe Stunt.

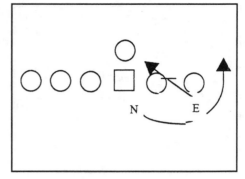

Diagram 4-62: Weak Toe (from nose).

- Now—A tackle slide stunt run from the 0 technique. The defensive nose tackle runs a weakside slide from the headup alignment. The letters of the word "now" have a significance. "No" stands for "nose" tackle, and "w" stands for "weak." The slide technique is detailed in the "Tim" stunt section.

- Now Slant—A "Now" stunt with a slant technique instead of a slide technique. The word "slant" added to the Nose call changes the slide of the Now call to a slant. The coaching points are identical to the "T" stunt. See the section on the "T" stunt for more details on slanting.

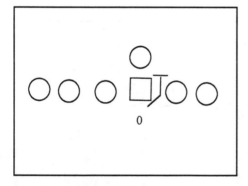

Diagram 4-63: Now stunt.

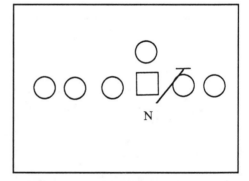

Diagram 4-64: Now Slant stunt.

- Nose—A tackle stunt run from the 0 technique. The defensive nose tackle runs a slide stunt to the strongside from a head-up alignment. The letters of the word "nose" have a special significance. "No" stands for "nose," and "s" stands for "strong."

- Nose Slant—A "Nose" stunt with a slant technique instead of a slide technique. The word "slant" added to the Nose call changes the slide of the Nose call to a slant. The coaching points are identical to the "T" stunt. See the section on the "T" stunt for more details on slanting.

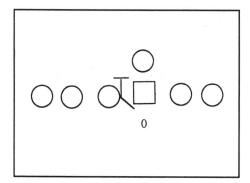

Diagram 4-65: Nose stunt.   **Diagram 4-66: Nose Slant stunt.**

- Wild—A weakside linebacker stunt through the gap for which the linebacker is primarily responsible. The weakside tackle runs a Tiger stunt from a shadow alignment. This combination tackle and linebacker stunt is usually run on passing downs.

- Sam—A strongside linebacker stunt through the gap for which the linebacker is primarily responsible. The strongside tackle runs a Tiger stunt from a shadow alignment. It is usually run in passing situations.

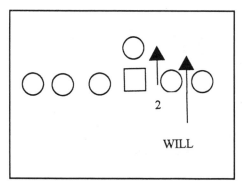
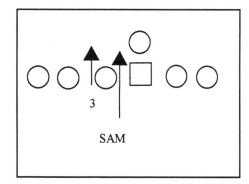

Diagram 4-67: Wild stunt.   **Diagram 4-68: Sam stunt.**

- Dog—A Dog stunt is a Wild and Sam stunt run together. Both tackles run Tiger stunts from the shadow alignment. The combination tackle and linebacker stunt is usually run in passing situations. The nose tackle will participate in a Dog as shown in Diagram 4-70.

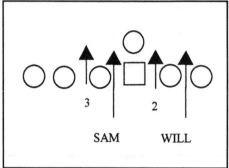

Diagram 4-69: Dog stunt.   **Diagram 4-70: Dog stunt (from nose).**

- Nose Sam Loop—The nose tackle runs a Nose stunt as the Sam linebacker loops through the weakside "A" gap.

- Now Will Loop—The nose tackle runs a Now stunt as the Will linebacker loops through the strongside "A" gap.

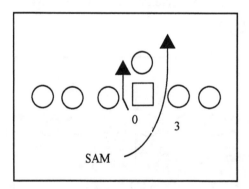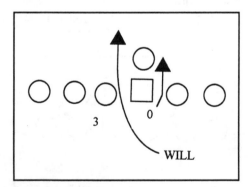

Diagram 4-71: Nose Sam Loop.   **Diagram 4-72: Now Will Loop.**

- Green—The Green call is not a stunt, rather, it is a defensive adjustment. When the defensive end who is aligned on the weakside recognizes a tight end, tight slot, or other third man outside of the tackle, he calls "green." The defensive end aligns in a 7 technique and runs a "blitz" stunt. The defensive tackle responds by sliding his alignment to a 1 technique and gap charging. The Will linebacker also adjusts his depth in accordance with the Green call game plan. A Green call is only made versus the weakside tight formation if the defensive tackle is originally aligned in a 0 technique.

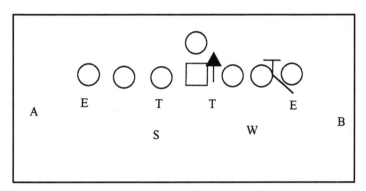

Diagram 4-73: Green adjustment.

CHAPTER 5

Defensive Ends

END CHARACTERISTICS

The Forty Nickel defensive end (DE) is either a fast tackle or a slower linebacker. We refer to him as the T-Rex of the defense. His role is to knock the tight end backward and ideally play both "C" and "D" gaps. His primary function is to turn back the offensive edge and allow the linebackers a downhill run at plays offtackle and wider.

Squat strength and bench strength are important factors in locating a defensive end. Bulk size is ideal along with height. The 40 speed for the high school defensive end should be under 5.2 seconds. The faster defensive end candidate is usually placed on the defensive right side.

END ALIGNMENT

The end's technique is determined by his near tackle's technique. If the defensive call is "32" and the strength is "Lou" (left), then the tackle will align in a 3 technique. The left end responds to the "Lou" by aligning in a 6 technique. The right end will respond to the right tackle's 2 technique by aligning in 7 technique.

END STANCE

Two-gap play from the defensive end is a trademark of the Forty Nickel base front. A defensive end aligned on the tight side will align in a three-point stance in order to more efficiently attack the "V."

The three-point defensive end should have his outside foot staggered behind the inside. A long stance is preferred with the back kept flat. It is desirable for the defensive end to possess sprinter's feel in his stance. The off hand should either be cocked near the knee or hanging loosely with the hand open. The eyes should focus on the screws of the blocker's facemask, but the ball is consciously kept in the peripheral vision, because the ball is the primary movement key. A three-point defensive end will attack the tight end or other third man set close to the formation.

Chart 5a: Defensive End Alignment Chart	
Tackle	End
0	Crotch 5 (depending upon ability, possibly a Shadow 5)
1	Crotch 7 (depending upon ability, possibly a Shadow 7)
2	Shade 7
3	6 (depending upon ability, possibly a Shade 7 tech.)
4	6
5	Crotch 9

Note: The defensive end aligned on the open end will align in a shadow or crotch 5 technique.

On the open side, the end will align in a two-point stance to key the triangle of the tackle, quarterback, and nearback. The feet may be staggered with the outside foot back in a four- to six-inch stagger. A forward lean of the torso is desired. The hands should be hanging loosely at the side of the quarterback. The defensive end should be light on his feet, similar to a boxer in the ring. He should have the "float like a butterfly, sting like a bee" mentality of the great boxer Muhammad Ali as he focuses on the big picture of the triangle.

Allowing a defensive end to stand in a two-point stance does not always receive a consensus by the staff. In many ways, the stance is a minor issue. The comfort and confidence of the player are more important to contemplate. If they do their job well, they can stand on their heads, although the coach may have some explaining to do at the next post-game press meeting.

END TECHNIQUE

The defensive end aligned on a blocker will have a staggered stance with the outside foot back about four inches. He will attack on the snap of the ball to either to the outside or inside "V" of the neck or the chin, depending on alignment technique. His responsibility is to create an offensive bubble at the edge of the offensive line by driving the tight end backward. Important to this concept is the throwing of the hands and separation with thumbs up. Shoulder pad leverage is least desired, especially at this position. The bench press technique coupled with driving legs is crucial to excellent end play.

As stated, the outside foot is back. The defensive end should contact the tight end after the third step. The first step with the outside foot is a maximum stride of four inches. The push foot, the inside foot pushes off and falls another four inches forward. The outside foot again power steps four inches. A total of twelve inches has been covered in three steps. It is most desirable for the defensive end to make contact on his third step and follow through the initial contact on his fourth step. Impossible? Yes, if there is not a daily commitment to drill, feedback and repetition of the footwork. Overcome the overstriding obstacle of defensive end play and your defensive ends will be the best in their area. Allow long, powerless strides and the defensive end will play like a wrestler with his feet in concrete, his feet stopping on contact with a narrow, elongated and unstable base. The power step movements are crucial to our scheme's success in playing two-gap control from the 6 technique. Without this footwork technique, we could not expect the defensive end to physically knock the end backward.

Should the defensive end be knocked back, creating a defensive bubble, the entire defensive front will be cutoff. (See defensive end guide sheet for details on technique responsibility against the various blocks.)

END STUNTS

BINGO	(Be Inside & Go) slant inside.
BLITZ	(Be Inside) slide inside.
BLUE	(Be Loose Upfield) slide outside.
BLOOD	(Be Loose Outside Of D gap). Align two yards outside end and run a lightning/lance (see OLB stunts).
BUT	(Be Upfield, make Tackle, put QB on his butt). Align one yard outside and rush two yards upfield on snap to get a jump on QB drop.

END COMBINATION STUNTS

CLUTCH	Means the DE will guard the TE on any vertical route.
CRASH	Means ends run bingo with OLB lightning (strong, weak, double).
DOG	(Linebacker stunt) means both DE's will run a BLUE.
GREEN	(Not called in huddle) an adjustment, means to run a BLITZ.
ME	(Not called in huddle) an adjustment, means to run a BLITZ.
STRONG BLUE LIGHTNING	(OLB) Means the strong DE will run a BLUE, OLB goes first.
STRONG BLUE THUNDER	(OLB) means the strong DE will run a BLUE, DE goes first.
TEXAS	A combination stunt with the tackles, means to dropstep and rush through "B" gap (only to 3-technique side).
TOE	A combination stunt with the tackles, means to run a BINGO (strong, weak, double).
WEAK BLUE LIGHTNING	(OLB) means the weak DE runs a BLUE, OLB goes first.
WEAK BLUE THUNDER	(OLB) means the weak DE runs a BLUE, DE goes 1st.
WILL	(Linebacker stunt) DE weakside runs a BLUE if in 5 technique.
YOU	(Not called in huddle) a reminder, means the ILB is running a stunt inside.

FIVE TECHNIQUE

The 5 technique is the base alignment of the weakside defensive end when he is aligned on the side of the open end. The 5 technique defensive end aligns in a crotch 5 technique but may loosen his alignment to a shadow 5 technique. The more talent and skill that a defensive end demonstrates in his play, the tighter his alignment may be. A defensive tackle may also play a 5 technique, but only on the 50 series fronts. The defensive tackle plays a shade alignment on the offensive tackle. The pass rush responsibility of a 5 technique differs from that of the 5-technique defensive end. The defensive end will usually pass rush with contain responsibility while the defensive tackle will push the middle through the "B" gap.

- Base Block—The 5 technique attacks the outside "V" and squeezes the blocker while keeping his shoulders parallel and his outside arm free.

- Cutoff Block—The 5 technique attacks the outside "V" of the tackle while keeping his outside shoulder free. He keeps his shoulders square and squeezes down the line of scrimmage to pursue the ballcarrier. If a tight end is aligned to his side, the 5 technique wishes to keep that tight end from cutting him off from the backside pursuit.

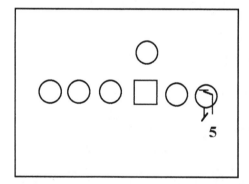

Diagram 5-1.

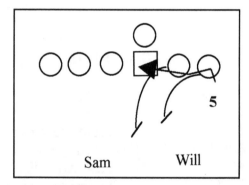

Diagram 5-2.

- Double Team Block—The 5 technique may be double-teamed by the tackle in conjunction with a slotback or tight end. He should attack the tackle (i.e., the post blocker) and hook his outside arm under the inside knee of the tight end or slotback while dipping his outside shoulder. He attempts to get his outside hip on the ground, make a pile, and pursue laterally to the outside. The 5 technique should always keep his feet churning to split the double team.

- Down Block—The 5 technique attacks the tackle. The down block is executed by the third blocker (e.g., the tight end or slotback). The 5 technique dips the outside shoulder and pursues behind the down blocker. An alternative technique is to cross the face of the down blocker. The appropriate technique is dependent upon the landmark of the blocker and the speed of recognition of the 5 technique. The 5 technique should dip and run around the down block only if the blocker overextends his landmark.

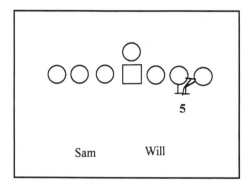

Diagram 5-3.

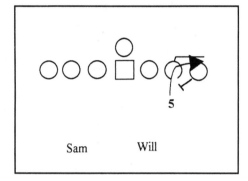

Diagram 5-4.

- Dropback Pass—The 5 technique attacks the outside "V" of the offensive tackle and uses a speed rush technique after getting three yards upfield. If the offensive tackle overextends on his pass protection set, the 5 technique may dip and rip underneath. A primary consideration of the 5 technique when pass rushing is to maintain outside leverage on the quarterback.

- Hinge Pass Block—The 5 technique pass rushes the quarterback. He trails the quarterback no deeper than one yard behind the level of the quarterback.

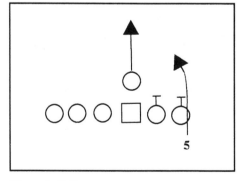

Diagram 5-5.

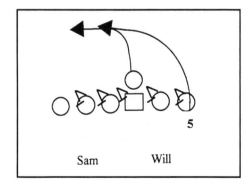

Diagram 5-6.

- Influence Block—The 5 technique attacks the outside "V" of the tackle. As the tackle sets and blocks out, the 5 technique throws his eyes inside to check for a trap blocker. As he recognizes the trap, the 5 technique attacks the trapping guard. His objective is to place the outside shoulder to the inside knee of the blocker.

- Inside Block—The 5 technique attacks the outside "V" of the tackle and squeezes in response to the target moving inside. He uses his hands to keep the tackle off the linebacker and attacks the trapper with his outside shoulder to the inside knee of the blocker.

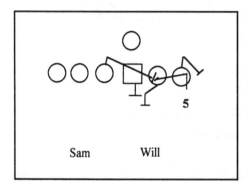

Diagram 5-7.

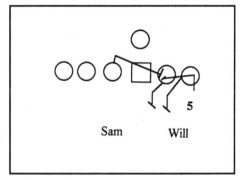

Diagram 5-8.

- Load Block—The 5 technique attacks the outside "V" of the tackle and closes the "B" gap as the tackle blocks inside. He comes off the hip of the offensive tackle as he focuses in the backfield to seek out the first threat. He reads the angle of the first threat (i.e., load blocker). Recognizing the load angle, the 5 technique attacks the load blocker while keeping his outside arm free. His objective is to force the contact deep in the backfield and make the quarterback run the bubble around the pile created by the contact. Ideally, the 5 technique keeps his outside arm free to sweep for the feet of the quarterback as he breaks outside of the load block.

- Reach Block—The 5 technique attacks the outside "V" of the tackle and stalemates his block. The defensive tackle attempts to maintain outside leverage and pursue laterally down the line of scrimmage.

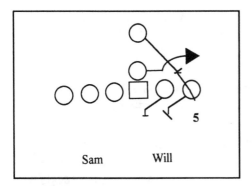

Diagram 5-9.

Diagram 5-10.

- Trey Block—The 5 technique attacks the outside "V" of the tackle and looks through to the backfield for a key to the quarterback bootleg. The 5 technique plays the bootleg unless he sees the ball handed off to a running back. If the ball is handed off to a running back, the 5 technique gets into the hip pocket of the pulling tackle. If a fullback attempts to block back on the 5 technique, the 5 technique uses the wrong shoulder technique to attack the fullback and cross his face to pursue the ballcarrier.

- Turnback Block—The 5 technique gains depth into the backfield and attacks the blocking back by focusing his vision on the headgear of the blocker. He drops his hands low to the ground and works upfield while keeping his outside arm free. The 5 technique keeps the quarterback in his peripheral vision so that he may maintain outside leverage on the quarterback.

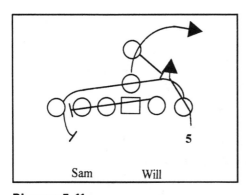

Diagram 5-11.

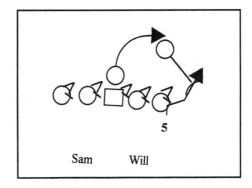

Diagram 5-12.

- Veer Block—The 5 technique attacks the outside "V" of the tackle and gets his eyes inside while throwing his hands to flatten the path of the offensive tackle. He comes off the hip of the inside block of the tackle and attacks the diveback while keeping his outside arm free. His objective is to wreck the mesh point by tackling the diveback with outside leverage, sweeping his outside arm for the legs of the quarterback as he pulls the ball on the veer option.

- Zone Block—The 5 technique's objective is to ride the block of the tackle and keep him from working to the second level. The zone block is defeated in exactly the same manner as the reach block. The 5 technique stalemates the tackle and pursues the ballcarrier by sliding down the line of scrimmage.

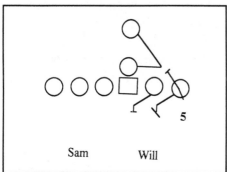

Diagram 5-13.

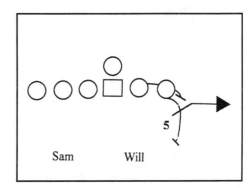

Diagram 5-14.

SEVEN TECHNIQUE

The 7 technique is responsible for the "C" gap. Although responsible for the same gap as the outside shade 5 technique, the 7 technique is an inside shade on the third man. The third man on which the 7 technique aligns is usually a tight end; however, the third man could also be an extra tackle aligned to that side or a slotback aligned off the line of scrimmage. The 7 technique is the only inside read technique regularly played in the Forty Nickel base package. The most common shade specification of the 7 technique is the tighter shade alignment. Defensive ends who are less talented or less physical and who may have greater difficulty in anchoring the "C" gap should use the more gap-conscious crotch or shadow alignment. In the Forty Nickel, only the defensive ends play a 7 technique. The 7 technique is played by the defensive end when his corresponding defensive tackle aligns in a 1 or 2 technique.

- Arc Block—If no dive threat exists, the defensive end widens the block of the tight end and sinks one yard off the line of scrimmage to slow-play the option. If a dive threat does exist, the defensive end tackles the diveback with outside leverage.

- Base Block—The defensive end attacks the inside "V" of the tight end while looking inside through the "C" gap. He anchors the "C" gap, but controls the blocker so that he is able to cross the face of the base blocker, should the ballcarrier bounce outside.

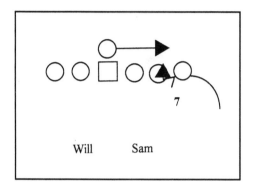

Diagram 5-15.

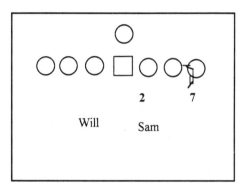

Diagram 5-16.

- Cutoff Block—The defensive end attacks the inside "V" of the tight end while looking inside through the "C" gap. He attempts to keep his inside arm free as he slides inside while keeping his shoulders parallel to the line of scrimmage. He is vigilant for the reverse or bootleg as he shuffles down the line of scrimmage. Once no threat of reverse or bootleg exists, the defensive end pursues on the proper path.

- Double Team Block—The defensive end attacks the post blocker (i.e., end) and dips the shoulder closest to the lead blocker (i.e., tackle). He hooks the lead blocker's outside leg with his inside arm. He makes a pile while churning his feet so that he may split the double team and rise to his feet to pursue the ballcarrier.

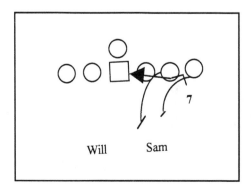

Diagram 5-17.

Diagram 5-18.

- Dropback Pass Block—The defensive tackle pushes the middle, using either the rip or swim technique to clear the blocker. He pressures the quarterback with at least one arm up, and tackles the quarterback using a drape technique.

- F or H Block—The defensive end attacks the inside "V" of the tight end while looking inside through the "C" gap. He throws his hands to flatten the tight end and uses his outside shoulder to attack the kick-out blocker.

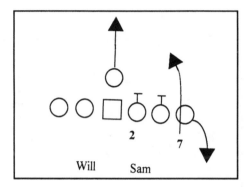

Diagram 5-19.

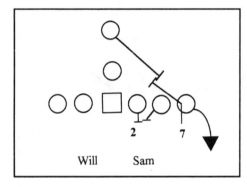

Diagram 5-20.

- G Block—The defensive end attacks the inside "V" of the tight end while looking inside through the "C" gap. He throws his hands to the tight end to flatten his path and attacks the guard. He places his outside pad to the inside knee of the pulling guard while attempting to keep his shoulders nearly parallel to the line of scrimmage.

- Hinge Pass Block—The defensive end pass rushes the quarterback. He trails the quarterback no deeper than one yard behind the level of the quarterback.

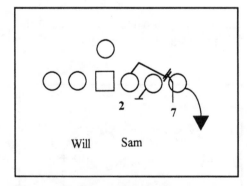

Diagram 5-21.

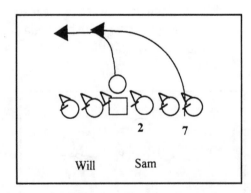

Diagram 5-22.

- Influence Block—The defensive end attacks the inside "V" of the tight end while looking inside through the "C" gap. He throws his hands to the tight end to flatten his path and attacks the guard. As he recognizes the trap, the 5 technique attacks the trapping guard. His objective is to place the outside shoulder to the inside knee of the blocker.

- Load Block—The defensive end attacks the inside "V" of the tight end while looking inside through the "C" gap. He reads the angle of the first threat, (i.e., load blocker). Recognizing the load angle, the 5 technique attacks the load blocker while keeping his outside arm free. His objective is to force the contact deep in the backfield and make the quarterback run the bubble around the pile created by the contact. Ideally, the 5 technique keeps his outside arm free to sweep for the feet of the quarterback as he breaks outside of the load block.

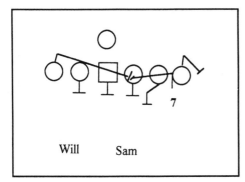

Diagram 5-23.

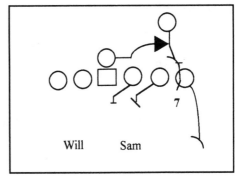

Diagram 5-24.

- Out Block—The defensive end attacks the inside "V" of the tight end while looking inside through the "C" gap. He stretches the release of the tight end. On recognition of the out block of the tackle, he attacks the tackle using the wrong shoulder technique. He should not run around the out block of the tackle.

- Trey Block—The defensive end attacks the inside "V" of the tight end while looking inside through to the backfield for a key to the quarterback bootleg. The defensive end plays the bootleg unless he sees the ball handed off to a running back. If the ball is handed off to a running back, the 5 technique gets into the hip pocket of the pulling tackle. If a fullback attempts to block back on the 5 technique, the defensive end uses the wrong shoulder technique to attack the fullback and cross his face to pursue the ballcarrier.

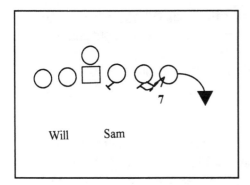

Will   Sam

Diagram 5-25.

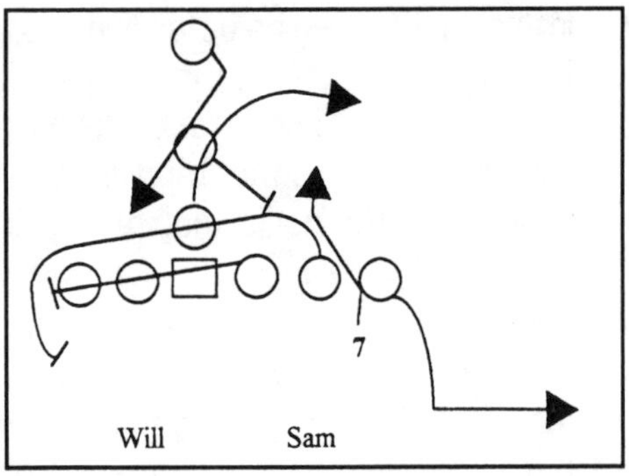

Will   Sam

Diagram 5-26.

- Turnback Block—After widening the release of the tight end, the defensive end gains depth into the backfield and attacks the blocking back by focusing his vision on the headgear of the blocker. He drops his hands low to the ground and works upfield while keeping his outside arm free. The defensive end keeps his quarterback in his peripheral vision so that he may maintain outside leverage on the quarterback.

- Veer Block—The defensive end attacks the inside "V" of the tight end and gets his eyes inside while throwing his hands to flatten the path of the tight end. He attacks the diveback while keeping his outside arm free. His objective is to wreck the mesh point by tackling the diveback with outside leverage—sweeping his outside arm for the legs of the quarterback as he pulls the ball on the veer option.

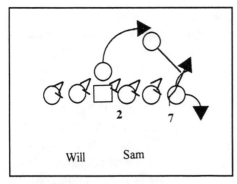

Will   Sam

Diagram 5-27.

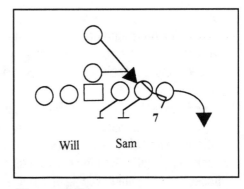

Will   Sam

Diagram 5-28.

- Zone Block—The defensive end's objective is to stretch the block of the tight end by using his hands. He reads the zone scheme of the interior linemen and the outside path of the running back. He stalemates the tight end and pursues the ballcarrier by sliding down the line of scrimmage.

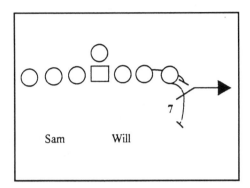

Diagram 5-29.

SIX TECHNIQUE

The 6-technique defensive end attacks the chin of the tight end. This technique is played from a toe-to-toe headup alignment. In order to play the 6 technique, the defensive end must be physically strong while exhibiting a dominating style of play versus the average tight end. If such a player does not exist at the defensive end, the recommended replacement technique is the 7 technique. The 6 technique is a two-gap control player with a primary responsibility of anchoring the "C" gap. Forty Nickel defensive ends play a 6 technique when the defensive tackle plays a 3 or 4 technique. Six technique play versus the various blocks is described below along with detailed diagrams showing the appropriate response.

- Arc block—The defensive end attacks the chin and responds to the arc block by throwing the hands into the tight end. He sinks two steps off the line of scrimmage if he reads option. If he reads a kick-out block by the nearback, then the arc block is a false key. He attacks the nearback using the wrong shoulder technique. If there is no kick-out threat and the ball is moving down the line of scrimmage, the defensive end extends his inside arm, drops his outside foot, and slowly shuffles outward. He takes care to keep his shoulders parallel to the line of scrimmage.

- Base block—The defensive end attacks the chin of the tight end and maintains outside leverage. He squeezes the turn-out block of the tight end. Keeping his shoulders square, the defensive end closes off the "C" gap and forces the ballcarrier to bounce outward or cut back. If the ball is moving down the line of scrimmage on the option, the defensive end defeats the blocker and takes the quarterback.

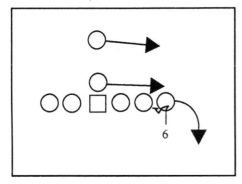

Diagram 5-30: Arc block.

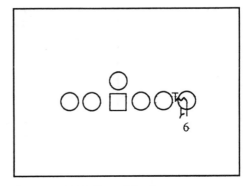

Diagram 5-31: Base block.

- Cut block—The defensive end attacks the chin of the tight end and flattens the path of the tight end's release. He attacks the blocker by focusing his eyes on the headgear of the blocker, seeing the quarterback in his secondary line of sight. He must work upfield while maintaining outside leverage.

- Cutoff block—The defensive end attacks the chin of the tight end and responds to the blocker by squeezing down the line of scrimmage. He keeps his shoulders parallel and looks for bootleg or reverse as he shuffles to the center area. Once no threat exists of bootleg or reverse, the defensive end takes a proper pursuit angle to the ballcarrier.

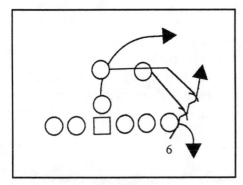

Diagram 5-32: Cut block.

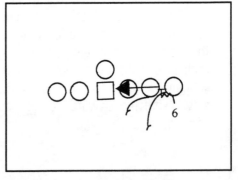

Diagram 5-33: Cutoff block.

- Double Team block—The defensive end attacks the tight end and dips to his outside hip. He gets to the ground by dropping his outside shoulder and twisting his upper body to the inside, thus reducing the blocking surface available to the lead blocker from the outside.

- Dropback Pass—The defensive end attacks the tight end to delay his release. He rushes the quarterback while maintaining outside leverage on the quarterback. Versus an inside release, the defensive end must be especially tough—he delays the tight end's release and widens his pass rush angle in order to regain outside leverage.

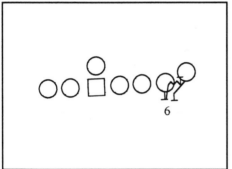

Diagram 5-34: Double Team block.   **Diagram 5-35: Dropback Pass block.**

- F or H block—The defensive end attacks the blocker with his outside shoulder to the inside knee of the blocker.

- G block—The defensive end attacks the guard. He places his outside shoulder to the inside knee of the pulling guard.

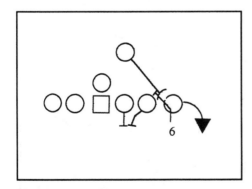 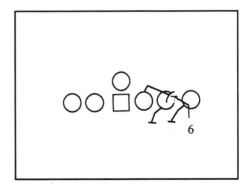

Diagram 5-36: F or H block.   **Diagram 5-37: G block.**

- Hinge block—The defensive end trails the quarterback no deeper than one yard behind the level of the quarterback.

- Influence block—The defensive end attacks the tight end. Upon recognition of the set by the tight end, the defensive end gets his eyes inside and recognizes the trap. He attacks the pulling blocker by putting his outside shoulder to the inside knee of the trapper.

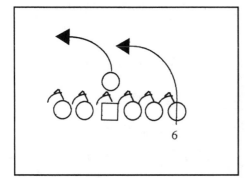

Diagram 5-38: Hinge block.   **Diagram 5-39: Influence block.**

- Load block—The defensive end stretches the release of the tight end and shifts his line of sight to the inside. He diagnoses the action of the triangle of the ball, the nearback and the blocker. Upon recognition of the load angle of the nearback, he attacks the back while keeping his outside arm free. He forces the quarterback to bubble around the pile and/or tackles the quarterback.

- Reach block—The defensive end attacks the chin of the tight end and pushes him upfield. He maintains a tight outside leverage on the blocker. He does not "float" outside, rather, he gains ground into the backfield as he works to keep outside leverage. He forces the ballcarrier to run the hump around the bubble.

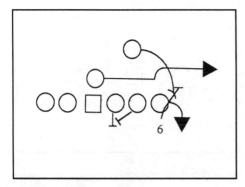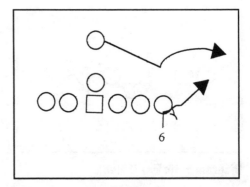

Diagram 5-40: Load block.   **Diagram 5-41: Reach block.**

- Trey block—The defensive end trails the offensive tackle, keeping outside leverage while checking the quarterback for bootleg. He attacks the fullback's block to keep him from slipping out into the flat. If he sees the ball handed to the tailback, the defensive end may wrong shoulder the fullback and pursue flat down the line of scrimmage.

- Veer block—The defensive end attacks the chin and flattens the path of the tight end. He physically closes the "C" gap and keeps his shoulders parallel to the line of scrimmage. His primary responsibility is to keep the tight end from reaching the linebacker. He attacks the diveback and wrecks the mesh point, keeping his outside arm free to sweep for the feet of the quarterback as the quarterback reads pull and comes off the mesh.

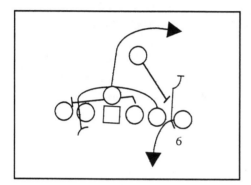

Diagram 5-42: Trey block.

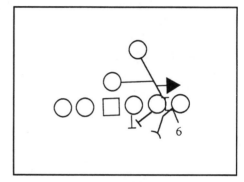

Diagram 5-43: Veer block.

- Zone block—The defensive end stretches the block of the tight end and pursues down the line of scrimmage. The zone block is successfully played by using the technique of defeating the reach block. Zone blocks may be expected when facing one-back sets in the offensive backfield.

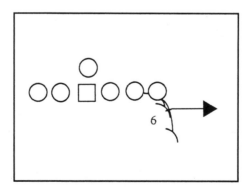

Diagram 5-44: Zone block.

NINE TECHNIQUE

The 9 technique defensive end attacks the outside "V" of the tight end. The base 9 technique is played from a crotch alignment, but may be played from a shade or shadow alignment. The 9 technique anchors the "D" gap. Forty Nickel defensive ends play a 9 technique when the defensive tackle plays a 5 technique. An outside linebacker plays a 9 technique on the Squeeze call. The 9 technique responsibilities and the coaching points for the two positions are identical with the difference being that the outside linebacker plays only a shadow 9 technique. Nine technique defensive end play versus the various blocks is described below, along with detailed diagrams showing the appropriate response.

- Arc block—The defensive end attacks outside the "V" and responds to the arc block by throwing the hands into the tight end. He sinks two steps off the line of scrimmage if he reads option. If he reads a kick-out block by the nearback, then the arc block is a false key. He attacks the nearback using the wrong shoulder technique. If there is no kick-out threat and the ball is moving down the line of scrimmage, the defensive end extends his inside arm, drops his outside foot, and slowly shuffles outward. He takes care to keep his shoulders parallel to the line of scrimmage.

- Base block—The defensive end attacks the outside "V" of the tight end and maintains outside leverage. He squeezes the turn-out block of the tight end. Keeping his shoulders square, the defensive end closes off the "C" gap and forces the ballcarrier to bounce outward or cut back. If the ball is moving down the line of scrimmage on the option, the defensive end defeats the blocker and takes the quarterback.

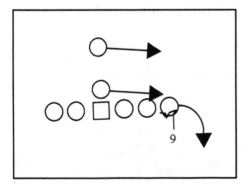

Diagram 5-45: Arc block.

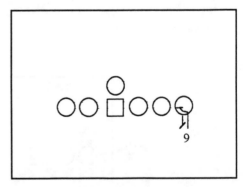

Diagram 5-46: Base block.

- Cut block—The defensive end attacks the outside "V" of the tight end and flattens the path of the tight end's release. He attacks the blocker by focusing his eyes on the headgear of the blocker, seeing the quarterback in his secondary line of sight. He must work upfield while maintaining outside leverage.

- Cutoff block—The defensive end attacks the outside "V" of the tight end and responds to the blocker by squeezing down the line of scrimmage. He keeps his shoulders parallel and looks for bootleg or reverse as he shuffles to the center area. Once no threat of bootleg or reverse exists, the defensive end takes a proper pursuit angle to the ballcarrier.

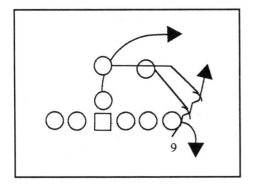

Diagram 5-47: Cut block.

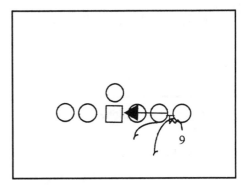

Diagram 5-48: Cutoff block.

- Double Team block—The defensive end attacks the outside "V" of the tight end and dips to his outside hip. He gets to the ground by dropping his outside shoulder and twisting his upper body to the inside, thus reducing the blocking surface available to the lead blocker from the outside.

- Dropback Pass—The defensive end attacks the outside "V" of the tight end to delay his release. He rushes the quarterback while maintaining outside leverage on the quarterback. Versus an inside release, the defensive end must be especially tough—he delays the tight end's release and widens his pass rush angle in order to regain outside leverage.

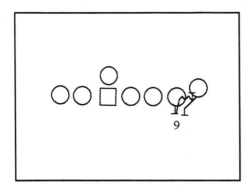

Diagram 5-49: Double Team block.

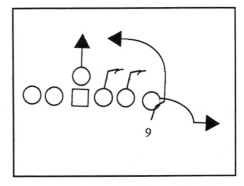

Diagram 5-50: Dropback Pass block.

- F or H block—The defensive end attacks the blocker with his outside shoulder to the inside knee of the blocker.

- G block—The defensive end attacks the guard. He places his outside shoulder to the inside knee of the pulling guard.

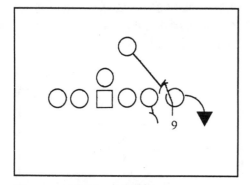

Diagram 5-51: F or H block.

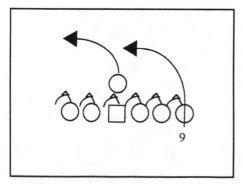

Diagram 5-52: G block.

- Hinge block—The defensive end trails the quarterback no deeper than one yard behind the level of the quarterback.

- Load block—The defensive end stretches the release of the tight end and shifts his line of sight to the inside. He diagnoses the action of the triangle of ball, nearback and blocker. Upon recognition of the load angle of the nearback, he attacks the back while keeping his outside arm free. He forces the quarterback to bubble around the pile and/or tackles the quarterback.

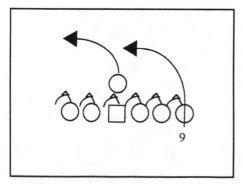

Diagram 5-53: Hinge block.

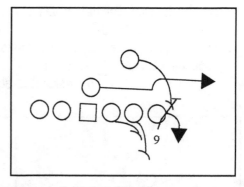

Diagram 5-54: Load block.

- Reach block—The defensive end attacks the outside "V" of the tight end and pushes him upfield. He maintains a tight outside leverage on the blocker. He does not "float" outside; rather, he gains ground into the backfield as he works to keep outside leverage. He forces the ballcarrier to run the hump around the bubble.

- Trey block—The defensive end trails the offensive tackle, keeping outside leverage while checking the quarterback for bootleg. He attacks the fullback's block to keep him from slipping out into the flat. If he sees the ball handed to the tailback, the defensive end may wrong shoulder the fullback and pursue flat down the line of scrimmage.

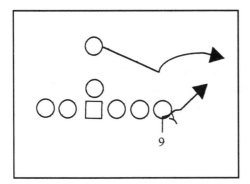

Diagram 5-55: Reach block.

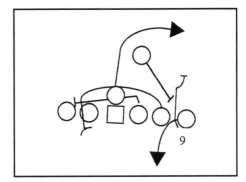

Diagram 5-56: Trey block.

- Veer block—The defensive end attacks the outside "V" and flattens the path of the tight end. He physically closes the "C" gap and keeps his shoulders parallel to the line of scrimmage. His primary responsibility is to keep the tight end from reaching the linebacker. He attacks the diveback and wrecks the mesh point, keeping his outside arm free to sweep for the feet of the quarterback as the quarterback reads pull and comes off the mesh.

- Zone block—The defensive end stretches the block of the tight end and pursues down the line of scrimmage. The zone block is successfully played by using the technique of defeating the reach block. Zone blocks may be expected when facing one-back sets in the offensive backfield.

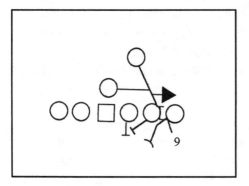

Diagram 5-57: Veer block.

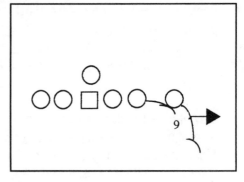

Diagram 5-58: Zone block.

DEFENSIVE END STUNTS

Defensive end stunt names begin with the letter "b." Combination defensive end stunts and defensive end adjustments may not begin with the letter "b." As with all stunts, the stunt is a strongside stunt if neither the word "weak" nor "double" precedes the stunt name. Defensive stunts are run from various techniques. A list of the Forty Nickel defensive end stunts along with the specific coaching points and their illustration follows.

- Bingo—An inside slant to the hip of the tackle. The letters of the name "Bingo" have specific meaning. "B" stands for the defensive end stunt, "i" for "inside," and "go" for "go." "Bingo" means " end inside—go." The coaching points of the slant stunt are discussed in more detail in the tackle stunt section of this text.

- Blitz—An inside slide to the aiming point. The aiming point of the slide is no deeper than six inches behind the tackle's stance. The coaching points of the slide stunt are discussed in more detail in the tackle stunt section of this text.

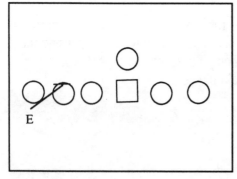

Diagram 5-59: Bingo stunt.

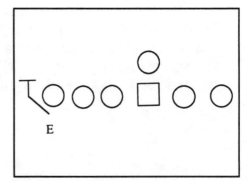

Diagram 5-60: Blue stunt.

- Blue—An outside slide to the aiming point. The aiming point is one yard outside the end man of the formation and one yard deep in the backfield. The letters and sounds of the name have special significance. "B" stands for the defensive end stunts "l" for "loose," "u" for "upfield," and "e" to remind the end to stunt outside of the "D" gap.

- Blue Spy—A wide slide to the outside. The aiming point of a Blue Spy is two yards outside the end man of the formation and two yards deep in the backfield. The primary responsibility of the Blue Spy stunting end is to take the option pitch and play the screen pass. The name "Blue" has the same significance as in the Blue stunt. "Spy" implies that the end should play cautious as he is spying to defend the screen.

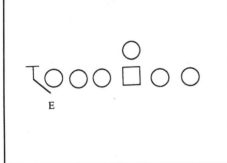

Diagram 5-61: Blue stunt.   **Diagram 5-62: Blue Spy stunt.**

- But—An upfield charge from a loose alignment. The stunting end aligns one yard outside the last man of the formation and charges to a point two yards upfield on the snap. Upon reaching that point, he finds the ball. The letters of the name have a special significance. "B" stands for the end stunt, "u" for "upfield" and "t" for "tackle" the quarterback. Another more humorous meaning of the stunt name that the athletes deem more descriptive of the stunt's intention is "knock the quarterback on his 'but'."

- Blue Lightning—A diagonal stunt to the head of the fullback by the outside linebacker in combination with a Blue stunt by the defensive end. See the outside linebacker section for more information on the Lightning stunt.

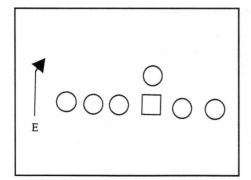

Diagram 5-63: But stunt.

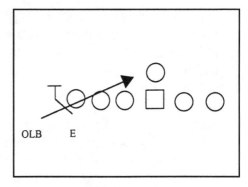

Diagram 5-64: Lightning stunt.

- Blue Thunder—An underneath looping stunt by the outside linebacker in combination with a Blue stunt by the defensive end. See the outside linebacker section for more information on the Thunder stunt.

- Crash—A combination of an outside linebacker Lightning stunt and a defensive end Bingo stunt.

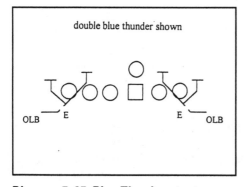

Diagram 5-65: Blue Thunder stunt.

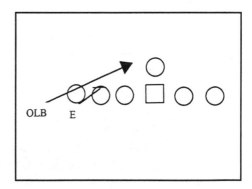

Diagram 5-66: Crash stunt.

- Double Blue Dog—A combination stunt in which both defensive ends run a Blue stunt while the two inside linebackers run a Dog stunt.

- Texas—A combination stunt in which the defensive end runs an underneath looping stunt as the tackle drives outside in front of the defensive end. For more details on the Texas stunt, see the tackle stunt section.

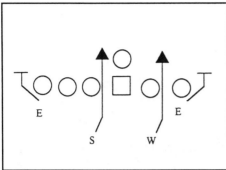

Diagram 5-67: Double Blue Dog stunt.

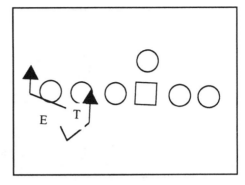

Diagram 5-68: Texas stunt.

- Toe—A combination stunt in which the defensive end runs a Bingo while the tackle loops behind the defensive end. For more details on the Toe stunt, see the tackle stunt section.

- Green—An adjustment of the defensive end technique. The defensive end calls "green" when a weakside tight flank (i.e., a weakside tight end, slotback, tackle over) exists and the defensive call resulted in the weakside tackle being aligned in a 0 technique (e.g., 20, 30, 40, or 50 front). The defensive end runs a Blitz stunt on a Green call. For more details on the Green call, see the defensive tackle stunt section.

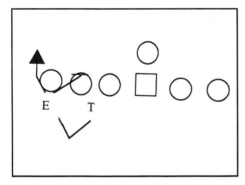

Diagram 5-69: Toe stunt.

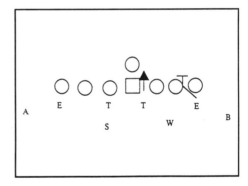

Diagram 5-70: Green adjustment.

- Squeeze—A defensive call usually received in the huddle. The Squeeze call can also be an alternative adjustment to the Green call versus a weakside tight flank. The defensive end aligns in a crotch 5 technique on a Squeeze call. When made in the huddle, "Squeeze" is a strongside alignment, "Weak Squeeze" is a weakside alignment, and "Double Squeeze" refers to both defensive ends. When called on the field as an adjustment, "Squeeze" refers only to the weakside. The outside linebacker to the side of a Squeeze aligns in a shadow 9 technique.

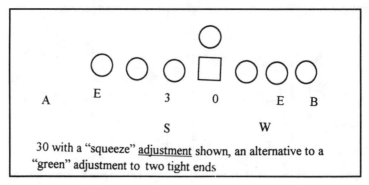

Diagram 5-71: Squeeze adjustment.

- Me—A defensive field call. If the linebacker makes a "me" call, the defensive end runs a blitz stunt from his 5-technique alignment.

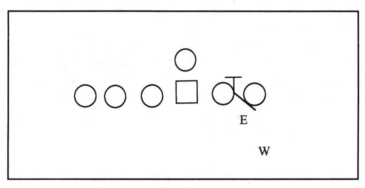

Diagram 5-72: "Me" call by linebacker.

- You—The antithesis of the "me" field call. If the linebacker makes a "you" call, the defensive end has containment responsibility. A less talented defensive end may respond to the "you" call by widening his alignment or even running a Blue stunt.

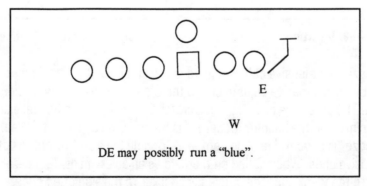

Diagram 5-73: "You" call by linebacker.

Outside Linebackers—Antler and Brave

INTERPRETATION OF BALL LEVEL AND FLOW

The ball moves through one of three levels: level one, level two, and level three. The direction of the ball is identified as either toward the respective defensive player or away from the defensive player. Direction is also known as flow (see the section on ball level identification).

Level-one ball action is a running play. The ball movement obtains level-one status if it moves down the line of scrimmage outside of the area behind the offensive tackle. The area behind the tackle is known as the tackle box. Level-one action—ball movement down the line of scrimmage outside the tackle box—will have a direction of toward the outside linebacker or away from the outside linebacker.

Level-two ball action is most often a sprint-out pass or roll-out pass. The quarterback rolls out to a point behind the tackle box or beyond. Level-two ball action will have a direction of either toward the outside linebacker or away from the outside linebacker. A ball moving down the line of scrimmage which has not moved outside the tackle box is also considered level-two action by the deep *zone coverage* personnel (man-to-man defenders do not presnap key the ball). For short zone defenders on the perimeter, the ball moving down the line of scrimmage inside the tackle box is a "no-level" read.

A "no-level" read means that the ball movement has not yet reached an identifiable level for the appropriate defensive reaction. The short zone defenders use this window of opportunity during the "no-level" action to jam receivers, read routes, or read other clues to the developing play.

Level-three ball action is a dropback pass. No ball direction or flow exists on level-three ball movement.

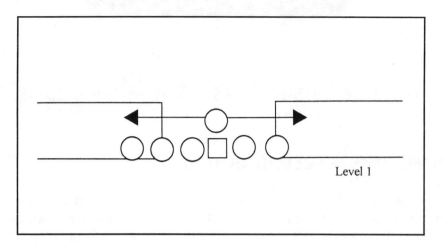

Diagram 6-1.

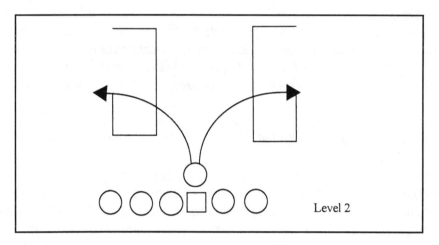

Diagram 6-2.

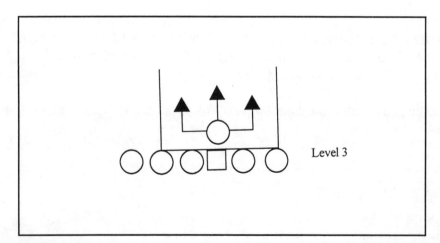

Diagram 6-3.

PERSONNEL CHARACTERISTICS

The outside linebacker is a linebacker-defensive back hybrid. A high school outside linebacker may run the forty-yard dash in 4.8 to 5.1 seconds. Agility is important at this position.

The benchmark from which an outside linebacker is selected includes the following abilities: the ability to defeat blockers both from the backfield and offensive line, the ability to cover running backs in a man-to-man scheme, the ability to disrupt the pass routes of wide receivers, the ability to play a defensive end shadow 9 technique, and the ability to read ball levels and pass routes. The outside linebacker must be an excellent tackler who is not afraid of attacking and funneling the sweep and other plays. Most quoted by coaches in discussing outside linebacker characteristics is the need for the outside linebacker to demonstrate a "recklessness under control" in his outside linebacker technique. The best outside linebacker is a usually a big-hitter who can run and who loves to play the game.

To be sure, the outside linebacker position is no place for the least athletic personnel on the team. Without aggressive, mobile, head-hunting people at the outside linebacker position, the Forty Nickel package will be immeasurably undermined. Ideally, the coach should search for two outside linebackers capable of performing the tasks required of both outside linebacker positions.

DESIGNATION

There are two outside linebackers in the Forty Nickel Defense. The outside linebacker who aligns with the defensive front call is named Antler. The outside linebacker who aligns opposite Antler is named Brave.

DECLARATION RULE

Brave is given no specific alignment instructions in regard to the declaration other than to align opposite Antler. This rule eliminates Antler and Brave aligning to the same side through a misinterpretation of the offensive formation presented.

Following the huddle break, the SAM yells "Ray" if the strength declaration is to the defensive right. "The SAM yells "Lou" if the strength declaration is to the defensive left. Other players along the defensive front will echo the call in acknowledgment of the call. The most common declaration rule which SAM uses is the declaration to the tight end, the "y" receiver.

Antler will declare his alignment with SAM's call. If the call is "Ray," Antler will align to the defensive right. If the call is "Lou," Antler will align to the defensive left. As mentioned earlier in the text, Brave aligns opposite Antler.

ALIGNMENT

The outside linebacker may align in several positions. As a member of the secondary corps, the outside linebacker aligns in a S1, S2 or 8 technique. As a member of the linebacker corps, the outside linebacker aligns in a crotch 9 technique, a stacked 50-gap technique, or even (in special circumstances) a 00 technique. Of all the positions in the Forty Nickel package, the outside linebacker has the most varied assignment possibilities.

STANCE

The outside linebacker aligns in one of three stances:

- the S1 technique stance

- the S2 technique stance

- the 8 technique stance

While playing a S1 technique, the outside linebacker will have a backpedaling stance *if* he has to cover a second receiver. If the does not have a second receiver to cover, the outside linebacker assumes his usual 8 technique stance. An outside linebacker may also use a S2 technique stance and an inside linebacker stance.

In the stance of a S1 technique, the feet are close together with the weight on the balls of the feet. The heels are off the ground while the feet point forward. No pronounced stagger of the feet exists. The shoulders are parallel to the line of scrimmage and the torso leans forward so that the shoulders are over the toes. The hands hang loosely outside the thighs.

The stance of a S2 and 8 technique are identical. The feet are set shoulder width apart, but turned in to the formation or the receiver to put the body at a forty-five-degree angle to the formation. The weight is firmly on the balls of the feet with a slight heel raise of each foot. The torso leans forward slightly as the athlete bends forward at the waist. The hands hang loosely outside the thighs.

The inside linebacker stance sets the feet close together. The toes are placed on an even horizontal plane. The weight should be slightly forward with only a slight heel raise. The torso bend is more pronounced than the secondary techniques so that the shoulders are low.

The hands hang loosely just outside the knees. The inside linebacker stance is used when the linebacker is playing a "Stack" defensive alignment using a 50-gap technique. The inside linebacker stance is also used on the rare occasion of playing a 00 technique against an empty set formation.

Stance variations are a key coaching point. By varying the stance for certain tasks, we reinforce the differences of one technique assignment from another. The physical act of assuming the proper stance is like the string on a finger; it helps the athlete remember his initial movement requirement and his responsibilities. The stance is closely linked to the assignment. For this reason, the staff continually reinforces the proper elements of each technique stance and does not allow a player to exhibit a poor stance.

OUTSIDE LINEBACKER ASSIGNMENT

The outside linebacker's primary role is determined by one of three factors:

- The front call—if the front call has the word "squeeze," "hold" or "stack" incorporated in the call, the outside linebacker's assignment is affected.

- An outside linebacker stunt call—follows the front call, as in "30 Lightning."

- The secondary call—the outside linebacker has specific roles dictated by the coverage which are only superseded by the outside linebacker stunt call.

The outside linebacker must listen to the front and secondary calls. Both calls may provide information to the outside linebacker regarding his assignment. For example, the call "30 Stack" refers to the alignment and front responsibility of the Antler. "30 Stack, Cover 3," the complete call, lets the Antler and Brave know the coverage is Cover 3. Each has specific duties in regard to Cover 3.

INITIAL MOVEMENT

The initial movement varies according to technique. The initial movement of the S1 technique is a backpedal. The athlete should keep his heels close together as he backpedals. The weight should remain forward with a forward lean of the torso.

The initial movement of the S2 and 8 techniques is a bounce movement. The outside linebacker will bounce on the balls of his feet upon the snap of the ball. He will neither gain ground nor retreat from the line of scrimmage. This movement is consistent regardless of the down and distance. The outside linebacker will adjust to downs with longer distances by aligning farther off the ball.

The initial movement of a reading inside linebacker is a step to stance. The linebacker steps laterally with the foot corresponding to the direction of the primary key. An outside linebacker may step with the outside foot to stance, since he has limited practice at stepping to stance. However, it is important that the outside linebacker assume the proper presnap stance with the feet close together. This stance will keep the outside linebacker from "side-straddling" on the snap.

With the feet wide prior to the snap, a player tends to snap them outward as in a "jumping jack" movement. This reaction is the result of uncertainty about what to do and the intimidation of being aligned inside. When the player side-straddles on the snap, he becomes a target with no leverage to deliver a blow.

For the Forty Nickel coach, the outside linebacker's unfamiliarity with being aligned inside is a consideration when making the "Stack" call. If the "Stack" call is to be used a great deal, then the outside linebackers should receive sufficient instruction on inside linebacker technique.

OUTSIDE LINEBACKER STUNTS

Weather terms are used in naming outside linebacker stunts.

LIGHTNING   "Light" up quarterback, align on the line of scrimmage at a position to stunt on a direct line to head of fullback, quarterback on option.

RAIN   "R" for "rush" upfield, align on the line of scrimmage at a position to stunt to heels of tailback, pitch on option—used for pass containment.

THUNDER   "Under" the tight end, align outside the defensive end or in the stack position and stunt through nearest gap inside of DE, QB on option—good for pass rush and causing misreads for option attack.

STRONGSIDE   If neither the word "weak" nor "double" precede the stunt, it is a strongside stunt—only Antler stunts.

LIGHTNING
RAIN
THUNDER

WEAKSIDE   "WEAK" is added to stunt when only the weakside outside linebacker stunts—only Brave stunts.

WEAK LIGHTNING
WEAK RAIN
WEAK THUNDER
WEAK STACK

DOUBLE   "DOUBLE" tells both outside linebackers to run the stunt.

DOUBLE LIGHTNING
DOUBLE RAIN
DOUBLE THUNDER

COMBINATION STUNTS

CRASH — A defensive end combination stunt; the strongside outside linebacker runs a lightning stunt; defensive end runs a bingo.

WEAK CRASH — A defensive end combination stunt; the weakside outside linebacker runs a lightning stunt; weakside defensive end runs a bingo.

DOUBLE CRASH — A defensive end combination stunt; both outside linebackers run a lightning stunt; both defensive ends run a bingo.

BLUE LIGHTNING — A defensive end combination stunt; the strongside outside linebacker, Antler, runs a lightning stunt; defensive end runs a blue.

WEAK BLUE LIGHTNING — A defensive end combination stunt; the weakside outside linebacker, Brave, runs a lightning stunt; weakside defensive end runs a blue.

DOUBLE BLUE LIGHTNING — A defensive end combination stunt; both outside linebackers run a lightning stunt; both defensive ends run a blue.

BLUE THUNDER — A defensive end combination stunt; the strongside outside linebacker, Antler, runs a thunder stunt; strongside defensive end runs a blue.

WEAK BLUE THUNDER — A defensive end combination stunt; the weakside outside linebacker, Brave, runs a thunder stunt; weakside defensive end runs a blue.

DOUBLE BLUE THUNDER — A defensive end combination stunt; both outside linebackers run a thunder stunt; both defensive ends run a blue.

SPY LIGHTNING — A strongside defensive end combination stunt; when used with an outside linebacker stunt, the name of the defensive end stunt, "blue spy," is shortened to "spy;" Antler runs a lightning stunt and strongside defensive end runs a "blue spy."

WEAK SPY LIGHTNING — A weakside defensive end combination stunt; when used with an outside linebacker stunt, the name of the defensive end stunt, "blue spy," is shortened to "spy;" Antler runs a lightning stunt and strongside defensive end runs a "blue spy."

DOUBLE SPY LIGHTNING — A weakside defensive end combination stunt; when used with an outside linebacker stunt, the name of the defensive end stunt, "blue spy," is shortened to "spy;" Antler runs a lightning stunt and strongside defensive end runs a "blue spy."

SPY THUNDER	A strongside defensive end combination stunt; when used with an outside linebacker stunt, the name of the defensive end stunt, "blue spy," is shortened to "spy;" Antler runs a lightning stunt and strongside defensive end runs a "blue spy."
WEAK SPY THUNDER	A defensive end combination stunt; the weakside outside linebacker, Brave, runs a thunder stunt; weakside defensive end runs a blue.
DOUBLE SPY THUNDER	A defensive end combination stunt; both outside linebackers run a thunder stunt; both defensive ends run a blue.

OUTSIDE LINEBACKER ADJUSTMENTS

SQUEEZE	The outside linebacker called by the Will linebacker to "Squeeze" will play a shadow 9 technique.

OTHER OUTSIDE LINEBACKER ASSIGNMENTS

HOLD	Outside linebacker to the strongside, Antler, plays a crotch 9 technique and covers the "y" receiver man-to-man.
SQUEEZE	Outside linebacker to the strongside, Antler, plays a shadow 9 technique.
WEAK SQUEEZE	Outside linebacker to the weakside, Brave, plays a shadow 9 technique.
DOUBLE SQUEEZE	Both outside linebackers play a shadow 9 technique.
STACK	Outside linebacker to the strongside, Antler, aligns in a 50-gap technique and executes a called stunt or plays the "at" and "out" inside linebacker reads.
WEAK STACK	Outside linebacker to the weakside, Brave, aligns in a 50-gap technique and executes a called stunt or plays the "at" and "out" inside linebacker reads.
DOUBLE STACK	Both outside linebackers align in a 50-gap technique and execute a called stunt or play the "at" and "out" inside linebacker reads.

Chart 6a: Outside Linebacker Alignment Techniques

SI Technique	Man-to-man on the number-two receiver from the outside, seven yards off the line of scrimmage and one yard outside.
S2 Technique	One yard off the line of scrimmage and one yard outside the number-one receiver.
S7 Technique	Man-to-man one yard off scrimmage and one yard inside receiver.
8 Technique	Three yards off the line of scrimmage and three yards outside the nub.
9 Technique	On the line of scrimmage in shadow 9 technique alignment on tight end or tight slot.
50-Gap Technique	An inside linebacker technique, three yards off the ball and in the gap between the tackle and end. Used on "stack" defenses.

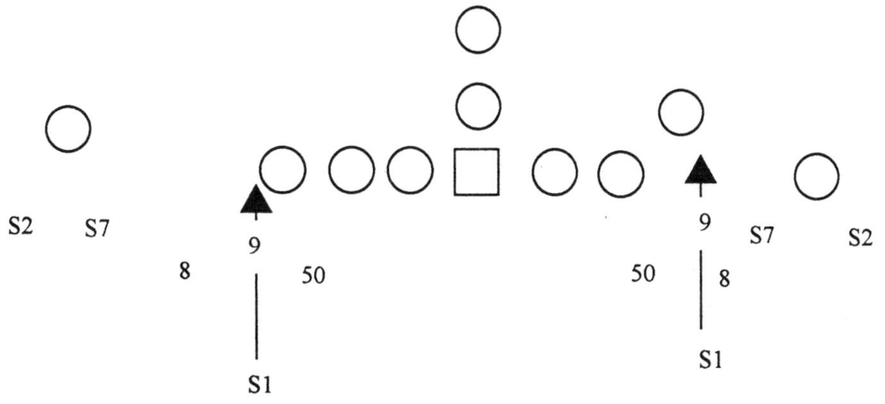

Additional details and diagrams for each stunt are as follows:

- Lightning—means to "light" up the quarterback. The landmark for the Lightning stunt is the head of the fullback or approximately two yards behind the quarterback. The Lightning angle adjusts to a Rain stunt angle versus a level-two or level-three pass. The aiming point on an offside counter trey play is outside of the upfield shoulder of the quarterback (i.e., shoulder farthest from the line of scrimmage). The Antler runs the Lightning; the Brave runs the Weak Lightning; and both Antler and Brave run the Double Lightning. The Lightning stunt runs a sharp angle and only tackles the diveback if the ball is seen to be handed off. Otherwise, the Lightning has the quarterback on a mesh point. Lightning stunts are usually called with Cover 1 and Cover 20, but may be called with Cover 3 and a defensive end Clutch call. Weak Lightning stunts are usually called with Cover 1 and Cover 20 Weak. Lightnings may be run with Cover 3, but both flat zones will be uncovered unless a linebacker adjustment is made. The outside linebacker never checks out of a Cover 1 Lightning unless called to the middle by the inside linebacker. This scenario will only occur versus an empty set (i.e., no-back set). A game plan may call for automatic Lightnings to the nub of a formation or in response to a specific formation. Special considerations of adjustment must also be made when a Lightning is called in the zone coverages such as Cover 3 and Cover 20.

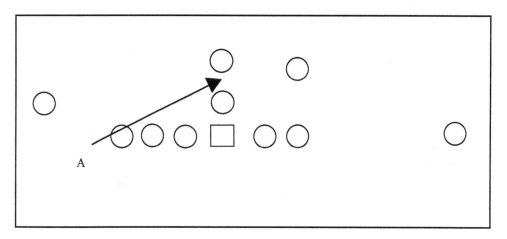

Diagram 6-4: Lightning.

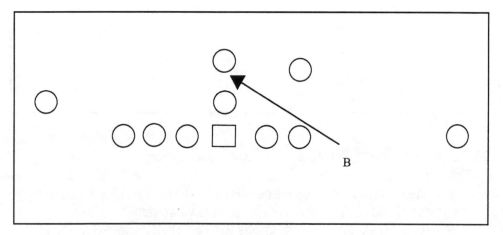

Diagram 6-5: Weak Lightning.

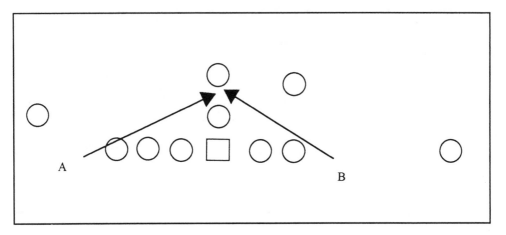

Diagram 6-6: Double Lightning.

- Rain—"Rain" means "rush" upfield. The initial steps of a Rain stunt are directed straight upfield. He takes three steps into the backfield as he reads the action of the play. If the action is a level-three pass or level-two pass, the stunting outside linebacker gets a jump on the passer. His pass rushing technique is a speed rush. He is expected to contain on level-two action toward him and trail as deep as the quarterback on level-three away from him. He has the pitch responsibility on the option. The Rain stunt is usually run from Cover 1, but can be run from the Cover 20 twin coverages (e.g., 20 and 20 Weak), as well as Cover 3. Special adjustment considerations are to be taken into account when running the Rain stunt from a zone coverage. These considerations are the same as the Lightning stunt considerations from a zone coverage. The coaching points for the Rain versus the counter trey are identical to the Lightning. A Rain stunt is run by the Antler; a Weak Rain stunt is run by the Brave; and a Double Rain stunt is run by both outside linebackers.

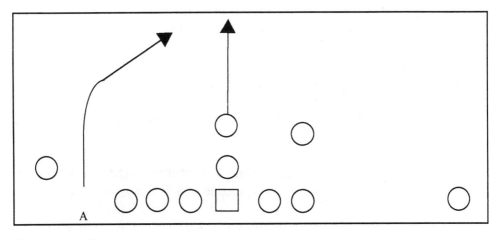

Diagram 6-7: Rain.

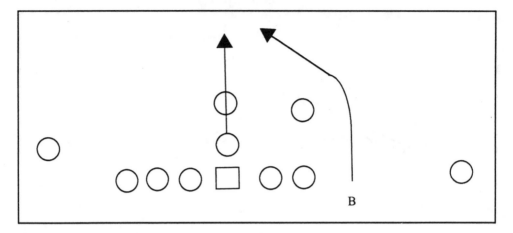

Diagram 6-8: Weak Rain.

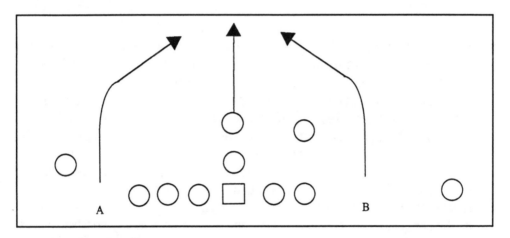

Diagram 6-9: Double Rain.

- Thunder—The name "Thunder" is used to cue the outside linebacker to go "under" the defensive end. The stunt is normally run from an alignment off the line of scrimmage and outside of the defensive end, although it can be run from the stack alignment and the squeeze alignment. An important coaching point for the outside linebacker is that he must adjust the angle of the stunt according to the blocking scheme. If the offensive tackle blocks inside and the "C" gap widens, the outside linebacker flattens his path. The Thunder landmark is the same landmark as the Lightning stunt. Versus a dive option, the Thunder stunting outside linebacker takes the first threat. If a back is diving at him, he takes the dive. If the offense is not using a diveback and the first threat is the quarterback, the Thunder stunting outside linebacker takes the quarterback. Thunder stunts are not called to the same side as a 5-technique tackle or 7-technique end, as this would place two defenders in the "C" gap. Compatible coverages from which the Thunder may be run are identical to the coverages from which the Lightning and Rain are run. The considerations of running the stunt from the zone coverages are identical to the considerations of running the Lightning and Rain stunts from zone coverages. The stunt is best run with a Blue or Blue Spy stunt by the corresponding defensive end. The nature and shape of the weakside of the formation are significant factors in the execution of the stunt. Versus the weakside tight flank with a 3-technique tackle, the outside linebacker runs a Thunder through the "C" gap. Versus the weakside open flank shown with a 1 technique tackle, the outside linebacker runs a Thunder through the "B" gap.

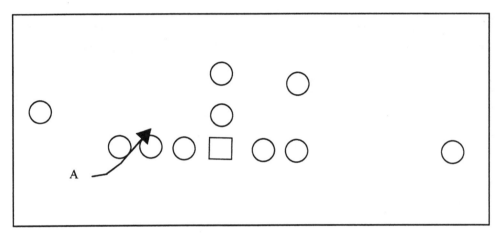

Diagram 6-10: Thunder.

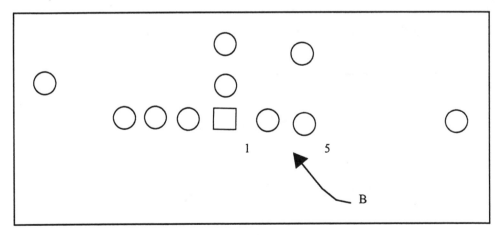

Diagram 6-11a: Weak Thunder to side of 1 technique tackle and 5 technique end.

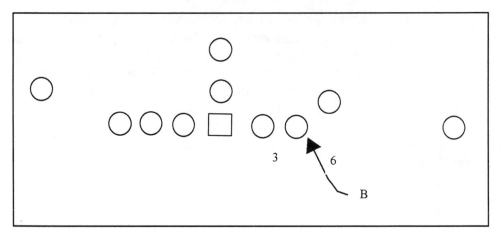

Diagram 6-11b: Weak Thunder to weakside tight flank and 3 technique and 6 technique.

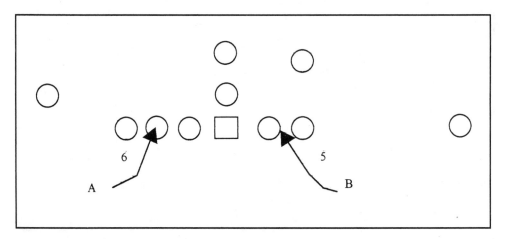

Diagram 6-12a: Double Thunder to both flanks; tight and open flanks.

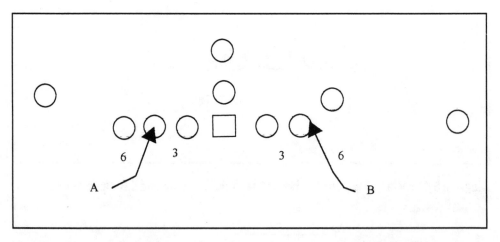

Diagram 6-12b: Double Thunder to both flanks; strongside tight and weakside tight flank.

- Blue Lightning—A combination stunt by the defensive end and outside linebacker. A Blue Lightning is a defensive end Blue stunt combined with an outside linebacker Lightning stunt. A Blue Lightning is run by the Antler and strongside end; a Weak Blue Lightning is run by the Brave and weakside end, and a Double Blue Lightning is run by both outside linebackers and both defensive ends.

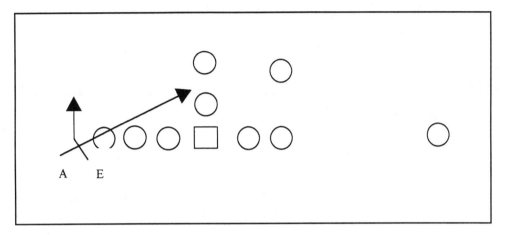

Diagram 6-13: Blue Lightning.

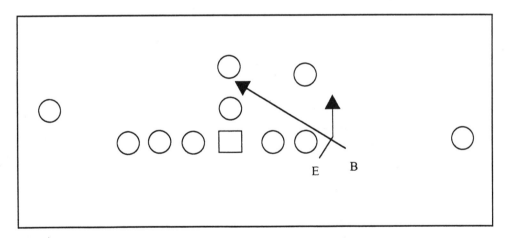

Diagram 6-14: Weak Blue Lightning.

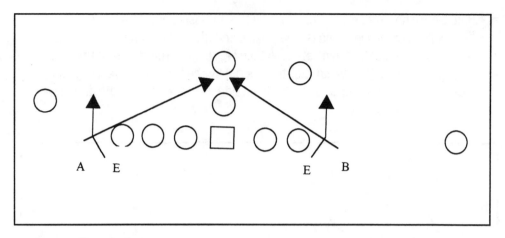

Diagram 6-15: Double Blue Lightning.

- Crash—A combination stunt by the defensive end and outside linebacker. A Crash is an outside linebacker Lightning run in combination with a defensive end Bingo. A Crash is run by the Antler and strongside end; a Weak Crash is run by the Brave and the weakside end; and a Double Crash is run by both outside linebackers and both defensive ends. The inside linebackers must be ready to quickly scrape to the outside when the Crash stunt is called.

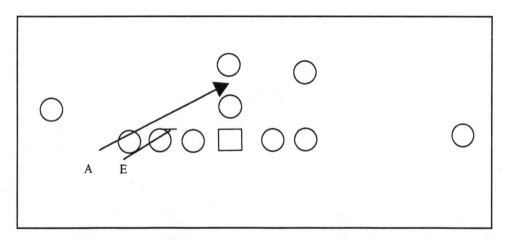

Diagram 6-16: Crash.

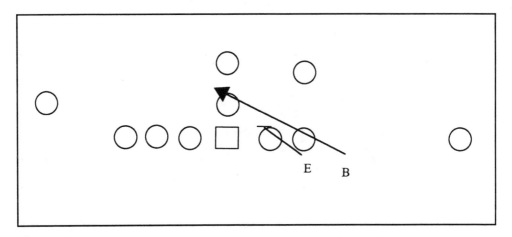

Diagram 6-17: Weak Crash.

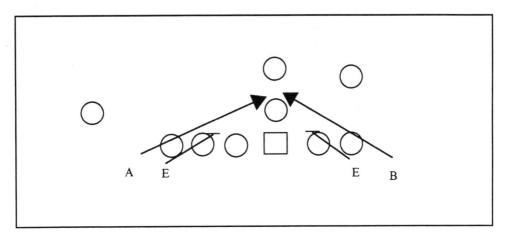

Diagram 6-18: Double Crash.

- Blue Thunder—A combination stunt by the defensive end and outside linebacker. A Blue Thunder is a defensive end Blue stunt combined with an outside linebacker Thunder stunt. A Blue Thunder is run by the Antler and the strongside defensive end; a Weak Blue Thunder is run by the Brave and the weakside defensive end; and a Double Blue Thunder is run by both defensive ends and both outside linebackers. The coaching points of running the Blue Thunder according to the type of flank and with regard to the nearside tackle technique are discussed in the previous section detailing the Thunder stunt.

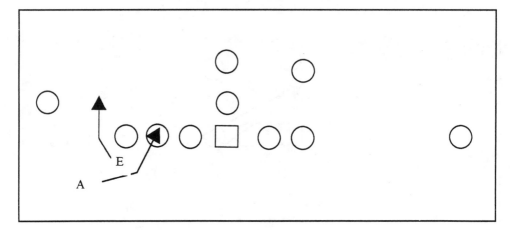

Diagram 6-19: Blue Thunder.

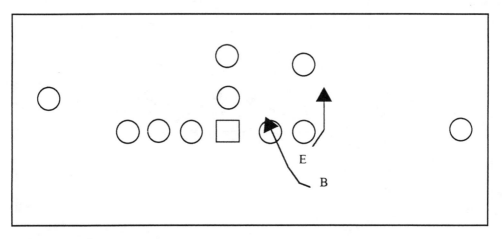

Diagram 6-20: Weak Blue Thunder.

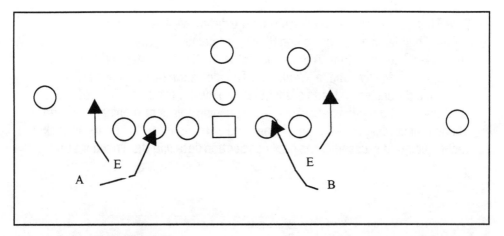

Diagram 6-21: Double Blue Thunder.

- Spy Thunder—A combination stunt by the defensive end and outside linebacker. On a Spy Thunder, the defensive end runs a Blue Spy in combination with the outside linebacker Thunder. A Spy Thunder is run by the Antler and the strongside defensive end; a Weak Spy Thunder is run by the Brave and the weakside defensive end; and a Double Spy Thunder is run by both defensive ends and both outside linebackers. The coaching points of running the Spy Thunder according to the type of flank and with regard to the nearside tackle technique are discussed in the previous section detailing the Thunder stunt.

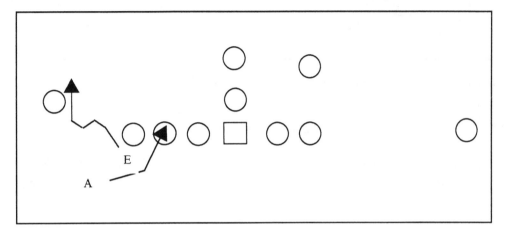

Diagram 6-22: Spy Thunder.

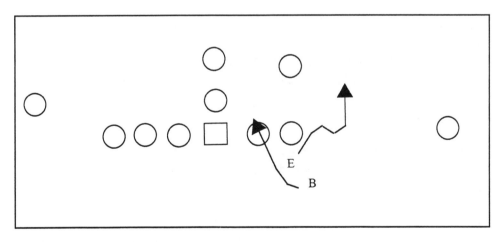

Diagram 6-23: Weak Spy Thunder.

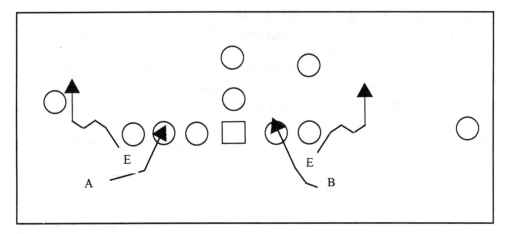

Diagram 6-23: Double Spy Thunder.

OUTSIDE LINEBACKER PLAY AS THE S1 TECHNIQUE

The outside linebacker plays a S1 technique in Cover 1 Free. A S1 technique is a man-to-man technique with an alignment cushion of about seven yards, depending on the down and distance.

The outside linebacker is responsible for covering the number-two receiver counting from the outside. If no second receiver exists, the outside linebacker is free.

Should a running back run a pass route to the single receiver side, the outside linebacker would cover him since the running back would be the number-two receiver. Consequently, the free outside linebacker must be on alert for a receiver slipping out of the backfield on a pass route.

S1 TECHNIQUE SPLIT RULE

The split is measured from the nearest lineman of the formation, the nub of the formation. The alignment depth, six to seven yards off the receiver, is unaffected by the split of the receiver, although some coaches do play an under-split receiver at five yards.

The split rule for a S1 Technique is simple. If the receiver is split over 8 yards from the nub of the formation, the S1 technique aligns one yard inside the receiver. If the receiver splits less than 8 yards from the nub, the S1 technique aligns one yard outside of the receiver.

When the receiver under-splits (splits less than eight yards), the S1 technique discourages the quick out route by alignment, but is in position to gain inside leverage should the receiver run a vertical route down the field. As the S1 technique backpedals, he weaves to a position headup to the receiver.

The alignment cushion is six to seven yards for a S1 technique. This cushion allows the S1 technique the opportunity to weave to a headup position as he backpedals.

THE FREE 8 TECHNIQUE ALIGNMENT

A free 8 technique alignment refers to an outside linebacker who is playing a S1 technique on the number-two receiver. The outside linebackers play a S1 technique in Cover 1 Free.

A free 8 technique is an 8 technique by alignment, but major differences exist between the two techniques. Regular 8 technique split rules do not apply to the free 8 technique. The free 8 is a S1 technique outside linebacker who only assumes the 8 technique alignment when he has no second receiver to cover. Without a second receiver to his side, the outside linebacker S1 technique is "free" for another assignment. When "free," the S1 technique outside linebacker assumes the alignment of an 8 technique and becomes a free 8 technique.

The free 8 technique is a man-to-man coverage technique and the 8 technique is a zone-coverage technique. The free 8 technique has the second receiver out to the same side as the outside linebacker's alignment. This receiver may come from across the formation or from out of the backfield. The free 8 technique has the second man out. If the offense has no second man out, the free 8 technique may cover level-two and level-three action according to regular 8 technique parameters.

The free 8 technique does not wheel, as would the 8 technique, on level-one flow away. Wheeling against level one with flow away is an unsound technique for a free 8 technique player. The free 8 technique should drop anchor and look for flashing colors.

A good technique is to have the free 8 technique widen against level-one away. This widening movement ensures the linebacker will not drift into the middle and puts him in good position to check for a back slipping out into the near flat on bootleg. Provided the ball has broken the line of scrimmage on level-one action away, the free 8 technique executes the proper 8 technique pursuit angle.

The free 8 technique attacks level-one action toward him in the same fashion as a regular 8 technique would attack. If no second receiver is aligned to his side and level one with action toward him shows, the free 8 technique will provide run support.

OUTSIDE LINEBACKER S1 TECHNIQUE MOTION ADJUSTMENT

When playing an S1 technique, the outside linebacker is not "locked" on the receiver. The outside receiver does not run across the ball with a number-two motion across the formation.

The S1 technique outside linebacker adjusts with the motion, keeping proper alignment until the outside linebacker reaches the nub of the formation. The outside linebacker then reverts to the free 8 technique alignment. The defense adjusts to the motion through the application of the Cover 1 Free coverage rules for the linebackers. The inside linebackers bump to cover through the use of their squirm adjustment technique. The outside linebackers do not run across the formation with the motion or pre-snap shift of the number-two receiver.

In Cover 1 Free, the free safety will convert his technique from a S6 technique to a S1 technique on the fourth receiver to either side, quads. Chart 8b shows the Cover 1 Free coverage rules.

Chart 6b

COVER 1 FREE COVERAGE RULES	
Antler	Number 2
Brave	Number 2
Sam	Number 3 strong* ... according to front strength
Will	Number 3 weak** ... according to front strength

* Sam may check to a "50 Clutch" defense instead of squirming to cover number 3 receiver to the strongside. Sam must call Will to middle when Sam squirms to cover the number 3 receiver strongside.

** Will must call Sam to the middle when Will squirms outside to cover the number 3 receiver to the weakside.

Diagram 6-25 shows the "Z" receiver motioning across a pro formation. The cornerback has number one in Cover 1 Free, so he bumps to a S1 technique on the nub end—in this case the "Y" receiver. Antler becomes free and aligns as an 8 technique. Brave, previously aligned as a free 8 technique, adjusts to a S1 technique on the "Z" receiver, as "Z" has become the number-two receiver to Brave's side.

Diagram 6-26 shows the "Z" receiver motioning across the formation from a twins formation. Brave adjusts with the "Z" receiver until the Brave reaches the nub of the formation. Once the Brave reaches the nub, he converts his technique to a free 8 technique. Antler recognizes the motion and converts his technique from a free 8 technique to a S1 technique on the "Y" receiver. The cornerback moves with the motion in proper S1 technique alignment as the cornerback bumps to cover the "Z."

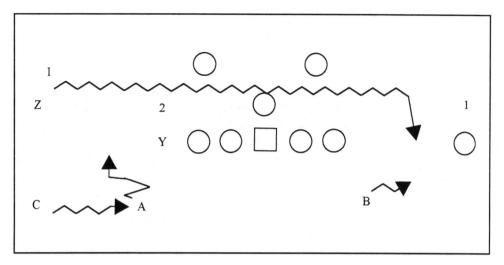

Diagram 6-25: Antler at S1 technique alignment on #2, Brave as free 8 technique.

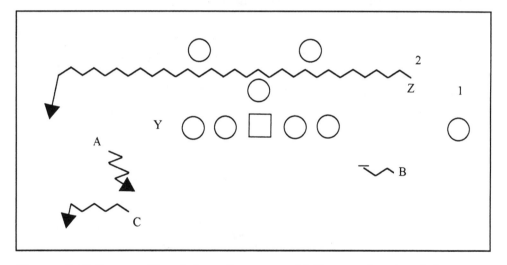

Diagram 6-26: Brave at S1 technique alignment on #2, Brave as free 8 technique.

SPLIT FLOW, THE NUMBER-TWO RECEIVER BLOCKING, AND DROPPING THE ANCHOR

The rule on man coverage is if the assigned man flows away, drop the anchor and look for "split flow." The S1 technique outside linebacker who is aligned as the free 8 technique should drop his anchor and sink in the throwback area upon recognizing level-one or level-two flow away 1) look for a back coming out of the backfield from across the formation; 2) look for a flashing color such as a lineman pulling out for a play-action screen pass; 3) look for the quarterback to run a naked bootleg; 4) sink in the curl and rob the weakside number-one receiver. This rule applies to both the Brave and the Antler. This four-part sequence must also be applied by the free 8 technique outside linebacker when the number-two receiver blocks.

Dropping and dragging the anchor are phrases used in coaching the outside linebacker to help the athlete understand the type of slow, cautious reaction desired of a S1 technique in his reaction to the blocking or split flow of the number-two receiver. The athlete is taught to imagine that he is dragging an anchor with him. The phrases "dropping the anchor" and "dragging the anchor" are also helpful in teaching inside linebacker play.

Antler must be acutely aware of the possibility of tight end delay patterns and tight end screens. Antler and Brave must both be vigilant for the reverse when playing a S1 technique and getting a split flow or block read from the pre-snap assignment. The eyes should focus inside as the number-two receiver flows to the other side of the formation. The outside linebacker should visually seek out the inside threat before the threat appears in the flat.

The outside linebacker must be careful to not run off when his presnap coverage assignment flows to the other side of the formation. The offense will use a good fake to help bait the Brave into drifting into the middle of the field, thus leaving the fullback open in the flat Drifting into the middle while playing a S1 technique, even when aligned as a free 8 technique, can result in a big play given up to the offense.

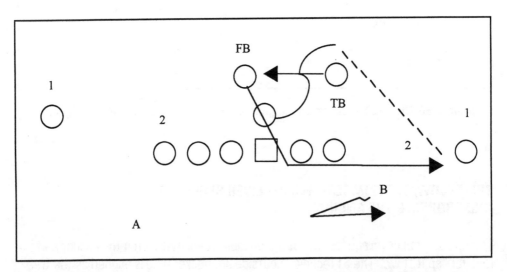

Diagram 6-27: Brave is incorrectly responding to flow away by the tailback.

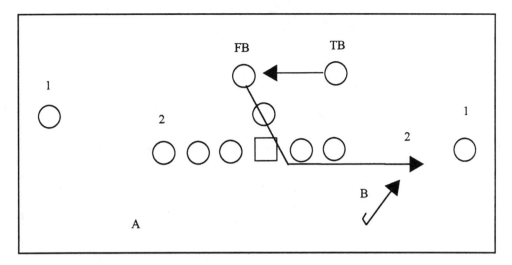

Diagram 6-28: Brave is correctly responding to flow away by the tailback.

The outside linebacker should never drift to the middle when playing a S1 technique. While the outside linebacker wheels to stop the cutback when playing an 8 technique, wheeling while playing a S1 technique is not a good reaction. Drifting to the ball flow is never a good movement, even when playing a zone coverage 8 technique. In Diagram 6-29, the number-two receiver blocks. Antler, who is playing a S1 technique, drifts to the middle after peeking to find the flow of the ball. The result could be a big play for the offense.

In Diagram 6-30, Antler makes the mistake of drifting into the middle because the number-two receiver, the fullback, appears to block.

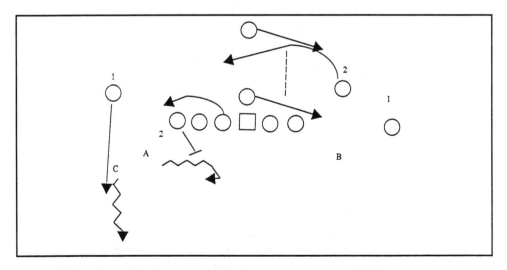

Diagram 6-29.

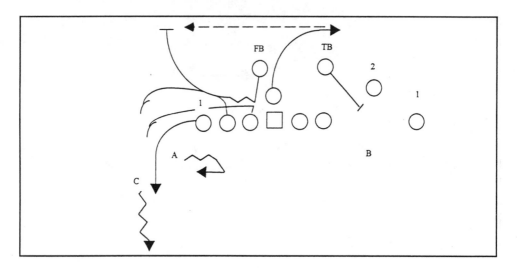

Diagram 6-30.

Both outside linebackers play a S2 technique in Cover 2 , Cover 3 Out and Cover 23. Antler plays a S2 technique in Cover 20 Weak and Brave plays a S2 technique in Cover 20.

Brave also makes an adjustment from an 8 technique to a S2 technique when checking from Cover 3 to Cover 3 Squat. This check is made to gain an advantage against an end-over attack. The result of the check means little to the Brave, since the S2 and 8 techniques are identical techniques when aligned on the nub of the formation.

The S2 technique is what is commonly known as a "hard corner." However, in the Forty Nickel defense, the "hard corner" is usually played by an outside linebacker. The idea of limiting the personnel who play the S2 technique to the outside linebackers fits well with the tenet that the outside linebackers are the athletes who provide perimeter run support and cover the flat zone. The S2 technique provides a funneling type of run support when the ball is on level-one action toward the S2 technique. The S2 is not usually the primary force, but the S2 can be the primary force in a coverage such as one of the "20" coverages.

On level-one and level-two ball flow away from the S2 technique, the S2 technique rolls back into the outside third of the field as he sinks underneath the route of the number-one receiver. The S2 technique covers the flat on ball level-two action toward him. Against level-three ball action, the S2 technique jams the number-one receiver, the outside receiver. As he jams the receiver in an attempt to prevent an outside release of the receiver, the S2 technique gets his eyes focused on the inside receiver, the number-two man. The S2 technique sinks under the outside receiver's route as long as no inside receiver threatens the flat. If an inside receiver runs a route to the flat zone, the outside linebacker stops sinking under the outside route and jumps the route of the receiver threatening the flat.

OUTSIDE LINEBACKER STANCE AS A S2 TECHNIQUE

In the stance of a S2 technique, the feet are set shoulder width apart, but turned in to the formation or receiver to put the body at a 45-degree angle to the formation. The weight is firmly on the balls of the feet with a slight heel raise of each foot. The torso leans forward slightly as the athlete bends forward at the waist. The hands hang loosely outside the thighs.

OUTSIDE LINEBACKER ALIGNMENT AS A S2 TECHNIQUE

The outside linebacker alignment in an S2 technique is one-and-one off the outermost wide receiver. This term translates as one yard outside the number-one receiver and one yard off the line of scrimmage.

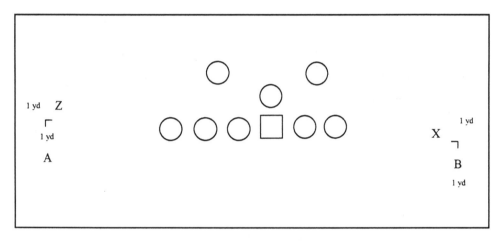

Diagram 6-31: S2 technique alignment against a pro formation.

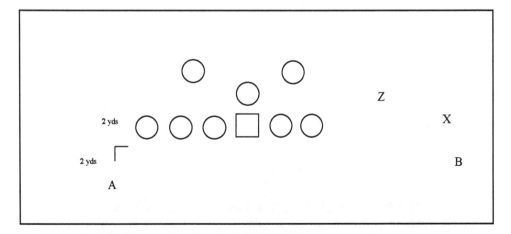

Diagram 6-32: S2 technique alignment against a twins formation. An outside line-backer modifies his S2 alignment technique to two-and-two against a nub end.

Unless special circumstances exist, the outside linebacker remains on the outside receiver, regardless of the arrangement of multiple receivers.

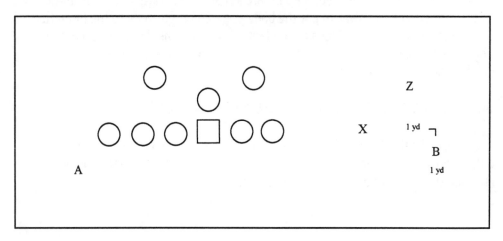

Diagram 6-33.

An example of special circumstances in which a S2 technique outside linebacker would adjust against multiple wide receivers is Cover 3 Out. An outside linebacker adjusts from a S2 technique to an 8 technique when facing multiple receivers while in Cover 3 Out.

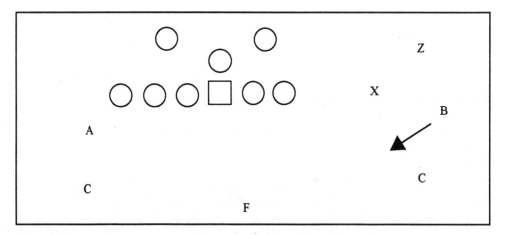

Diagram 6-34.

OUTSIDE LINEBACKER SPLIT RULE AS A S2 TECHNIQUE

The S2 technique does not align closer than five yards to the sideline, regardless of the outside receiver's proximity to the sideline. If the outside receiver aligns within five yards of the sideline, the S2 technique aligns five yards from the sideline with a cushion of four to six yards. The closer the receiver aligns to the sideline, the greater the depth of the S2 technique's alignment. When playing an oversplit receiver, the S2 technique squares his stance slightly so that the S2 technique may gain peripheral vision of the outside receiver's movement.

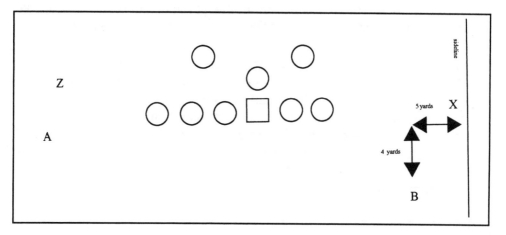

Diagram 6-35.

S2 TECHNIQUE KEYS

As stated earlier in the text, the S2 technique outside linebacker keys the inside receiver if the ball goes to level three. If the ball goes to level-two, the outside linebacker properly reacts to the ball flow. If the ball proceeds down level one, the S2 technique linebacker funnels the ball into the front pursuit.

Thus, the primary key for the S2 technique is ball movement. The primary key on the open end side of the formation is ball level movement. On the tight side of a formation, the primary key of the S2 is the movement of the end man on the line of scrimmage. The end man on the line of scrimmage is referred to as the nub of the formation. Incorporated within the outside linebacker's read is the triangle of the lineman, the nearback and the ball.

The movement of the nearback in conjunction with the action of the nub player will alert the S2 technique to the nature of the play prior to the play's actual execution. For example, if the nearback flows away from the S2 technique on level-one action, the outside linebacker looks for a "flashing color" coming from the other side of the ball. "Flashing color" is a descriptive phrase normally used in teaching inside linebacker play. A flashing color is an offensive player pulling or moving against the flow of the primary key. The flashing color, when recognized, overrides the movement of the primary key in identifying a particular play. In other words, the flashing color's movement takes the defense to the ball.

Should a "flashing color" be seen, the S2 technique stops sinking under the outside receiver's route and closes ground to funnel the running play or cover a threat to the flat zone. Should the ball redirect its flow toward the S2 technique, the outside linebacker stops sinking and looks for a shallow dragging route from the nub end or from across the field. Upon recognition of the dragging route, the outside linebacker attacks the route, timing his arrival to coincide with the arrival of the thrown pass.

The S2 technique also sinks to the outside third zone when the ball moves down level-two away from the S2 technique. As the S2 technique linebacker sinks underneath the outside receiver to this outside deep zone, the outside linebacker keeps his eyes inside to the action of the nearback and the player on the nub. On reacting to level-three action, the S2 technique is aware of the action of the tight end or nearback. Even on level three, the S2 technique is aware of the supplemental triangle keys. Integrating the keys of the nub, the nearback and the ball movement is called keying the triangle.

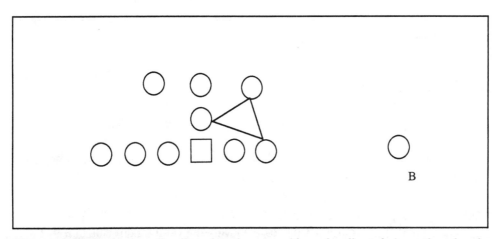

Diagram 6-36: Brave, usually aligned to the open side, subordinately keys the triangle of the nearback, the tackle, and the ball.

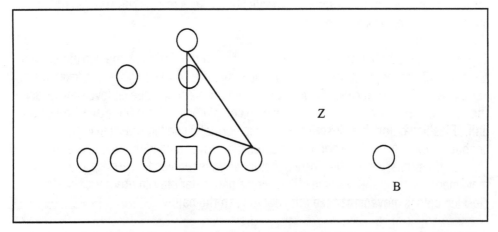

Diagram 6-37: Even though the "Z" receiver is a nearback, the triangle includes only backs who are between the tackles or in a position to take a handoff.

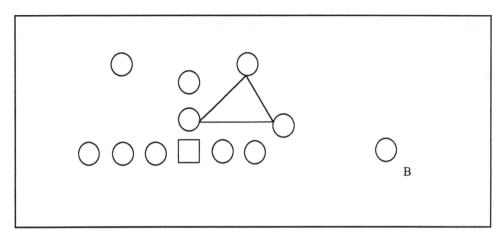

Diagram 6-38: A tight slot is considered a tight end for the purpose of keying the triangle.

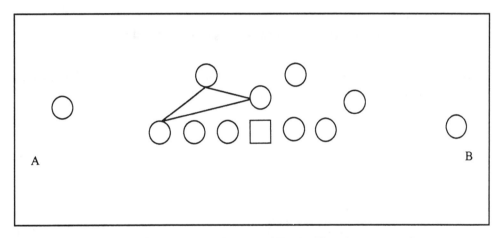

Diagram 6-39: Antler, who is usually aligned to the tight end side, subordinately keys the triangle of the tight end, the nearback and the ball.

PLAYING A S2 TECHNIQUE ON THE NUB END OF THE FORMATION

The outside linebacker aligns at two-and-two on an undersplit receiver (wingback) or the nub end of the formation. The primary key against a wing set or other undersplit receiver is the nearest lineman. The S2 technique keys the tight end in a wingback-tight end combination. When a tight slot is set on the nub side of end-over formation, the S2 technique will key the tackle.

When aligned on a nub end, the outside linebacker also changes his presnap key from ball movement to man. The man from which the S2 technique receives his initial run-pass key is the nearest lineman. If the nub is the tight end, then the presnap key is the tight end. If the nub is a tackle, as in an end-over formation, the S2 technique keys the triangle of the tackle, nearback and quarterback. Antler aligns two yards off the line of scrimmage and two yards outside the end man on the line of scrimmage when facing a nub end.

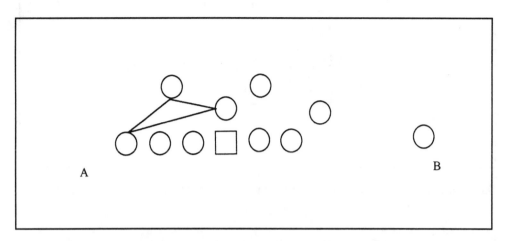

Diagram 6-40: The subordinate triangle key versus a nub end is shown.

Antler aligns two yards off the line of scrimmage and two yards outside the outside receiver when facing an undersplit receiver such as a wingback.

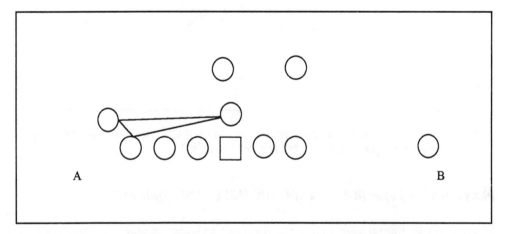

Diagram 6-41: The subordinate triangle key versus a wingback is shown.

S2 TECHNIQUE REACTION TO LEVEL ONE

Level-one ball movement toward the S2 technique cues the S2 technique to funnel the ballcarrier inside to the pursuit of the front. A factor in reacting to level-one movement from the S2 technique position is the diagnosis of the type of running play coming toward the defender. Level-one movement with flow toward the S2 technique can be classified as option or sweep. The identification of the play as a sweep or an option requires further diagnosis by the S2 technique.

Options are divided into three classifications: lead option, load option, and speed option. Sweeps are subtly different in many ways. A sweep may be an I-formation toss sweep, a wing-T attack sweep, or a quick toss sweep to the nearback. Identifying and playing lead, load, and speed option from the S2 technique position is covered in detail later in this text. Sweeps are all played in basically the same manner. The S2 technique outside linebacker must close the running alley as he keeps outside leverage. A quick read of ball level and direction is important to effectively closing the alley.

The coach may give the S2 technique tips to help the athlete react quickly to level one toward the defender. For example, we tell our outside linebacker that if the quarterback reverses-out and tosses to the ball to an I-formation tailback, the outside linebacker is to sprint to the upfield shoulder of the I-back and close the alley. The angle of the outside linebacker's path should lead him to a depth of less than three yards into the backfield, at which point the outside linebacker assumes the proper open field tackling position with outside leverage. We have been successful in funneling the talented I-formation tailbacks in the past through the use of this coaching point. To the offensive coach, the reaction of the S2 technique to the I-formation toss sweep often appears as if we are stunting the S2 technique on the snap of the ball. Since the S2 technique is a short-zone player, the reward of playing the toss sweep aggressively outweighs the risk. A defensive coach can take greater liberty in coaching the short zone defensive secondary techniques to be aggressive.

SQUEEZING THE ALLEY

The alley which the outside linebacker must squeeze may be a wide alley, as in an alley to the split end or wide side. The alley may also be very tight, as an alley to the tight side of the formation. Shown below in Diagram 6-42 are the approximate alley areas.

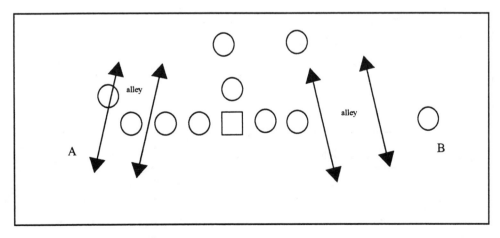

Diagram 6-42: The two alleys.

Both outside linebackers must quickly narrow the width of the alley by funneling the ball carrier inside. In Diagram 6-43, Brave defeats the block of the "X" and closes the alley while keeping outside leverage. The outside linebacker should try to keep his shoulders parallel or nearly parallel to the line of scrimmage when funneling the ballcarrier.

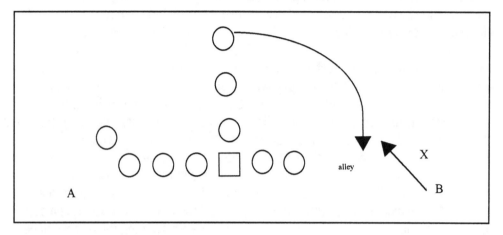

Diagram 6-43: Funneling the ball carrier.

The funneling outside linebacker must not help "create an alley" by vertically penetrating into the backfield. This concern occurs at the S2 technique position when aligned on the tight side of the formation. In Diagram 6-44, Antler goes upfield and fails to squeeze, or narrow, the alley.

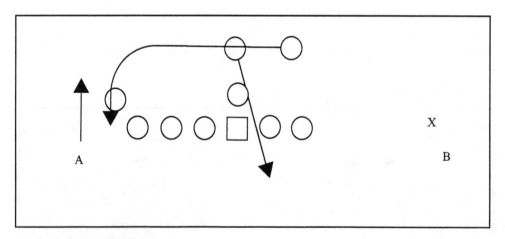

Diagram 6-44: Creating an alley.

The outside linebacker's reaction should lead him no deeper than two and a half yards behind the line of scrimmage. Deep penetration can allow the running back to break underneath a brush block and get back into the alley with no outside containment. Brave beats the block of the "X" but penetrates at too slight an angle and goes too deep into the backfield. The running back dips under a brush block and now has an alley with the sideline boundary as the outer edge.

THE COVER 2 STRONGSIDE ADVANTAGE

Cover 2 presents an advantage to the S2 technique on the strongside. The free safety plays a S5 technique in Cover 2. Thus, by alignment, the free safety is sitting in the middle of the alley to the open side of the formation, the split end side. As an S5 technique to the closed side, or tight end side of a pro formation, the free safety is aligned on the tight end, again aligned in the alley.

Knowing the responsibility of the S5 technique allows the S2 technique aligned in conjunction with the free safety to play the sweep more cautiously. The S2 technique does not have to sprint to the upfield shoulder of the I-formation running back on the toss sweep. With the aid of the S5 technique free safety, the S2 technique may funnel the play in a less urgent manner. While the fact that the S2 technique narrows the alley against the sweep is still important, the outside linebacker's primary objective is to maintain outside leverage. The angle of attack for the S2 technique does not change due to the presence of the S5 technique. If anything, too much penetration into the backfield is more dangerous when aligned with the S5 technique. The free safety will play to make the tackle. Keeping outside leverage is not a priority in the reaction of the S5 technique to the sweep.

In Cover 2, the S5 is referred to as the primary force. The S2 technique is called the secondary force. The running back will attempt to hit the crease between the S2 and S5 techniques. Both techniques are outside leverage techniques, but the main responsibility for squeezing the alley belongs to the S2 technique outside linebacker. Diagram 6-45 shows Cover 2 alignment against a twins formation. The free safety is aligned in the alley. Brave can funnel with a priority on outside leverage.

Diagram 6-46 illustrates the strength of Cover 2 versus the pro formation. The free safety is aligned in the alley. Antler can funnel with a priority on outside leverage.

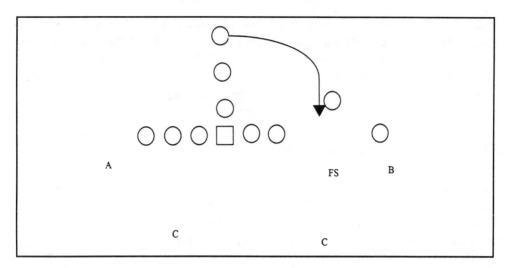

Diagram 6-45.

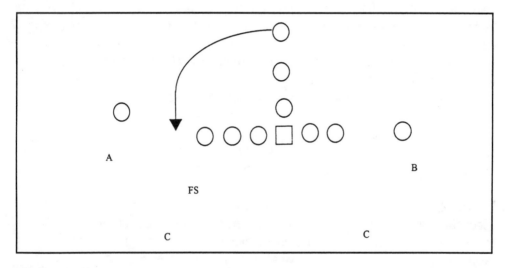

Diagram 6-46.

S2 TECHNIQUE LEVEL-TWO REACTION

On level-two flow toward the him, the S2 technique outside linebacker disrupts the route of the receiver as he sits on the rail. For the S2 technique, the rail is a point of reference, an imaginary horizontal line running parallel to the line of scrimmage. This line runs across the defensive side of the ballfield at a depth of five yards. The S2 technique defender may gain width to a position at which he is underneath the out route, or in the line of sight between the quarterback and the wide receiver's out route. The S2 technique reads through the number-two receiver to the formation and quarterback as he sinks and gains the appropriate width. Should any inside receiver threaten the flat, the S2 technique will break up to cover the threat.

Down and distance are factors in defending level-two action, as they are always a factor to front and secondary personnel on every down. If level-two action shows on a third and medium to long (possession down), the S2 technique will play soft under the out route and break up on the bench or flare route only when the ball is thrown.

Game planning can have an effect on the rapidity in which the S2 technique jumps the bench and flare route out of the backfield. If the offense features a premier "go-to guy" in the backfield and tries to get him open in the broken field, the offense may like to flare him out in the flat or hit him on a quick bench route. The plan may prioritize shutting off any opportunities for the back to touch the ball. This approach would necessitate sitting on the rail and not cushioning under the out route of the wide receiver. By sitting on a four-yard rail across the field, the S2 technique may provide the defensive with a big play, should a flair or bench route be attempted. In Diagram 6-47, Brave cushions the out route to a six- to seven-yard rail and forces the quarterback to hit the bench route. Brave comes up and makes the tackle on the back out of the backfield for a gain that is short of the first down.

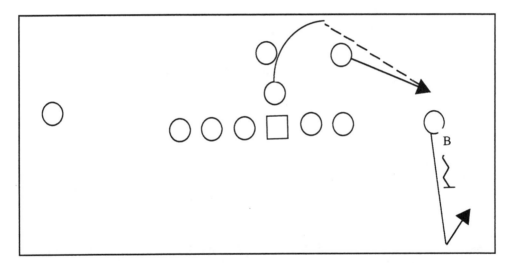

Diagram 6-47: Down and distance = third and seven. Brave cushions the out route to a six- to seven-yard rail and forces the quarterback to hit the bench route. Brave comes up and makes the tackle on the back out of the backfield for a gain that is short of the first down.

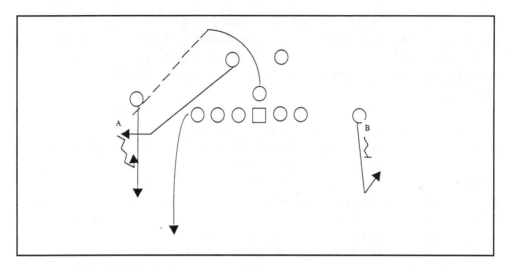

Diagram 6-48: Antler jams the outside receiver's route and sinks against level two. Antler reads through the number-two receiver to the ball and recognizes the fullback's out route. Antler breaks up on the route.

THE COVER 2 ADVANTAGE AGAINST LEVEL TWO

As shown in the previous diagram, an S2 technique will read through the second receiver and break up on the route which threatens the flat. And as discussed earlier in the text, the speed in reacting to the threat is dictated by down and distance. In Cover 2, the strongside S2 technique has an additional coaching point. Since Cover 2 is basically a squat coverage, the defense has three defenders on the two widest receivers. This numbers advantage allows for a more aggressive flat coverage by the strongside S2 technique. The weakside S2 technique does not have this advantage. Nor does either S2 technique have the numbers advantage in the Cover 20 tandem coverages, 20 and 20 Weak.

By playing on the squat side, the strongside S2 technique can break off his cushion without hesitation. The same coaching point holds true for a S2 technique playing Cover 3 Out. It is a minor coaching point but nevertheless something of which the coach may make the athlete aware.

Cover 2 offers a great advantage against the strongside running and passing attack. For more information on Cover 2, see the secondary section of the text.

An important consideration in playing the S2 technique is the fact that sometimes it is best for the S2 technique to react to level-two action as a run. Some very successful teams who use the quarterback extensively as a ballcarrier. These teams like to run student-body sweeps with the quarterback carrying the ball deep around the edge. By definition, the ball off the line of scrimmage in a path down the line is level two. And level two is a pass read to the coverage defenders and linebackers. However, in the instance mentioned above, the quarterback clearly has no intention to pass the ball. Everyone is running interference for the quarterback as he rounds the end deep in the backfield with the ball tucked under his arm. In this case, this play and action are read as level one.

One should take heed in attending to this coaching point. The interpretation of reading level two as level one cannot be accomplished in a chalk talk. Hopefully a S2 technique has been drilled daily on reading level-two action as pass. A great amount of repetition is needed to temporarily unlearn this pass read and read level two as run. With practice, the S2 technique can become aggressive against a level-two run read. Scouting and teaching the athletes the down and distance tendencies attains a greater importance when facing such a contradiction in the run-pass recognition reads.

ADDITIONAL S2 TECHNIQUE COACHING POINTS

If reading level three, the S2 technique sinks and disrupts the wide receiver. The S2 can then pattern read the single receiver route. In Diagram 6-49 below, Brave begins to sink to the outside third zone when the "X" breaks the route off on a curl. By keeping his eyes inside to the ball, Brave is able to determine that no threat to his flat zone exists, nor does a rail threat out of the backfield. Making this read allows Brave to get underneath the curl route of the "X." This read is extremely helpful since it allows the inside linebacker to settle in the hook or wall the second receiver's vertical route. A circle route is shown by the nearback. The inside linebacker is free to sit on the circle route, because the outside linebacker pattern reads with no threat to either the flat or the outside third. Blanket zone coverage can be achieved with pattern reads taught and practiced.

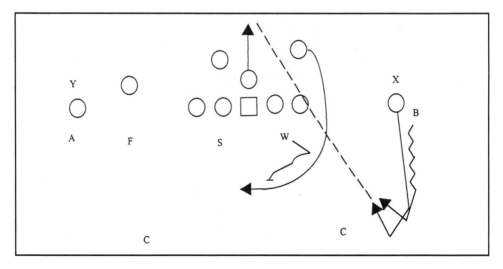

Diagram 6-49.

READING THE INSIDE RECEIVER WITH LEVEL THREE

Level three is dropback pass. The outside linebacker playing the S2 technique must read the inside receiver's movement if the ball moves to level three. In the simplest scenario, it is the inside receiver who is the number-two receiver. If the number-two receiver does not run an out-breaking pattern such as a bench or out route, the outside linebacker continues to read through the number-two receiver to a third or fourth receiver. If the outside linebacker sees no threat to the flat zone, the outside linebacker sinks to the outside deep third zone. Should any inside receiver threaten the flat, the outside linebacker will break off his sinking movement into the outside third and cover the threat.

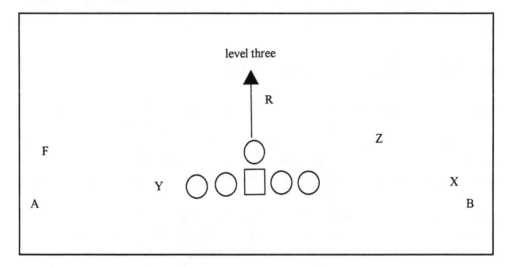

Diagram 6-50: Antler reads through the "Y" receiver on level-three ball action. Brave reads through the "Z" receiver.

In Diagram 6-51, the route run by the "R" back is called a bench route, so named because the receiver takes a direct path to the bench. Coaches sometimes call the bench route a spear route, or an arrow. The bench route is converted to a rail (wheel) if the receiver continues upfield in the outside third zone. The "Z" and "X" are running vertical routes, routes straight down the field. In the following diagram, Brave is fortunate enough to be able to jam the "X" and force an inside path. Brave reads level three. Number two, "Z," is running a vertical. As Brave sinks under the outside receiver route to the outside deep third zone, Brave keeps his eyes inside and reads through number two to the ball. Brave recognizes the "R" back threatening the flat and breaks off the sink to meet the threat.

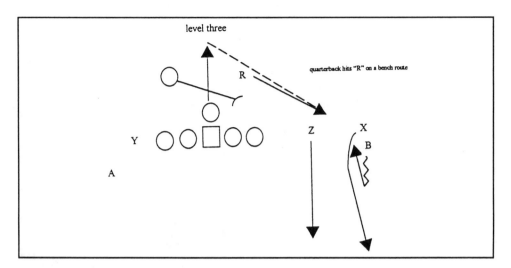

Diagram 6-51.

If a second receiver runs a route behind the clearance of another receiver's route, the second receiver's route is called a trail. In diagram 6-52, the "R" is converting his bench route to a rail. This particular route is also a trail route as the "X" has cleared the outside zone for the "R" receiver's rail. Brave must not drop the anchor when defending the route shown below. "R" may continue down the field on a "rail route" trailing the "X." If the quarterback has time, the "R" will turn up the field on a pump fake. Brave must cover the "R" in a trail coverage technique if the "R" converts the bench route to a trailing rail route. In Diagram 6-53, the "R" back converts the bench route into a rail behind the vertical route of the "X." This is called a trail route. Brave dropped his anchor and settled in the flat for the bench route. The result is a long pass completion to the "R" receiver. Brave must be ready to cover the unexpected conversion.

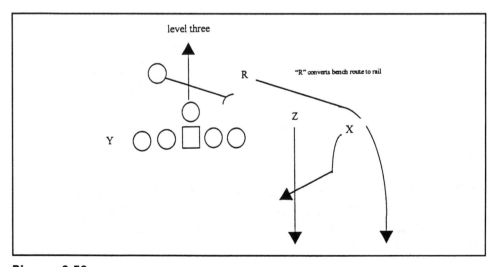

Diagram 6-52.

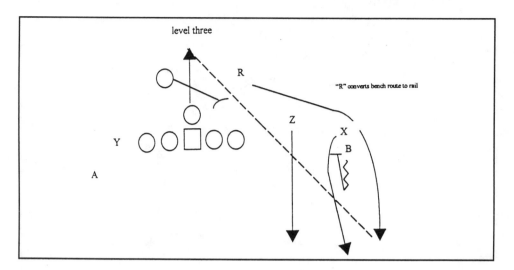

Diagram 6-53.

In Diagram 6-54, Brave is ready for the bench to rail conversion of the "R" back and walls out the "R" back by using the defensive trail coverage technique. See the cornerback section of this text for more information on the "trail technique" of covering receivers.

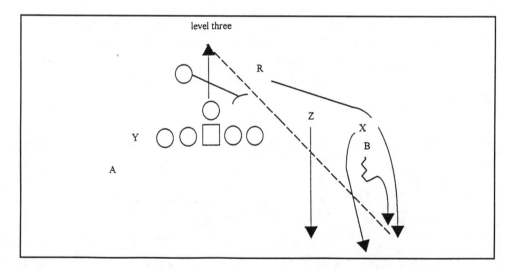

Diagram 6-54. ·

The S2 techniques need weekly practice time allotted for covering the curl-rail and post-rail combination routes. In Diagram 6-55, the wheel combination (e.g., curl-rail, etc.) is shown from the twins set, while in Diagram 6-56, the combination is seen from a nub end and nearback.

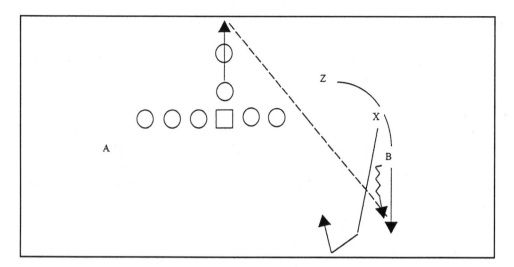

Diagram 6-55.

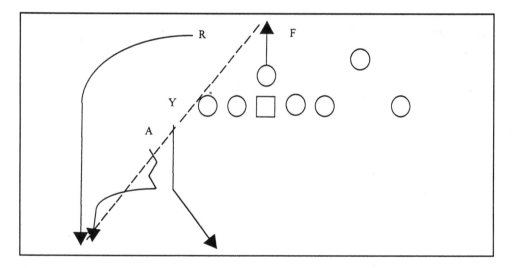

Diagram 6-56.

A rail route is a route describing the path of the inside receiver as he attempts to run a vertical route to an outside zone. The rail is usually run in combination with an outside receiver's inward breaking route. Some coaches call the rail a "banana," because of the shape of the route when diagrammed. The curl-rail is a common combination route from the twins formation. In Diagram 6-55 below, the "X" receiver runs a curl route and the "Z" runs a rail route behind the "X." Brave reads level-three action as he disrupts the release of the "X." Coached to read through the number-two receiver to the formation, Brave sees the "Z" running a rail route. Brave breaks off his squeezing outside-in coverage of the "X" receiver's route and walls out the rail route of the "Z" receiver from inside-out. Brave pivots to the outside in a whirling motion to his right shoulder. Should Brave roll to the inside toward his left shoulder, Brave would momentarily lose sight of the ball and the "Z" receiver. Brave uses the outside shoulder to press the "Z" into the boundary as he runs with the "Z." Brave may also place slight pressure with the back of his left hand on the inside hip of the "Z." This coverage by "feel" helps the Brave to be able to glance over his right shoulder to find the ball without the consequence of losing coverage.

In the latter diagram, the "R" back runs the rail and the "Y" runs a skinny post. The S2 technique should be well versed on recognizing this backfield set and formation as a good arrangement to run the post-rail combination route. In Diagram 6-56, Antler sinks with the number-one receiver, "Y," as he reads level-three ball action. Antler looks through the number-two receiver and sees the "R" back running the rail route. Antler pivots and opens to the sideline as he moves to cover the "R" back in a man principle within the zone. Antler attempts to wall the "R" receiver as Antler uses the back of his right hand to press into the inside hip of the "R" receiver. This hand check is slight but useful in helping the Antler "feel" the route of the "R." By "feeling" the route, Antler is able to keep close coverage on the "R," while peeking over his left shoulder for the ball.

8 TECHNIQUE ALIGNMENT

The 8 technique is the hub of the technique number system. Because it is the numbered technique at which the secondary and front techniques connect, the 8 technique is not designated as an "S" technique. The base alignment of an 8 technique is three yards off the line of scrimmage at a position three yards outside the near lineman. Against a wing set, the 8 technique may align two yards off the line of scrimmage at a position two yards outside of the tight end. An 8 technique

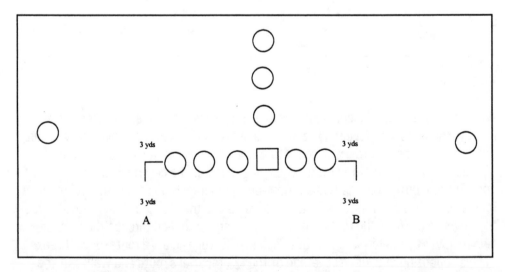

Diagram 6-57: Standard 8 technique alignment; Antler on the closed end, Brave on the open end of the formation.

aligned on the nub end of a formation takes a position of one yard outside the nub and one yard of the line of scrimmage. An 8 technique may auto-lightning if the ball flows away with level-two action. The standard alignment of the 8 technique in most eight-man front packages is four and four, four yards off the line of scrimmage and four yards outside the near lineman. Our experience at the high-school level leads us to believe a tighter alignment helps us to defend the running game.

The four-and-four alignment is used when facing teams who are better at passing teams than running. Also, the more aggressive personnel use the standard four and four alignment. Four and four is a good rule of thumb for any level of competition. Because the 8 technique's initial movement is to bounce, four and four is also an acceptable base alignment. The 8 technique should be well-coached on applying down and distance situations to his own alignment depth and width. Down and distance are important considerations for proper alignment. Another consideration in aligning the 8 technique is the nature and talent of the defender who plays the 8 technique. The more aggressive player may align farther off the ball. Plainly speaking, proper alignment is simply the alignment which puts the player in the best position to execute the assignment.

Diagram 6-58 shows the standard 8 technique alignment against a wingback at two and two. Note this alignment places Antler in a shadow alignment on the wing at a depth of two yards from the line of scrimmage. (The 8 technique is aligned on the line of scrimmage against some power wing formation running attacks.)

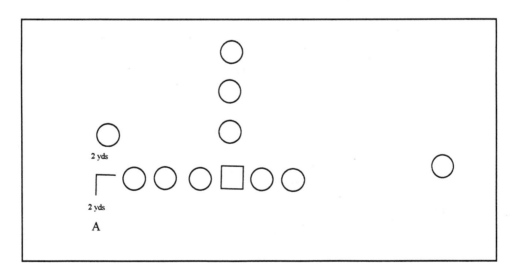

Diagram 6-58.

8 TECHNIQUE SPLIT RULE

The 8 technique rarely aligns wider than eight yards from the nub of a formation. Proper alignment against an under-split receiver dictates that the 8 technique assume the "squeeze" alignment. The squeeze adjustment alignment for an 8 technique is at a shadow 9 technique on the under-split receiver. The 8 technique defender will "squeeze" play the under-split receiver until the receiver reaches a distance greater than eight yards from the line of scrimmage.

Once the single receiver reaches a distance of greater than eight yards, the outside linebacker begins to adjust his alignment inward to the formation. The outside linebacker uses the eight-yard axis as the reference point for adjusting his depth off the line of scrimmage. If the receiver is close to the eight-yard axis, the outside linebacker aligns close to the line of scrimmage. For example, a receiver aligned nine to ten yards from the nub is in a good position to crack block the outside linebacker. The outside linebacker recognizes the close split and aligns at a depth from zero to one yard off the line of scrimmage. If the receiver moves out to a distance of eleven to twelve yards, the outside linebacker may deepen his alignment and move closer to the base alignment on the nub.

In summary, the 8 technique's width is related to the split of the single receiver. If the receiver is split eight yards or less, the 8 technique aligns as a shadow 9 technique on the receiver. As the receiver moves outward, the 8 technique tightens his alignment to the nub and gains depth. If the receiver is no longer a threat to crack block the 8 technique at his normal alignment, the 8 technique returns to his base alignment of three and three from the nub.

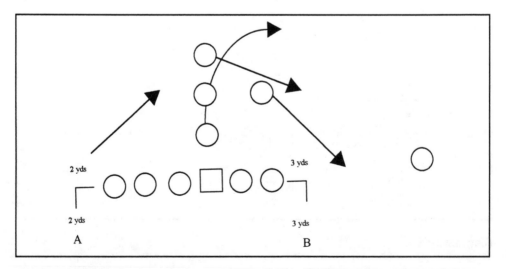

Diagram 6-59: Antler auto-lightnings against a nub end with level-two and full flow away. The lightning path is adjusted to the deeper rain stunt path against level two.

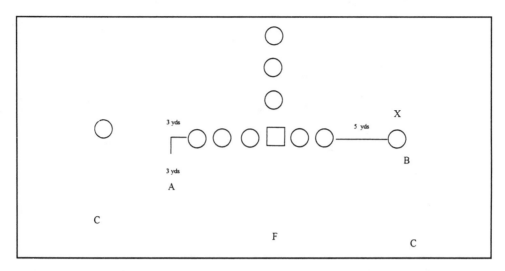

Diagram 6-60: The "X" aligns five yards. This is too wide for a "green" adjustment by the Will linebacker. Brave applies the "squeeze" adjustment guideline and aligns at shadow 9 technique on the "X."

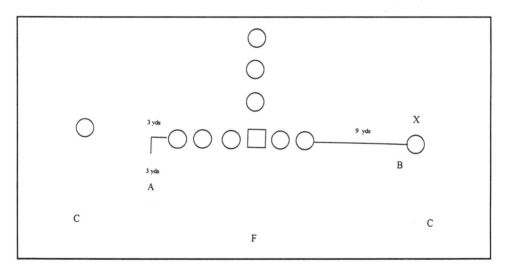

Diagram 6-61: "X" aligns at nine yards, one yard outside the 8 technique maximum width. Brave aligns on the line of scrimmage in an inside shadow alignment.

The defensive coach may want to adjust the stance to a square stance when playing an inside shadow on the closely split single receiver. Another philosophy is to turn inside with the back to the "X." Each have their good and bad points. We prefer to square the stance when aligned in a shadow technique, no matter if the shadow is an inside or outside shadow.

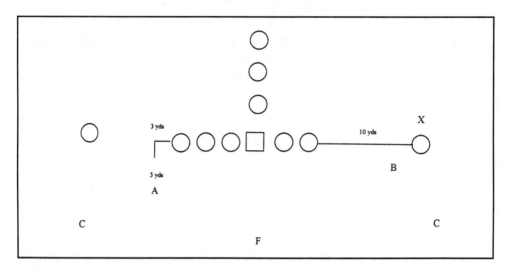

Diagram 6-62: "X" splits ten yards. Brave aligns near the line of scrimmage at the eight yard maximum width.

In Diagram 6-63, "X" receiver splits eleven to twelve yards, one to two yards *inside* the eight-yard axis. Brave moves to seven to six yards from the nub, one to two yards *outside* the nub. In this case, Brave would align about two yards off the line of scrimmage.

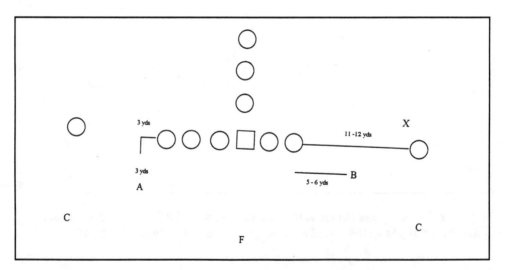

Diagram 6-63.

ALIGNING AGAINST TWINS

Twins presents special circumstances to the 8-technique's split rule. One coaching point to consider in aligning the 8 technique to twins is the depth of the 8-technique alignment. Another point is strict adherence to not aligning outside the eight-yard maximum split.

Twins is a formation which many teams use to run to the weakside off-tackle hole. The twins formation is designed to remove the force so that the weakside off-tackle hole has no outside support. For this reason, we restrict the alignment of our 8 technique against twins to the area inside the eight-yard axis.

Twins should also require the 8 technique to be more considerate of the coverage of the inside receiver. Our Brave should align at the eight-yard axis with enough depth to discourage the quick vertical route to the inside receiver. A "Z" receiver set in the slot of the twins formation will align off the line of scrimmage. This depth benefits the 8 technique. Because the "Z" aligns off the line of scrimmage, the 8 technique has a built-in cushion to read the ball level and junction the "Z"' receiver's route. Junctioning and disrupting the route of the twins formation's inside receiver is a major objective of the 8 technique. If the twins formation inside receiver is an "X" or "Y" receiver, the inside receiver will be on the line of scrimmage. The 8 technique must deepen his split rule alignment to a position at which he may be able to junction the receiver's route. Because junctioning the inside receiver is not the only concern of an 8 technique, the 8 technique should not align deeper than four yards from the line of scrimmage.

What is the bottom line when assessing the split rule to twins? When facing a twins receiver, the 8 technique should align three to four yards off the line of scrimmage, but not wider than the eight-yard axis. The rule of squeeze playing the receiver with an eight-yard or less split still applies to the twins formation.

ALIGNING AGAINST TRIPS AND QUADS

When facing widely spread multiple receivers in trips and quads formations, the 8 technique aligns on a vertical plane dissecting the split of the widest receiver and the nub. When facing multiple receiver clusters bunched together near the sideline, the 8 technique may extend his width beyond the eight-yard axis. The 8 technique should be closest to the most dangerous threat. Wide multiple receiver clusters from the bunch set pose a greater threat than the running game, so the outside linebacker may use the common sense rule of alignment.

THE COMMON SENSE SPLIT RULE

When in doubt as to where to align, the 8 technique may always use the common sense rule of alignment. The common sense rule states, "If you don't know where to align, how far out you should go, or how far off you should align, line up where you can get the job done."

Athletes often have a knack for understanding what their individual role is; they know their job and they have an idea of how to get it done. The common sense rule is the backbone of the alignment coaching points in the Forty Nickel defense. If for some reason the technical, prescribed plan fails, common sense doesn't. In Diagram 6-64, the "Z" receiver is split eleven to twelve yards. Brave aligns at the eight-yard axis against a twins receiver. Brave keeps his normal three yard depth but may align slightly closer to the line since the "Z" receiver is off the line of scrimmage.

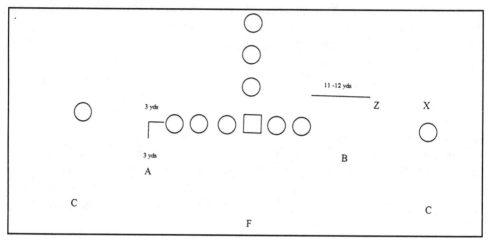

Diagram 6-64.

In Diagram 6-65, the "Z" is the outside receiver; the "X" receiver is in the slot. Since the inside receiver is on the line of scrimmage, Brave must deepen his alignment to four yards and stay on the eight-yard axis. By aligning at four yards instead of three, Brave gains ball-level recognition time.

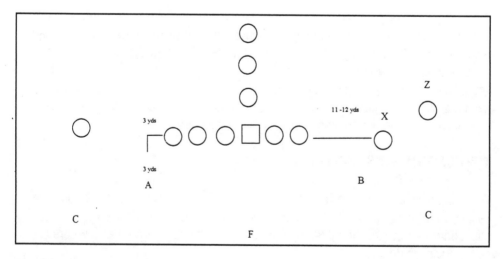

Diagram 6-65.

Open trips is shown in Diagram 6-66. Brave takes a position which is approximately midway between the outside receiver "X" and the nub. Brave aligns at normal depth since the receivers in the slot are off the line of scrimmage.

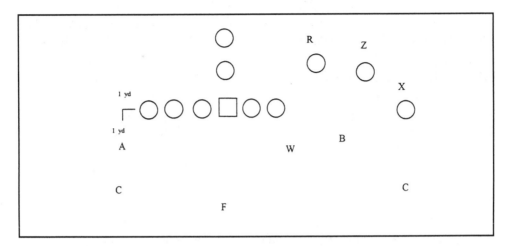

Diagram 6-66: Open Trips.

8-TECHNIQUE PLAY AGAINST LEVEL ONE

Level-one ball action with flow toward the 8 technique prompts the 8 technique player to provide run support. Like the S2 technique, the 8 technique provides run support. Unlike the S2 technique, the 8 technique is always the primary force player.

Understanding that the role of the force is to provide a defensive edge and funnel the ballcarrier, the 8 technique is to respond aggressively to run keys. Like the S2 technique, the 8 technique is turned in to the ball at a forty-five-degree angle, and like a S2 technique, the 8 technique bounces on the snap of the ball. The 8 technique provides run support in exactly the same manner as a S2 technique defender except for the following considerations:

- The 8 technique is tighter to the ball and must react quicker than the S2 technique to level-one action.

- The 8 technique has an advantage in playing the sweep because of his proximity to the formation.

- The 8 technique has an alignment conducive to slow-playing the load option.

- The 8 technique's tight alignment provides the lead option blocker with an advantage in attempting to arc block the defender.

- The 8 technique is responsible for "wheeling" and stopping the cutback run on level-one flow away.

8-TECHNIQUE PLAY AGAINST THE SWEEP

Being tighter to the ball allows the defender to attack the sweep with a more vertical attack angle than the S2 technique. One of the more difficult concepts for the athlete to master when playing the 8 technique is the principle of squeezing the alley from the 8-technique position. Because the 8 technique is aligned only three yards from the nub, the athlete often feels that he must fly straight upfield in order to keep outside leverage against the sweep. This misconception leads to the athlete attacking the sweep at a point too deep in the backfield. Penetrating too deeply into the backfield allows the lead sweep blocker to simply brush block the defender outside as the running back dips under the block and sprints to the sideline. This technique is so effective against the undisciplined 8 technique who over-penetrates that the scenario is a standard practice drill for most wing-T teams.

Eddie Robinson of Grambling has given clinics on the finer points of executing a blocking technique which allows the defender to keep his outside leverage but prevents him from properly squeezing the alley and defending the sweep. The block is called a "hammer" block. Successfully attacking the hammer block calls for the 8 technique's angle to be sharp to the upfield shoulder of the ballcarrier. An even more important coaching point for the 8 technique is to not get deeper than two yards in the backfield. Any penetration deeper than two yards behind the line of scrimmage opens a seam between the front and the force through which the ballcarrier may dip through and hit the alley—an alley with the outermost boundary as the sideline.

In Diagram 6-67, Antler attacks the sweep with a poor angle and too much penetration. The ballcarrier dips under and hits the sideline.

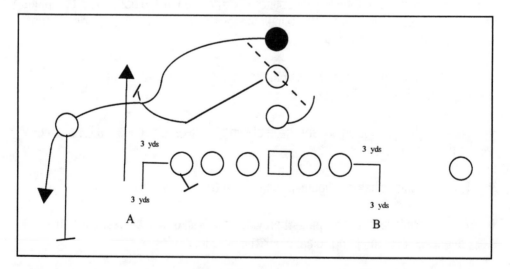

Diagram 6-67.

In Diagram 6-68, Antler attacks the sweep using correct technique. Antler does not penetrate too deep and squeezes the alley by staying under control and playing off the fullback's block near the line of scrimmage.

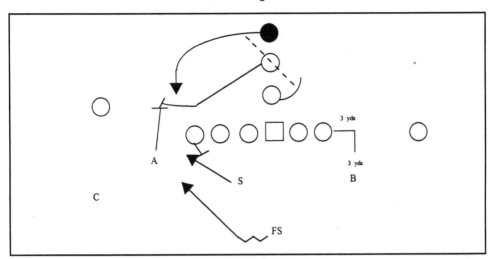

Diagram 6-68.

8-TECHNIQUE PLAY AGAINST THE OPTION

The 8 technique plays the option just as the S2 technique plays the option. The 8 technique slow-plays the quarterback on load option, dumps the lead option, and slow-plays the quarterback on speed option. Due to the tighter alignment of the formation, the outside linebacker is able to slow-play the load option quite easily. The 8 technique needs only to close the distance to the quarterback upon recognition of load option. The alignment depth of an 8 technique puts him in the perfect "off the line" position needed to slow-play the quarterback. See the section on outside linebacker play against the option for more details on slow-playing the quarterback and pitch.

Lead options are played much like the sweep. The 8 technique may be more aggressive against a lead option blocker than a sweep blocker. The reason for the opportunity for a more aggressive reaction is the fact that the trailing pitchman does not have access to the tight alley off tackle. The I-formation tailback and the wing-T formation halfback both have repetitions in practice on the skill of digging and hitting the tight crease. Both also have the opportunity to make the cut, since neither has to keep pitch relationship to the quarterback.

Knowing the limitations for the pitchman, the 8 technique may "kamikaze" the lead blocker with outside leverage. Against lead option blockers, the hesitant 8 technique is a blocked 8 technique. With this one exception, the coaching points for playing lead option are the same for the sweep. Maintaining outside leverage on the lead blocker, staying on the feet, and gauging the speed of the pitchman in order to maintain correct tackling leverage are the three main points to defending the lead option. In Diagram 6-69, Antler reads lead option and dumps (i.e., attacks) the lead blocker. An outside linebacker must be extremely aggressive when attacking the lead blocker.

Diagram 6-70 shows the 8 technique slow-playing the quarterback on load option. The 8 technique also slow-plays the quarterback on speed option.

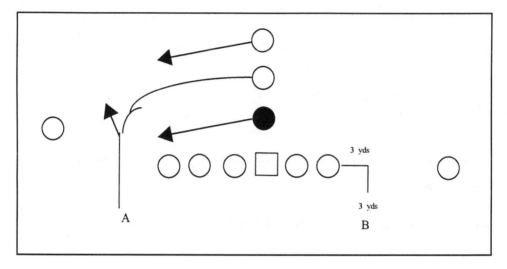

Diagram 6-69.

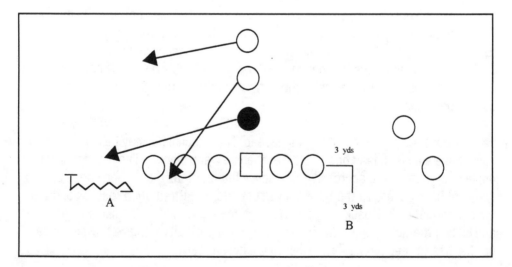

Diagram 6-70.

WHEELING THE 8 TECHNIQUE

When level-one action with flow away shows, the 8 technique reaction is called a "wheel." The outside linebacker bounces on the snap of the ball. As the ball moves down the line away from him, the outside linebacker sinks two steps in a shuffling motion. The outside linebacker must keep his shoulders parallel to the line of scrimmage during the brief shuffle.

The 8 technique outside linebacker shuffles backward because the ball has not yet achieved a level. Remember that a ball moving down the line is a "no-level" read for short-zone personnel when the ball is behind the center and guard. As the ball approaches the tackle box, the linebacker continues his shuffle three steps to the inside. Again, the shoulders will remain parallel to the line of scrimmage as the eyes look inside and scan for a flashing color.

If no opposition's color flashes across the 8 technique's face, the defender sits "in the hole" looking for a cutback. Patience is the key to executing the wheel technique. The outside linebacker must be disciplined to keep the shoulders square and not float to the middle. Neither can the outside linebacker bail out too early and take his pursuit angle downfield.

Abandoning the wheel move too early is probably the most common error in executing this maneuver. The phrases "dropping the anchor" and "dragging the anchor" are effective metaphors to use in coaching the wheel from the 8 technique alignment. The outside linebacker must seek out any flashing color while he waits for what seems to him an interminable amount of time to break into his downfield pursuit angle.

If a flashing color should appear during the wheel, the 8 technique outside linebacker should drive off his inside foot to contain the reversing path of the ballcarrier. If the ball is reversing at level two as in a bootleg, the outside linebacker sprints for width and to gain outside leverage on the ball. If the level-two action pulls up as the 8 technique is gaining the width, the 8 technique squares up, gets his head on a swivel and peeks for a crossing route from the inside. If the crossing route is seen, the outside linebacker floats to intercept the line of sight between the crossing receiver and quarterback, all the time keeping the shoulders square. The outside linebacker reads the eyes of the quarterback and only breaks up to tackle the quarterback if:

- The quarterback tucks the ball and attacks the line of scrimmage.

- The quarterback is standing outside the defensive edge with no pressure forthcoming.

An outside linebacker who executes the wheel technique provides the defensive front with an extra linebacker. Wheeling puts the outside linebacker in a position to compensate for the over-pursuit of the Will linebacker. Wheeling also compensates for the weakside end who failed to close laterally down the line of scrimmage. If the defensive end is left "on the island" as the pursuit moves to the strongside, the wheeling outside linebacker is able to close the hole by his inward shuffle. Keeping the shoulders square enables the outside linebacker to play cutback and ball reversals. Mastery of the wheel technique is vital for maintaining defensive continuity.

8-TECHNIQUE PURSUIT ANGLE

Taking a pursuit angle refers to getting to a location to tackle the ballcarrier before he scores. The pursuit angle of an 8 technique leads him to be the last defender to make the tackle on a long run. Teaching the 8 technique pursuit angle involves two elements.

The first element in teaching 8 technique pursuit is linked to proper execution of the wheel maneuver. As the linebacker becomes positive that no immediate cutback threat exists, the 8 technique shuffles backward or backpedals until the ball crosses the line of scrimmage. At that point the second element of the pursuit angle is undertaken. Once the ballcarrier has crossed the line of scrimmage and is a threat to get down the sideline, the outside linebacker breaks from his backward shuffle to take the long pursuit angle to save the touchdown. The outside linebacker must be disciplined in his angle.

If the ballcarrier cuts back against the grain, the outside linebacker will likely be ahead of the ballcarrier at that point. The most effective reaction to a back cutting back against the grain is for the 8 technique to break off the pursuit angle and again begin to backpedal or shuffle. The running back will often break into a position in which the outside linebacker may tackle him. By getting back into the backpedal or shuffle, the shoulders become square and the outside linebacker will be more likely to get an opportunity to tackle the ballcarrier. The "backpedal—sprint to pursue—backpedal—sprint to pursue" sequence may actually occur more than once in the season for the outside linebacker. Hopefully, it is not a common occurrence. As a defensive staff, we acknowledge that several instances will arise in which a player will save a touchdown by taking a proper pursuit angle.

During a season, a coach will likely see a well-executed offensive play now and then along with a fair share of defensive breakdowns. However, we believe firmly that the great defense does not surrender the big play and the long touchdown run. We will knock the ballcarrier out of bounds at the one- or two-yard line, and we will get into our goal-line package.

Pride in your goal-line package must be promoted to your athletes. Team confidence in the goal-line package is directly linked to the players executing their pursuit angle assignments. By building confidence in your goal line defensive abilities, you provide motivation for your players to go full speed into their pursuit angles. No defender has a larger role in assuring the defense of the second chance than the 8 technique in his proper pursuit angle. In Diagram 6-71, Brave sinks and shuffles inward as he executes the "wheel" maneuver. The area between the dotted lines illustrates the field of vision of which Brave is aware as he wheels inside.

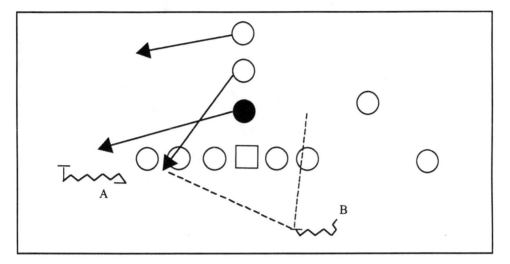

Diagram 6-71.

Diagram 6-72 shows the tailback cutting back. Because the 8 technique Brave properly wheeled on the level-one flow away, Brave stopped him for a short gain.

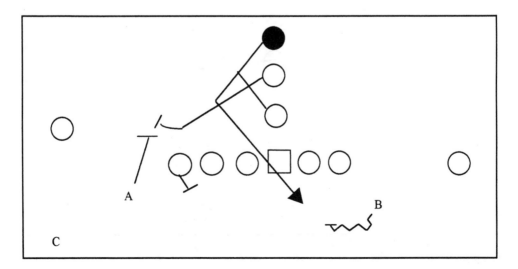

Diagram 6-72.

In Diagram 6-73, Brave starts to wheel but sees one of two flashing colors, the backside guard pulling and the fullback slipping out for the pass route. Ideally, Brave knocks the fullback to the ground and eliminates the flat route. If knocking the fullback down is not possible, Brave covers the fullback. The pursuit will adjust and pressure the quarterback.

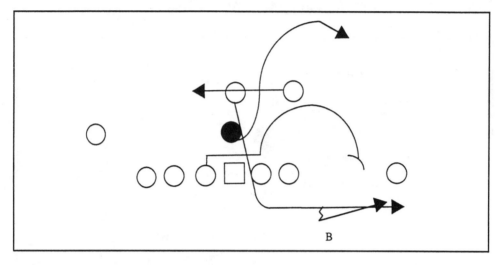

Diagram 6-73.

In Diagram 6-74, the ball reverses back to the Brave. Because the Brave wheeled with his shoulders square, Brave T-steps and redirects to make the tackle.

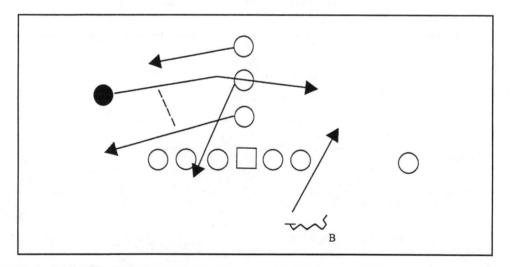

Diagram 6-74.

In Diagram 6-75, Brave wheels and takes the pursuit angle. The proper pursuit angle allows Brave to be the defender who makes the touchdown-saving tackle.

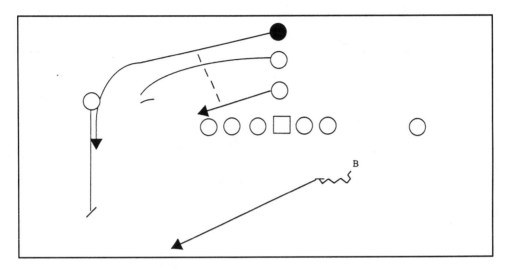

Diagram 6-75.

In Diagram 6-76, Brave drags the anchor in his wheel. As the ball continues to move down level one, Brave backpedals. When the ball gets to the line of scrimmage, Brave breaks into his pursuit angle. The ballcarrier breaks back across the grain and Brave squares his shoulders and again backpedals. The proper broken field pursuit tackling technique is for the Brave to let the ballcarrier come toward him.

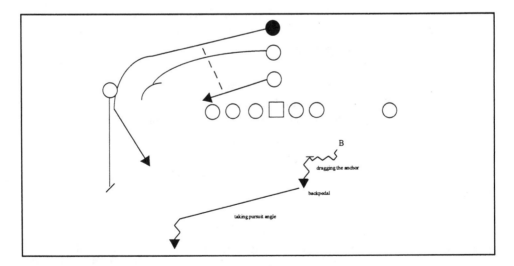

Diagram 6-76.

In Diagram 6-77, Brave reads level one and drops the anchor. As the ball flows away, Brave drags the anchor as he wheels. The concept of dragging an anchor helps the player to understand the relative speed he possesses in executing the wheel technique.

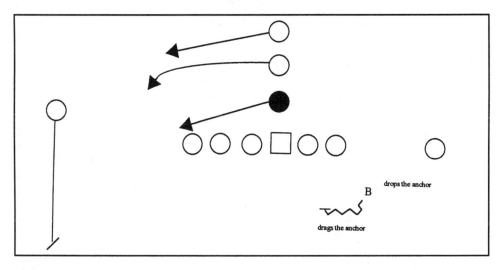

Diagram 6-77.

8-TECHNIQUE REACTION TO LEVEL THREE

The 8 technique has the same level-three assignment as the S2 technique. The 8 technique is responsible for the flat zone on level-three action. Unlike his alignment on the wide receiver in a S2 technique, the outside linebacker aligned in an 8 technique must sprint to gain width if level three shows. Like the S2 technique, the 8 technique is always concerned with the route of the number-two receiver as he looks through the number-two receiver to the ball. And like the S2 technique, the 8 technique breaks off any sinking action if he reads any inside receiver running a route which threatens the flat. The S2 technique usually has the luxury of the number-one receiver being aligned within the S2 technique's field of vision. An 8 technique must sneak a peek at the number-one receiver as the 8 technique sprints to cover the flat zone. The 8 technique "sneaks a peak" because, as with any zone-playing pass defender, the 8 technique's main focus is the line of sight to the quarterback.

By sneaking a peak at the number-one receiver's route, the 8 technique will be able to read the number-one receiver. The advantage of route reading against the number-one receiver prevents the 8 technique from being wasted in the flat zone. If, on level three, no inside receiver threat to the flat exists and the number-one receiver runs a curl or other inside breaking route, the 8 technique may sink into the curl zone.

If the number-one receiver runs an out, hitch, or such other pattern in the flat, the 8 technique continues his sprint to cover the flat zone. The 8 technique's alignment is not conducive to defending the wide receiver out route, quick fade, or hitch. The 8 technique's base alignment leaves the defense vulnerable to these routes. However, the defender aligned as an 8 can provide immediate support to the cornerback by sprinting to the flat zone.

The goal of an 8 technique in defending the wide receiver perimeter routes is to get underneath the route. Getting underneath the out route entails the 8 technique sprinting to the flat in such a manner as to intersect the line of sight between the quarterback and the receiver—another good reason to sneak a peek. The 8 technique must be aware of the wide receiver's route to intersect the line of sight. By intersecting the line of sight, the 8 technique is in position to intercept the poorly thrown pass. As a defensive staff, we can guarantee the opportunity to pick off a pass to the athlete who consistently intersects the out route. The odds are against seeing a season of perfect passes to the wide receiver. Down and distance are enormous considerations in defending the pass from the 8 technique. If the down and distance permits, we allow the 8 technique to widen and deepen his alignment. In defending long-distance possession downs, our 8 technique may align as wide as five yards from the nub of the single-receiver side and as deep as five yards from the line of scrimmage. In special circumstances such as panic downs for the offense, we have allowed the 8 technique to align at the eight-yard axis on the single-receiver side. If an 8 technique needs to align wider than eight yards to stop the outside route, the Forty Nickel coach should call Cover 3 Out. Cover 3 Out is a three-deep coverage.

On Cover 3 Out, the outside linebacker aligns as a S2 technique instead of the 8-technique alignment of Cover 3. Cover 3 Out allows for the outside linebacker to be in position to stop the out route to the single-receiver side. If more than one receiver is split against Cover 3 Out, the S2 technique linebacker converts to an 8 technique.

JUNCTIONING NUMBER TWO

If level three shows to the two-receiver side, the outside linebacker junctions the number-two receiver's route. If the number-two receiver fails to go out on a pattern, the outside linebacker will revert to his technique of sneaking a peek at number one as the 8 technique linebacker sprints to the flat zone. In most cases of level-three action, the second receiver will run a pass route. A "Y" receiver aligned as number two in a pro formation may release inside or outside the defensive end. If the "Y" releases outside the defensive end on a vertical route, the path of the "Y" will bring him through the position of the 8 technique's base alignment.

Much like the S2 technique, the 8 technique seeks out the number-two receiver on level-three action. As a pro formation's "Y" receiver releases upfield, the 8 technique (usually Antler) junctions the "Y," disrupting his route. When junctioning the path of a "Y" or other under-split inside receiver, the 8 technique keeps his shoulders parallel to the line of scrimmage while maintaining outside leverage. After junctioning the route with one solid hit on the receiver, the 8 technique sprints to the flat zone. As the 8 technique sprints to the flat, he sneaks a peek at the number-one receiver. The 8 technique sneaks a peek because the vertical route of the number-two receiver discounts the inside receiver as a threat to the flat.

Once an inside receiver has shown verticality in his pattern, the 8 technique may revert to his route reading technique of play on the single receiver side. If a "Y" receiver or other such grossly under-split receiver releases inside the defensive end, junctioning the path of the receiver is not feasible. Most under-split receivers release inside in order to run a route across the field. The 8 technique discounts the route of an inside-releasing player from the tight end or tight slot position and reverts to his single receiver technique of coverage.

A "Z" receiver in the slot of a twins formation is also to be junctioned. Junctioning a wide receiver is more difficult than junctioning the tight receiver. In junctioning the wide receiver, the 8 technique should drop his hips and extend both arms to the upper torso of the receiver. Prior to this contact, the 8 technique must sight the receiver by momentarily shifting his focus from the quarterback to the receiver. As contact is made, the 8 technique brings his focus back to the quarterback. If a wide receiver has to "swim" around to the outside, the 8 technique was successful in his junction. The pattern is read as a vertical and the 8 technique returns to his route reading of the outside receiver as the 8 technique sprints to the flat.

If a wide receiver attempts to "swim" inside the 8 technique, the defender attempts to pin the receiver inside by jamming the outside arm under the outside armpit of the receiver. The 8 technique attempts to topple the receiver to the inside with a forceful ride. The outside arm acts as a lifting lever to the outside shoulder of the receiver. Once the receiver has fallen or cleared, the 8 technique reverts to his route reading technique of the outside receiver and proceeds directly to the flat.

8-TECHNIQUE PLAY AGAINST LEVEL TWO

The 8-technique gains immediate width against level-two action with flow toward him. The 8 technique jumps the route of any receiver crossing his face to threaten the flat.

The 8-technique linebacker does not provide secondary containment should the quarterback break initial containment. Secondary level-two containment responsibility belongs to the inside linebackers. Secondary containment will be provided by the frontside linebacker when the defense is facing a running quarterback. Secondary containment will be provided by the backside linebacker if the defense is facing a quarterback who looks to throw the ball on level two.

Should the 8 technique get to the flat and settle but read no flat-threatening route, the 8 technique will float to the line of sight between the curl route and quarterback. However, in floating to the line of sight, the 8 technique should keep an outside-in relationship to the quarterback. Keeping an outside-in relationship allows the 8 technique to fulfill his role as the guardian of the edge of the defense. Even a passing quarterback can break secondary containment, particularly when the backside inside linebacker is the secondary containment. If secondary containment is lost, the 8 technique must make the tackle for a two- to three-yard gain. To accomplish this task, the 8 technique must never float inside so far as to lose outside leverage on the quarterback. A good general rule calls for the 8 technique to shuffle only two to three steps when floating inside to the curl.

If covered, the curling receiver will in many cases break to the sideline when the quarterback breaks containment. It would be a shame for the 8 technique to float too far inside for supplemental help on the curl and leave the sideline (his primary area of coverage) open. When floating inside, even if only for a few steps, the 8 technique must keep his head on a swivel and feel the receiver's route, should the receiver break behind the 8 technique to the sideline.

Level-two action away from the 8 technique calls for the outside linebacker to sink with the shoulders square. The 8 technique sinks or backpedals two to three yards while looking for a throwback screen or handback draw. The 8 technique keeps his shoulders square while backpedaling. A level-two throwback screen is a rarely run but effective play. The quarterback will roll out to level two away from the 8 technique, stop, and throw a screen pass back to the side of the 8 technique. Hence the name, throwback screen. Any pass in which the quarterback rolls level two in one direction and passes the ball back across the midline of the formation is called a throwback. It is the job of the 8 technique to guard against shallow throwback routes on level-two action.

An 8 technique aligned on the "Y" receiver of a pro formation seeks out the "Y" on any level-two action weakside. It can be said that the 8 technique's style of play is a man-to-man technique on the "Y" when the ball moves to level-two away. If the "Y" blocks, the 8 technique, usually Antler, sinks and hangs to ensure that the "Y" doesn't spin out for a tight end screen. Another good route for the "Y" on level-two away is to block and delay. After the "Y" delays for a two count, the "Y" releases on a shallow route replacing the inside linebackers who ran to coverage against the level-two action.

The 8 technique must stop this route. An 8 technique aligned to the open side of the formation will be able to sink underneath and rob the drag route of the wide receiver. The outside linebacker may sneak the peek at the number one as the ball goes to level two with flow away. If the wide receiver is running a flat post or drag, the 8 technique may sink and settle to junction the route. If the wide receiver runs a skinny post, the 8 technique may sink underneath the route. However, unlike the level-two action away from a pro formation "Y" receiver or tight slot, the 8 technique does not use a man-to-man coverage technique on the open side (although a tight slot is on the open side of the formation, a tight slot is considered a tight end by an 8 technique.)

Another tricky route is a delayed rail by the number-two receiver. The ball will move to level-two away from the 8 technique and the number-two receiver will delay for a two count and run a rail route. This route will usually be run with a skinny post by the backside wide receiver. The cornerback will squeeze the skinny post, as he should. To allow for the cornerback to safely squeeze the skinny post on level-two action away from the cornerback, the 8 technique applies his man-to-man coverage principle in covering the number-two receiver.

Even though the 8 technique is a short *zone* the man-coverage principle on a tight receiver calls for the 8 technique to cover the delay rail route by the tight end, tight slot, or nearback. As the receiver rails, the 8 technique covers him man-to-man using the trail technique to wall the receiver from the inside. The trail coverage technique allows the 8 technique to stay in the line of sight between the quarterback and the receiver. This quirk of coverage responsibility for the 8 technique—man principle the tight number-two receiver on level-two away—fortifies the three-deep coverage defense. This strengthening also affords the Forty Nickel coach confidence in the generic safety of the strategy of running the base three-deep coverage against the exotic but well-coached passing teams.

THE FREE 8-TECHNIQUE ALIGNMENT

A free 8-technique alignment refers to an outside linebacker who is playing a S1 technique on the number-two receiver. The outside linebackers play a S1 technique in Cover 1 Free. A free 8 technique is an 8 technique by alignment, but no major differences exist between the two techniques. Regular 8 technique split rules do not apply to the free 8 technique. The free 8 is a S1 technique outside linebacker who only assumes the 8-technique alignment when he does not have a second receiver to cover. Without a second receiver to his side, the outside linebacker S1 technique is "free" for another assignment. When "free," the S1 technique outside linebacker assumes the alignment of an 8 technique and becomes a free 8 technique.

The free 8 technique is a man-to-man coverage technique and the 8 technique is a zone-coverage technique. The free 8 technique has the second receiver out to the same side as the outside linebacker's alignment. This receiver may come from across the formation or from the backfield. The free 8 technique has the second man out. If the offense has no second man out, the free 8 technique may cover level-two and level-three action according to regular 8 technique parameters.

The free 8 technique does not wheel, as would the 8 technique, on level-one flow away. Wheeling against level one with flow away is an unsound technique for a free 8-technique player. The free 8 technique should drop anchor and look for flashing colors. A good technique is to have the free 8 technique widen against level-one away. This widening movement ensures the linebacker will not drift into the middle and puts him in good position to check for a back slipping out into the near flat on bootleg. Provided the ball has broken the line of scrimmage on level-one action away, the free 8 technique executes the proper 8 technique pursuit angle. The free 8 technique attacks level-one action toward him in the same fashion as a regular 8 technique would attack. If no second receiver is aligned to his side and level one with action toward him shows, the free 8 technique will provide run support. In Diagram 6-78, the number-two receiver, "Y," releases outside with level-three action. Antler junctions the route and goes to the flat. Antler starts to cover the flat but recognizes the curl route after sneaking a peek at the "Z."

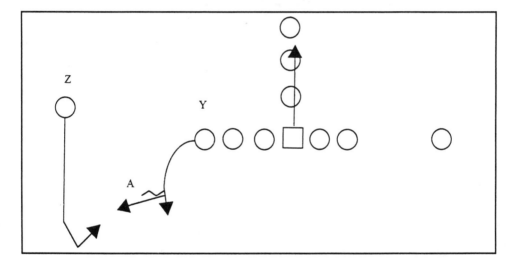

Diagram 6-78.

In Diagram 6-79, the number-two receiver, "Y," releases outside with level-three action. Antler junctions the route and goes to the flat. Antler continues to flat after sneaking a peek and seeing number one on an out route.

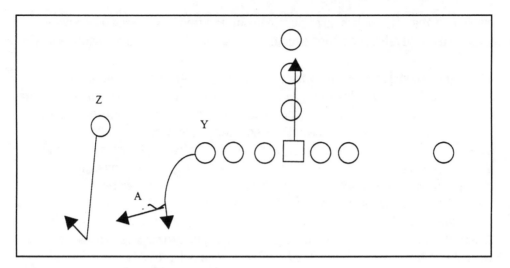

Diagram 6-79.

Shown in Diagram 6-80, is level-two action toward the 8 technique. Antler immediately gains width and sneaks a peek at the route of "Z."

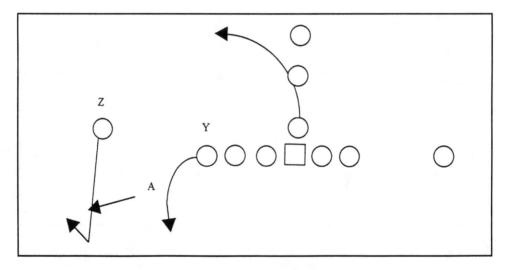

Diagram 6-80.

In Diagram 6-81, Antler reads level two toward him. Antler opens and sprints to the flat. After the 8 technique Antler sneaks a peek at the route of the "Z," Antler recognizes no threat to the flat and sinks under the curl route of the "Z."

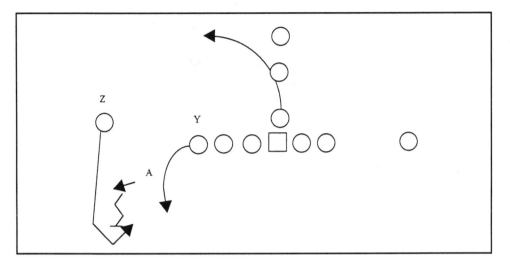

Diagram 6-81.

In Diagram 6-82, Antler reads level two toward him. Antler opens and sprints to the flat. After the 8 technique Antler sneaks a peek at the route of the "Z," Antler recognizes no threat to the flat and sinks under the curl route of the "Z." Antler moves back to the sideline as quarterback breaks secondary containment and "Z" is felt sliding to the sideline.

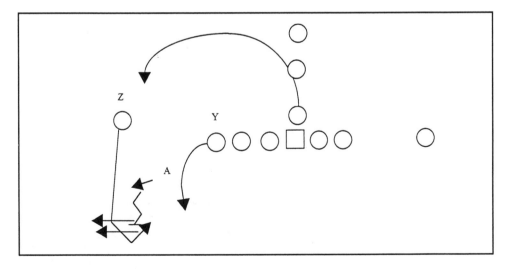

Diagram 6-82.

Level-two away from the 8 technique Antler is shown in Diagram 6-83, Antler covers the number-two receiver, "Y," using man-to-man principle.

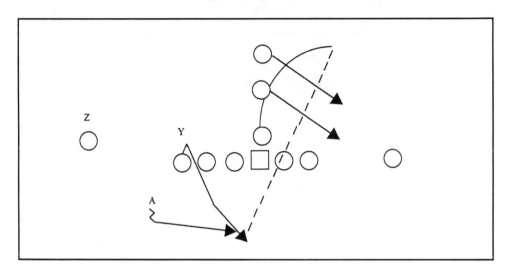

Diagram 6-83.

In Diagram 6-84, level-two flow away is shown. The 8 technique Antler applies man-to-man coverage principles to the route of the "Y" receiver. Antler covers the "Y" delayed rail by using the trail-coverage technique.

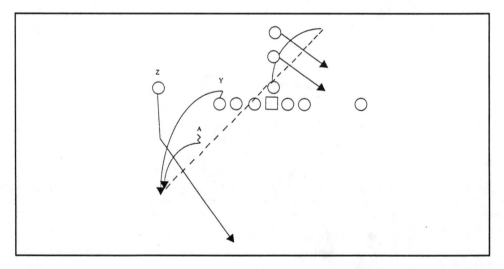

Diagram 6-84.

CHAPTER 7

Cornerbacks

CORNERBACK CHARACTERISTICS

The cornerback is a sure-footed high tackler with excellent hip flexibility. He must be able to backpedal and must enjoy the pressure of man-to-man coverage on the edge of the defense. The cornerback has the best speed on the defense and loves to hawk the ball. Cornerbacks go up for the ball and are counted on to provide game-saving, not necessarily hard-hitting, tackles. They are expected to grab cloth when they tackle. A cornerback should practice daily on the "tomahawk" technique of stripping the ball. The tomahawk technique is discussed in the section on outside linebacker play.

CORNERBACK STANCE

The cornerback keeps an ankle-to-ankle stance with a stagger of four inches. The stagger depends on the secondary technique which the cornerback is playing. A S1 technique plays with the inside foot back of the front foot. A S3 or S4 technique plays with an outside foot stagger; the outside foot is back of the front.

The cornerback has a forward lean with his hands just above and slightly outside his knees. His knees are bent. His back foot has a slight heel raise while the body weight is placed over the front foot. Placing the weight over the front foot allows the cornerback to push off to backpedal.

Assuming the proper stance is an important part of playing an defensive position. For the cornerback, an incorrect stance leads to a poor initial movement, backpedal. Fractions of seconds mean the difference between an iron curtain secondary and a porous secondary. The athletes who demonstrate the proper stance in the individual and group drills should be liberally praised. Conversely, a cornerback who refuses to assume the correct stance is passed over and not allowed his turn to participate in a drill. This type of vigilant support of the proper stance of the athlete ensures that the athlete develops a disciplined stance and style of play.

Chart 7a: Cornerback alignment techniques.

S1 Technique	Man-to-man on he number one receiver from the outside, seven yards off the line of scrimmage and one yard inside.
S2 Technique	One yard off the line of scrimmage and one yard outside the receiver.
S3 Technique	Seven yards off the line of scrimmage and one yard outside the receiver.
S4 Technique	Eight to ten yards off the line of scrimmage; four yards outside the hash, over the tackle when aligned on a nub.
5-Quarter	Five yards off the line of scrimmage, three yards outside the nub (alignment same as S5 technique shown).
S7 Technique	Man-to-man, one yard off the line of scrimmage and one yard inside receiver.
S9 Technique	Five yards off the line of scrimmage and three yards outside the nub end (not shown).

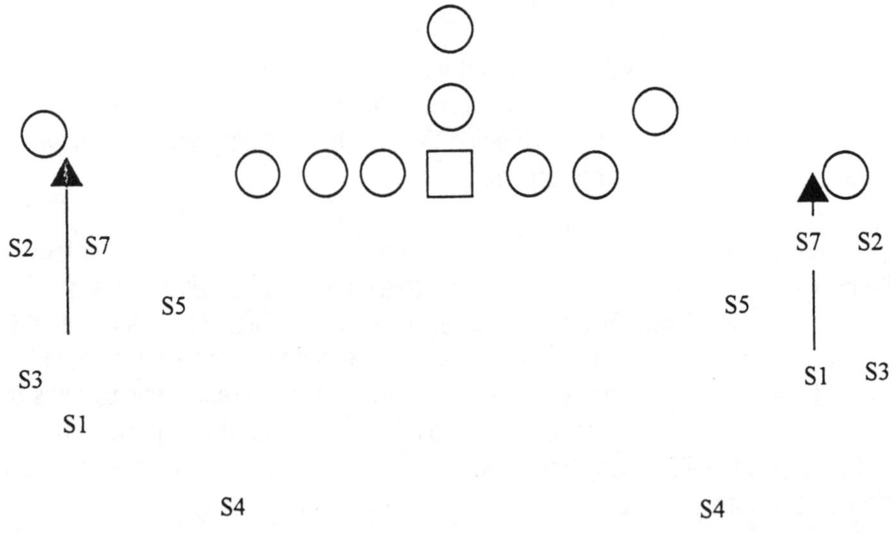

S2   S7   S7   S2

        S5   S5

S3   S1   S3

    S1

        S4   S4

Chart 7b: S9 technique alignment.

The cornerback plays a S9 technique on a nub end *if* the outside linebacker aligns as a squeezed 9 technique.

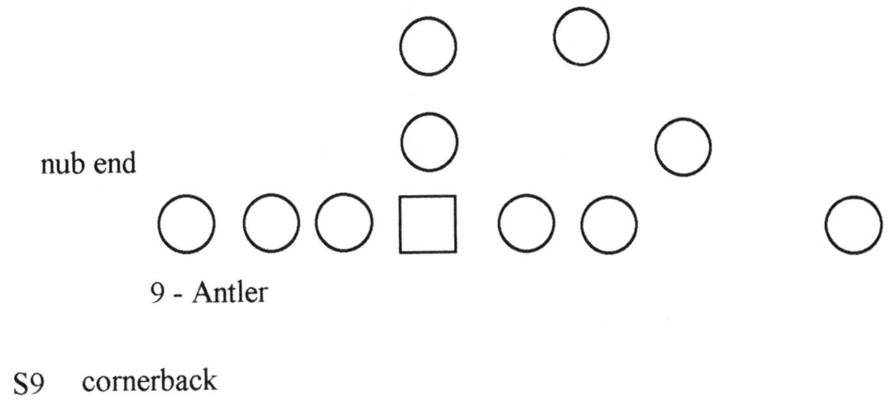

nub end

9 - Antler

S9   cornerback

CORNERBACK TECHNIQUE OVERVIEW

The cornerback will make a large percentage of tackles coming from the side of the ball carrier. The cornerback will usually be the second or third contact on a ballcarrier, arriving just before the ballcarrier goes down. The second and successive tacklers are expected to take every opportunity to strip the ball from the ballcarrier. The cornerback has the opportunity to strip the ball from the stalemated ballcarrier before the whistle is blown or the running back goes down. Cornerbacks will make tackles in the open field usually from the side or slightly behind the ballcarrier, and are then expected to strip the ball as they tackle the ballcarrier in the open field. This technique is practiced daily.

The cornerback will also be involved in tackling wide receivers. We teach the cornerback to be alert for opportunities to strip the ball from the receivers. Our cornerbacks are sold on the belief that receivers will usually be concerned with breaking the tackle rather than protecting the ball. Forty Nickel cornerbacks know it is part of their job to look for opportunities to strip the ball. Cornerbacks rarely cover underneath zones. Usually, cornerbacks cover the deep zones or play man-to-man. A "tight" call will tell the S3 technique to tighten his alignment and challenge the short routes. Interceptions are expected from the cornerback position. An excellent cornerback should deliver interceptions to the defense. Interceptions occur when a cornerback understands his coverage responsibility and believes the ball to be "his" when it goes over 15 yards in the air.

Cornerbacks usually play either S1, S3, or S4 techniques in the secondary. An athlete is selected to play cornerback because of his deep coverage ability. The cornerback position may be the place the coach can hide the athlete who demonstrates a distaste for hard contact, but who is an excellent athlete who likes to play pass coverage technique. The cornerback sometimes plays a 5-quarters technique as an adjustment technique from to a specific formation or motion. The 5-quarters technique is a secondary technique, but the usual denotation "S" for "secondary" is not necessary when discussing the 5-quarters technique. This lack of denotation is because there is no 5-quarters technique defensive line technique. The strongside cornerback in Cover 3 Squat will also play a S2 technique. The S2 technique is the only dual short zone and perimeter run support technique the cornerback will play. Finally, cornerbacks recognize nub ends and learn to play a S9 technique when facing a nub end with a "squeeze" adjustment from the outside linebacker. The S9 is basically a S3 technique but with run support responsibility. Alignment and nub end responsibility of the S9 technique are detailed further in the secondary section of this text.

THE S1 TECHNIQUE KEYS

The S1 aligned on a split receiver focuses on the quarterback to start his backpedal. Although the responsibility of a S1 technique is man-to-man, keying the quarterback for an initial read will give the cornerback a read as to the forthcoming short route from the receiver. The S1 technique wants to stop all routes, not just the deep route. The S1 technique will use the quarterback to decide if the cornerback should settle and break on the receiver's first cut. As the man-to-man technique has his bright lights on the quarterback, the defender is cognizant of the receiver's movement. If the quarterback drops with a low back shoulder, the drop will be a deep drop; consequently, the receiver will run a deep route. The S1 technique will throw his eyes to the receiver and attempt to maintain cushion and leverage. If the quarterback drops back with a high upfield (back) shoulder, then he will settle at three steps or less to throw the quick game.

When the S1 technique recognizes the quick game, he chops his backpedal and sinks his hip to settle as he throws the bright lights on the receiver. The S1 technique focuses his attention at the navel of the receiver's stomach, the belly button. This focus must be continually reinforced, as the novice cornerback will often throw his eyes inside but see the whole body of the receiver, or focus on the receiver's entire upper body. Failing to focus on the belly button will cause the receiver to lose intensity and become vulnerable to the moves of the receiver. Focusing on the belly button reminds the defensive back to keep his head low as he cushions the receiver.

Recognition of the three-step drop will tell the cornerback to jump the first cut of the receiver. Recognition of the deeper drop mechanics by the quarterback will cue the cornerback to stay off the first cut, but maintain cushion leverage on the cutting receiver. In other words, if the drop is shown to be greater than five yards, the defensive back should squeeze any first cut in order to maintain leverage to cover the deep route coming off the first cut. After all, the S1 technique is man-to-man. He has to keep position to play the cornerback on all cuts. It is the recognition of the three-step drop mechanics which will cue him to *challenge* the first cut.

The S1 technique should be coached to keep in mind the fact that his teammates are applying significant pressure to the quarterback. In most cases, the S1 technique and man-to-man coverage are principal parts to a pressure package. This knowledge allows the S1 technique the confidence to defend the receiver and not just watch the receiver.

DEFENDING THE RECEIVER AND MAKING THE PICK

Different styles are taught for allowing the man-to-man coverage technique the opportunity to intercept the ball. The S1 technique may sneak a peek for the ball, once he has obtained the high ground on the receiver. Some coaches tell the defender to watch the eyes of the receiver—the eyes will "get big" as the ball nears the receiver. Coaches tell the defender to watch for the receiver's hands reaching for the ball. These points are all good coaching points.

As the ball is nearing the "go" route receiver, the S1 technique has kept inside leverage and is pressing the receiver to the sideline. The S1 technique used one of the above methods to recognize the flight of the ball. As the receiver reaches to catch the ball, the S1 technique uses his arm closest to the receiver to reach *through* the grasp of the receiver. The S1 technique reaches through the receiver underneath the receiver's arm closest to the defender. The S1 technique next uses his hand to deflect the ball from the receiver. If the receiver maintains the concentration to catch the ball with two hands, the defender uses that same arm to jerk the outside arm of the receiver downward.

The arm farthest from the receiver comes around to grasp the receiver about the upper body. This arm provides the tackling safety measure in case the ball is not knocked from the receiver's grasp. If the receiver has broken on an in-breaking route such as a post, the same technique can be used if the defensive back has no chance for the two-handed interception. Naturally, if the defensive back goes for the interception, the safety of the tackling arm technique is lost as he reaches the off hand under the receiver to make the catch. If the S1 technique has no chance to intercept the short to intermediate route, he can drive through the upfield shoulder to make the tackle. At the moment of contact, the S1 technique should grab with the near arm and tomahawk strip with the other arm.

S1 TECHNIQUE CUSHION

Since the initial alignment of the S1 technique is seven yards off and one yard inside, the maximum cushion is seven yards. A common error is to allow the S1 technique to keep a huge cushion and not actually defend the route. This type of play negates the pressure from the front. The worst thing for our pressure front is to continually see the short pass thrown in front to the defensive back with the large cushion. This concern is the principal supporting fact for reading the quarterback's drop. The ultimate factor in alignment depth is the defensive back's ability. If the defensive back has excellent transition skills, speed turning ability to break out of the backpedal, the cushion may be less than seven yards.

PLAYING THE UNDERSPLIT RECEIVER

The S1 technique adjusts his alignment to headup at the eight-yard axis. The eight-yard axis is a point eight yards from the nub of the formation. As the receiver aligns closer to the formation, the S1 technique adjusts to an outside alignment. The maximum outside alignment is two yards on a close set receiver such as a wingback. The standard outside alignment is one yard outside the receiver, including the "Y" receiver. Against an under-split wide receiver, the S1 technique now has the advantage of looking through his man-coverage responsibility to the quarterback. Again, his bright lights are on the quarterback, but the receiver is now within his line of sight. The S1 technique may widen with the outward movement of the receiver as the quarterback mechanics reveal the depth of the drop and the consequential route options. The under-split receiver has few route options. He can either go straight upfield, slant across the linebacker minefield, make a cut, or immediately drive for the outside. The outside alignment facilitates defending the outbreak option. Our standard man coverage, Cover 1 Free, also gives the S1-technique free safety help in the middle.

PLAYING THE CLOSE-SPLIT RECEIVER OF THE WING-T

A close-split or close-set receiver is a wingback, tight end or tight slot. The Wing-T offense uses superior ball fakes to hide the ball and deceive the secondary coverage personnel. A good Wing-T offense will fake to make every pass look like a run. This faking accomplishes two things. First, run support from the zone package is affected, at least psychologically. The 8 technique may read run and come up only to see the ball looped over his head to the flat. The S6-technique free safety may read run and be caught in no man's land as the ball sails overhead to a naked receiver on the post route. The fear of this situation occurring intimidates the secondary personnel and undermines their confidence in reading run. Thus, they support a step slower and the defensive edge becomes soft against the run. Second, the great faking undermines the zone coverage through using the aggressive tendency of a player against him. Once the offensive coach is confident the free safety is actively making hits near the line of scrimmage, the coach calls for a good fake and a post route behind the free safety. The patient faking of the Wing-T will eventually catch the zone player out of position and make a big play.

In the Forty Nickel scheme, man-to-man is the preferred coverage against the Wing-T. Man-to-man coverage allows our S1 techniques to focus on the receiver and not the quarterback. This focus protects the S1 technique from the deception of the misdirection fakes prior to the play-action pass. The man-to-man coverage technique is altered slightly versus the tight formation. The defensive back does not focus on the quarterback versus a tight formation. Instead, the man-to-man technique looks at the defender he is responsible for covering. Bright lights are usually put on the quarterback when playing S1 technique, but not against the Wing-T attack. When facing a Wing-T which relies on ball faking, the S1 technique abandons the quarterback read and burns his eyes into the close-set receiver. Putting the bright lights on the receiver eliminates the deception of the ball fakes in the backfield.

By focusing on the receiver, the S1 technique will also get an accurate and immediate run-pass key. If the receiver blocks, the S1 technique drives out of his backpedal and provides run support. If the receiver releases, the S1 technique gains leverage on the route and covers the receiver. The block and release move by the wing or tight end is not a factor to us. We feel the defensive back can be trained to recognize the intensity and the follow-through of the block. Once again, the S1 technique comes out of his backpedal and provides run support upon recognition of the receiver *blocking*, not pretending to block. The S1 technique comes up after he is positive the potential receiver is a blocker.

Putting the bright lights on the receiver instead of the quarterback allows us to be more aggressive in playing the run. We find we get better run support against the Wing-T team when we play man-to-man. Our concept of keying the receiver and the triangle at the 2-technique nub and the 8 technique developed from the inconsistency of 8-technique play against the Wing-T when the 8 technique looked at the quarterback for a ball-level key. By the time the ball showed a level, the 8 technique was out of position for playing either run or pass.

The S1 technique can benefit from placing the bright lights on the quarterback any time he is aligned on a close-set receiver. The limited options of the close-split receiver demand no special emphasis being placed on the quarterback mechanics. The close-set receiver such as a tight end or wingback does not place the S1 technique on the island as does the wide set receiver.

RUN SUPPORT FROM THE S1 TECHNIQUE

The S1 technique has limited run support responsibility. When aligned on a split receiver, the S1 technique will provide secondary perimeter support as the ballcarrier approaches the line of scrimmage. The catch-22 is the fact that the S1 technique may not have visual contact with the ball if the receiver breaks cushion or makes a cut to take the S1 technique's line of sight from the ball. Keep in mind, the S1 technique does not peer into the backfield; he shifts his focus to the receiver after getting the initial read from the quarterback mechanics.

It is the quarterback mechanics which again aid the S1 technique in supporting the run. If the quarterback shows no level to the secondary (no level to deep techniques is the ball on the line of scrimmage inside the tackle box), the S1 technique responds to the "no level" as he would respond to the three-step mechanics. The S1 technique should sink the hips and chop the backpedal as he shifts his bright lights to the receiver. If the receiver is coming off with a choppy stride with his eyes focused on the defensive back, the receiver is gathering himself to stalk block the defensive back. The S1 technique moves to gain outside leverage on the stalk blocker. The defensive back then bench presses the stalk blocker, maintaining hip flexibility as he makes the final determination of run or pass.

As the ball approaches the line of scrimmage, the defensive back breaks up to make the tackle for a four- to five-yard gain. The allowance for the gain of the yardage is a significant coaching point, particularly at the high-school level. We do not want our S1 techniques bailing out of their man coverage responsibility too soon. When playing a S1 technique versus a wide receiver, the defensive back should err on the side of caution in regard to providing secondary run support.

The S1 technique facing a wingback or tight end can be more aggressive than his counterpart man-to-man on the wide receiver. Cover 1 and Cover 1 Free are good coverages against Wing-T teams who fake the ball well and hit the receiver either in the flat or in the dead areas between the zones.

THE S3 TECHNIQUE KEYS

The secondary coach has two options to use as a primary key for the S3 technique. The first option is the ball movement. The S3 technique is a three-deep zone cornerback technique, so keying the ball fits with the coverage philosophy: zone—key ball; man—key man. Also, keying the ball for the initial movement allows the cornerback to easily read the mechanics of the quarterback drop. Another supporting statement for the S3 technique keying the ball is the fact that the S1 technique also keys the ball against a wide receiver. This similarity allows for more consistency in the teaching of the techniques. As all coaches agree, consistency in teaching is a key to mastery of execution.

The main reason for supporting the S3 technique to key the receiver is the jump the cornerback gets into his backpedal. The numerous philosophies of alignment of the deep-third cornerback put him anywhere from five to nine yards deep off the line of scrimmage. For the aficionados of the deep alignment, keying the receiver movement would add to the already substantial cushion. For the devotees of the tight alignment of the deep-third cornerback, keying the receiver would allow them to guarantee the five-yard cushion on the snap. Keying the receiver means the cornerback will focus on the feet of the receiver. At the moment of the jump of the receiver, the cornerback throws his eyes inside to the quarterback.

Upon sighting the quarterback, the cornerback then reads the mechanics of the drop. Critics of this style of teaching state the that cornerback will lose his ability to read the quarterback mechanics if the cornerback is focused on the feet of the receiver. Supporters of the methodology point out that the ball is not initially in the quarterback's grasp at the moment of the center snap. In this window of time, the receiver—who has a clear view of the ball—gets a one-and-a-half step jump on the cushion of the cornerback. Couple this accepted fact with the physiological reaction time of the cornerback; instead of a five-yard cushion, the cornerback now has a three-and-a-half yard cushion. Even the tight alignment campers agree that a cushion of less than five yards for a deep-third responsible player is an uncomfortably tight cushion.

The Forty Nickel philosophy is a compromise between the two lines of thought. Since the S3 technique is outside in our scheme, we may be able to see the feet of the receiver in our dim light focus and still keep our bright lights on the quarterback. The argument for the consistency of looking at the quarterback for both the S1 and S3 techniques has some support. The value of looking at the quarterback is a greater ability to maintain the cushion, particularly in the "tight" alignment at five yards. For the standard S3-technique alignment the consistency argument wins us over to putting the bright lights on the quarterback. A seven-yard alignment allows the defensive back to intensely read the quarterback mechanics and still keep a comfortable five-yard cushion on the receiver.

In reality, the Forty Nickel coverage philosophy is not zone—key ball, man—key man, because we key the ball on both man and zone. Like the S1 technique, the S3 technique will read the quarterback mechanics for a tip of the route depth. Unlike the S1 technique, the S3 technique is a zone, played from outside-in. Many excellent coaches play the S3 technique from inside-out. They feel it resembles a man read to the receiver and the alignment limits the available routes to the outside cuts. These are excellent points to consider, but we prefer to keep outside leverage in order to guarantee secondary run support, as well as provide an alternative to the inside-out man coverage of the S1 technique. Additionally, the outside leverage alignment allows us to see the movement of the receiver when focusing the bright lights on the quarterback. Hence, the support for the aforementioned compromise philosophy of pre-snap keys from the cornerback position.

THE TIGHT ALIGNMENT AND KEYS

The tight call tells the S3 technique to align at a depth of five yards instead of the usual seven. A tight call alerts the S3 technique to challenge all short routes. Because we want to challenge the short route, the S3 technique tight player keys the quarterback just as the regular S3 technique. The S1 technique tight cornerback remains a backpedaling technique. All parameters of the S1 technique are intact except the alignment is closer in the tight call. With a S6 technique free safety, the tight call also allows for a tougher run support from the cornerback. However, a tight call used with a "cheat" puts the cornerback on an island similar to Cover 1. The free safety moves to a S5 alignment on a cheat call.

S3 TECHNIQUE SPLIT RULE

The S3 technique, being a zone technique, has a split rule. The split rule calls for the S3 technique to never align wider than eight yards from the sideline. Aligning at eight yards puts the S3 technique directly in the middle of the outside one-third fraction of the field. The preferred alignment of the Forty Nickel places the S3 technique aligned midway between the edges of his zone. Should the S3 technique apply his split rule to a wide receiver, the S3 technique burns his eyes into the quarterback for a read. The pre-snap key compromise is shelved. If a receiver splits out to a point within four yards of the sideline, the S3 technique will be seven yards off the line of scrimmage and four yards inside the receiver. He will key the quarterback and sneak a peek at the receiver, much like the S1 technique would sneak a peek at the ball.

The reasoning for the split rule is the compression factor. Expanding the free safety's universe to a point to where he is easy prey for the four vertical routes is a prime objective of the spread formation. The Forty Nickel three-deep philosophy ensures an equal share in the deep responsibilities with the S6 technique free safety. The concept of Cover 3 is three *equal* parts. Forty Nickel cornerbacks are not forced to the outer edge versus an over-split receiver. They will not leave a grand expanse of area in the middle for the free safety to cover. If not for the split rule, the cornerbacks could leave the free safety with three fourths of the field to cover instead of his fair share of one third.

THE STAY CALL

A "stay" call can be added to the entire coverage. The call is used for Cover 3 and applies to the S3-technique cornerbacks and free safety. The word "stay" means the S3 technique is to ignore the receiver cuts and backpedal down the vertical midline of the outside third zone. The S3 technique is to let the receiver routes break to him and not squeeze any receiver cuts. If a single receiver breaks for a post, the cornerback will ignore his break and look for the wheel route or the post corner move from the post receiver. The "stay" call helps the inexperienced or undisciplined cornerback play the smash combination. On the smash, the outside receiver will snap off a curl in front of the defensive back and an inside receiver will break a vertical into a corner route behind the defensive back. A "stay" call insures the cornerback does not sink his hips to play the curl as the corner route breaks behind him. The "stay" also helps stop the transcontinental route as well as solidify the S6 technique's responsibility of staying deep as the deepest in his zone. When given a "stay" call, the cornerback should intently scan for the combination routes from the inside.

PLAYING THE NUB END

When the S3 technique aligns on the nub end, he first takes notice of whether the outside linebacker is in a "squeeze" technique on the end or if the outside linebacker is an 8 technique. If the outside linebacker is not squeezed to a 9 technique on the end, the S3 technique will keep his normal alignment depth and width. His technique will remain the same except that the S3 technique, like the S1 technique, may now key the tight end instead of the quarterback.

Since no wide receiver threat exists and the tight end's options are limited, the S3 technique may put the bright lights on the tight end for the quick run-pass key. If the tight end releases, the S3 technique should quickly get his eyes inside to find ball level and the number two receiver. If the number two receiver is in a strong set, the wheel route from the number two receiver is a threat. This route is a favorite route from this set with a nub end and is usually run with play action away from the tight end. The S3 technique must be careful about honing in on the tight end vertical route on flow away. The nearback in the strong set can wheel out down the sideline.

If the outside linebacker is aligned in the squeeze alignment as a 9 technique, the cornerback moves to a five-and-three alignment. This alignment at five yards off the line of scrimmage and three yards outside the nub is called a S9 technique. We give the technique a new designation because of the increased responsibility of run support. With the outside linebacker squeezed, the S3 technique must now be the primary run support on the perimeter. A S3 technique is a secondary run support force, thus the new designation of S9 technique. The S9 technique is still a deep one-third responsible technique. For all concerns, the S9 technique keys the nub as a man-to-man technique. Keying the tight end provides an immediate run-pass key. By keying the tight end, the S9 cannot be deceived by a good ball fake. Also, the S9 is a backpedaling technique. Another reason to key the tight end is that a backpedaling technique could drift too deep for adequate run support if he did not get a quick run-pass key. In all respects, a S9 is close cousin to the S3. The significant difference is the force responsibility of the S9 technique. Because this coaching point is significant, the alignment of the S3 technique changes when he converts to the S9 technique. The five-and-three alignment better suits the role of providing primary level-one run support.

Should the ball go level three toward the S9 technique, the cornerback will cover deep as the deepest in his zone, weaving to the eight-yard split rule limit of his zone with a man-to-man principle of coverage on the threatening receiver. Should the ball go level two away from the S9 technique, the S9 technique plays a man-to-man coverage on the nub end. The outside linebacker will have throwback screen to the nub side. Versus level three, the S9 technique will drop to his deep one-third zone, keeping the man-to-man principle of coverage within his zone. One note: Should the coverage call be Cover 3 Stay and the cornerback converts to a S9 technique, the cornerback will drop to the split of his zone and ignore the route of the nub. At the least, he will ignore the route of the tight end to the point that he will not chase him across the field on level two. A favorite route against this alignment is the play fake to the S9 technique and the tight end corner route. The offensive coordinator will get the S9 technique to fly up and then show the good sweep fake and hit the corner route behind him.

RUN SUPPORT FROM THE S3 TECHNIQUE

The S3 technique provides secondary (supplemental) run support. The outside linebacker provides primary run support. The S3 technique will provide a layered perimeter support slightly behind and outside of the Antler or Brave. The defensive back attempts to gain a position which is tight to the outside shoulder of the outside linebacker. The position should be less than three yards outside of the Antler or Brave support. This snug relationship prevents a second alley from developing between the cornerback and the outside linebacker. By being slightly behind the primary support, the cornerback will be able to make the tackle on the outside, should the ballcarrier break primary containment. Also, by being behind the force, the cornerback will be the sentry of the defensive edge.

The role of the sentry is to guard against a breakout. If the force were to exhibit poor technique and get too much penetration, the cornerback would form a second edge of the alley near the line of scrimmage. If the ballcarrier were to get under the force and attempt to hit the sideline, the cornerback would be at a point behind the outside linebacker to force the ballcarrier back on a vertical path, denying him the sideline.

Denying a running back the sideline is the run support role of the S3 technique. If the cornerback is on an even plane with the forcing outside linebacker, the cornerback is too deep and is of limited value as a supplemental force. The S9 technique should never make the mistake of "sticking his nose inside" the alley. The cornerback should never penetrate the alley. He should always be at a position outside of the alley.

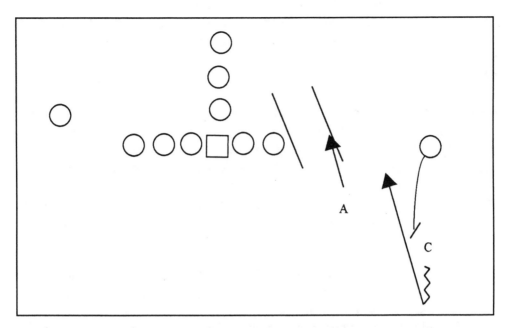

Diagram 7-1: The cornerback keeps a snug relationship with the outside linebacker and sets up the sentry position slightly behind the outside linebacker.

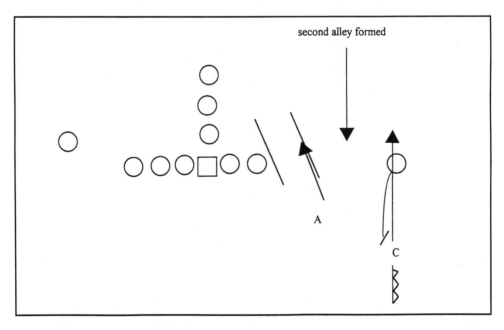

Diagram 7-2: The cornerback does not keep a tight relationship to the outside linebacker. Although the cornerback has outside leverage on the ballcarrier, the gap between the outside linebacker and the cornerback is too wide. A second alley is formed.

The S9 technique may make the tackle as the running back breaks through the alley to hit the sideline, but he may not enter the alley. For more information on the parameters of the alley, see the section on outside linebacker play against level one.

Level-one flow away from the S3 technique will cause him to squeeze the backside receiver, peeking into the backfield for a reverse or other trick. Once the ball approaches the line of scrimmage, the backside S3 technique sinks his hips and begins to backpedal lazily. The cornerback should not take off on the pursuit angle upon recognition of the ballcarrier's intentions to continue downfield. This reasoning comes from the fact that the cornerback is already 10 to 20 yards downfield in front of the ballcarrier. Sprinting to the far sideline would entail taking a sharp angle to the sideline. This type of perpendicular path to the ballcarrier would make the cornerback's pursuit almost useless, as the ballcarrier could make an eighth grade cut as the cornerback would fly past him. The backpedaling technique should place the cornerback near the same vertical plane as the backside outside linebacker. The backside outside linebacker also performs the backpedal technique if he gets too far ahead of the ball. With both players backpedaling 15 to 20 yards ahead of the ball, the pursuit has the opportunity to stop the cut against the grain. When the cornerback feels the angle is being lost, the cornerback will flip out of his backpedal and sprint on proper pursuit angle to stop the touchdown run.

READING THE SHOULDER TILT

A useful skill for the S3 technique and the S4 technique is reading the shoulder tilt of the quarterback. Once the quarterback sets his feet, the cornerback may measure the tilt of the shoulder to determine the expected depth of the pass. This technique would not be feasible in Cover 3, but it would be helpful in Cover 3 Stay. The Cover 3 cornerback plays the route of the receiver but the "stay" call allows the cornerback to keep his focus on the quarterback. A high front and low back shoulder gives away the impending deep ball. Level shoulders indicate an intermediate route. Combined with the steps of the drop, this coaching point gives a cornerback more opportunity to get a read on the upcoming pass.

BREAKING ON THE BALL

The route-reading 3 technique from Cover Three needs no specific break on the ball. He reads the quarterback for an initial calculation of the depth of the route and squeezes the receiver's route appropriately. The Cover Three Stay 3 technique cornerback may use some other clues to the timing of the release. The standard rule is for deep players to break on the ball's release, and short zone players to break on the eyes and shoulder of the quarterback.

Some throwing mechanics allow the deep player to differentiate between the pump fake and the upcoming release of the ball. On a pump fake, the quarterback will keep his front shoulder closed. When the ball comes thrown, the quarterback will open his front shoulder as the ball is motion forward. Another point of interest is the thumb of the off hand. If the thumb of the off hand is down as the ball is cocked, the ball will be thrown, not faked. Pronation of the off hand is a dead key for the ball being thrown. Pronation of the front hand leads to the thumb being pointed downward. These keys, as all keys, should be confirmed by intensive film study of the opponent. Conscientious film study will reveal other individual factors which will allow the cornerback to get a jump on the ball.

The pure zone cornerback technique should not wait until the ball is in the air to break on a route. We want an edge. However, all our little "cheat" keys are confirmed as 100 percent accurate before their implementation. During the preseason, we teach the little keys mentioned above, the thumb down, and the shoulder tilt. Learning to recognize these things helps the cornerback become better at the game. Each week our secondary coach studies the film along with our players and allows the players to search for the little cheat keys. In his role of teacher, the secondary coach confirms the athlete's observations as valid. This type of teaching and player participation is one more thing we do to make the players feel as if they are part of the game and not just our robots. Again, these cues are only available to pure zone players, the S3 technique in Cover 3 Stay and the S4 technique.

THE T-STEP

The backpedaling S1 and S3 techniques should be instructed in the T-step as part of their fundamental skills. The principle of the T-step is similar to the principle of the runner on first base who attempts to steal second base. As most baseball fans and coaches know, when a runner attempts to steal second base, he doesn't take a lead step to second base, he takes a crossover step. If the runner were to take a lead step, the back foot would be his push foot. And if the back foot is the push foot, that means his force is not underneath his body. His push force is extended outside the body. By having the push foot behind the body instead of under the body, the actual propulsion time provided by the back foot is lessened because the push must leave the ground sooner than if it were under the body. Furthermore, having the push foot behind the body prevents the full force of the body being exerted upon it; thus, less force may be exerted on the ground with the push foot. Less force equals less movement.

In recognition of this concept of the push foot needing to be under the body near the center of gravity, a defensive back technique was developed. The technique, called the T-step, allows the defensive back to keep his push foot underneath his body as he drives out of his backpedal.

The step is actually a heel-to-instep point of the foot to the side of the receiver's cut. In responding to an outside cut, the letter "T" is formed by the heel of the right foot to the instep of the left foot. Once the "T" is formed, the defensive back pushes off the right foot in a crossover move to the cut of the receiver. Like the baseball runner going to first base, the T-step allows the force foot to be under the player's center of gravity and stay in contact with the ground longer. This technique provides greater propulsion for the defensive back to drive toward the cut of the receiver.

The T-step is taught to both the Forty Nickel defensive backs and outside linebackers. Although the outside linebackers should use the step in redirecting after a wheel, we expect our defensive backs to master the technique. The technique provides for more deflections, more interceptions and less run-after-the-catch yardage for the receiver.

THE S4-TECHNIQUE STANCE

Although an acceptable stance for the S4 technique is a squared stance, we use the stance of S1 and S3 techniques. This approach gives us consistency for the three deep cornerback techniques.

THE S4-TECHNIQUE ALIGNMENT

When facing a split receiver to his side the S4 technique aligns at a depth of ten yards from the line of scrimmage, not wider than four yards outside the hash. Against a tight receiver or a nub, the S4 technique aligns over the offensive tackle at a depth of eight to ten yards.

S4-TECHNIQUE SPLIT RULE

The S4 technique uses a depth adjustment in response to a wide split of the receiver. If the receiver splits to a distance at which the S4 technique may not cover him on a fade route to the void, the S4 technique aligns at a depth which will allow him more leverage to cover the route. The closer the S4 is to the line of scrimmage, the less leverage he has to cover the fade. Many secondary coaches support moving the S4 technique to a point midway between the wide receiver and the nub, but keeping the depth at ten yards. In our philosophy, we do not want to evacuate the middle of the field. This evacuation would make our front more vulnerable to trap and other plays which could break into the second level. We prefer to deepen our alignment to give the S4 technique a better angle on the over-split receiver.

The S2 technique will respond to an over-split receiver by aligning at the four yard "sink" call depth. This cushion by the S2 technique will allow a safety zone against the fade stop and the short void route—routes which the deep S4 technique could not reach. Given level three and a go route out of the number one over-split receiver, the S4 technique should take a flatter path to cut off the route near the sideline. The common sense split rule is also used in the S4 technique alignment. When in doubt, the S4 technique takes an alignment, deep or wide, to be able to cover the number one receiver on a go route. If the S4 technique cornerback feels he must widen to cover the receiver, he may widen. However, our preferred adjustment is for the cornerback to simply deepen his alignment against the over-split wide receiver.

S4 TECHNIQUE KEYS

The S4-technique player focuses on the quarterback. He attempts to gain a read of the ball level and get a clue to the depth of an attempted route. The S4 technique backpedals as long as the ball has shown no level. Remember that "no level" is the ball moving in a direction on the line of scrimmage, but not yet at the tackle box. The S4 technique weaves his backpedal in the direction of "no-level" flow, but does not commit to his level-one reaction.

A supplemental key to the quarterback on level-three action is the route of the number-one receiver. If the number-one receiver breaks on an outbreak, the S4 technique realizes that number two could be a threat to make the corner route cut or continue on a vertical. If the number-one receiver makes an inbreak, the cut naturally brings the S4 technique's line of sight to the number-two receiver, particularly if the number-two receiver is running an outbreak in combination with the number-one receiver. An inbreak from the number-one receiver can indicate a corner route by the number-two receiver. Since the primary responsibility of the S4 technique is the deep half, the smash route combination is something for which the S4 technique should be alert.

S4-TECHNIQUE LEVEL-ONE REACTION

The S4 technique should overlap the force on level one toward the cornerback. The S4 technique will have a S2 technique to his side providing the primary force. Upon recognition of level one with flow toward him, the S4 technique takes a near vertical angle to the outer third of the alley. At the moment of recognition, this path would actually put the cornerback inside of the forcing S2 technique. However, the S2 technique will sprint to squeeze the alley.

At the moment of the S4 technique's arrival near the line of scrimmage, the S2 technique should have closed to force the edge of the alley. The S4 technique then continues to a snug relationship *outside* of the S2 technique. Like his S3 technique supplemental force responsibility, the S4 technique hopes to be outside and slightly behind the force.

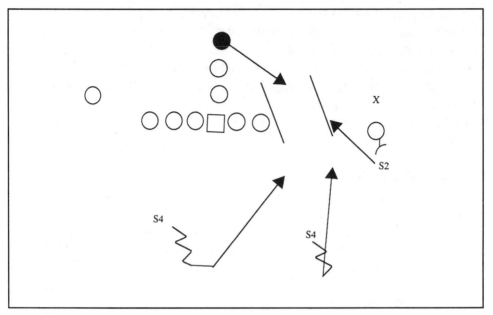

Diagram 7-3: Level-one flow to the defensive right. The right S4 technique checks the "X" and then comes up as supplemental force, snug to the S2 technique. The left S4 technique checks the middle and them sprints to the alley.

As the S4 technique recognizes level one and proceeds to the outer third fraction of the alley, the S4 technique may continue to see grass in front of him. In this case, the S2 technique did not complete his mission of squeezing the alley. The S2 technique may have been blocked and sealed from the alley's edge. If he sees grass in front of him, the S4 technique must now be the primary force, replacing the S2 technique. Granted, the coach does not want the S4 technique making tackles at the line of scrimmage, but the S4 technique may actually make the tackle on the ballcarrier, if the S2 technique fails to squeeze the alley. In this scenario, one can expect a short to medium gain. We would huddle and regroup without any significant damage done. Should the S4 technique overrun his angle, the ballcarrier would hit the seam without having to cut back to the alley-filling backside S4 technique. Attempting to keep a snug relationship to the S2 technique is a priority in providing supplemental force support against level one with flow toward the cornerback.

The playside S4 technique is also responsible for recognizing the threat of the halfback pass. When weaving on the "no-level" flow toward him, the S4 technique should peek at the number-one receiver. If the number-one receiver is not committed to blocking the S2 technique the S4 technique must overlap to the outer edge of the zone and cover the halfback pass. The key coaching point of the S4 technique on flow toward him is to always check number one. If number one is clearly committed to blocking the S2 technique, then the S4 technique is free to provide supplemental force. The S4 technique reading level-one flow away from the defender will attempt to fill the alley. Should the alley be formed by the S2 technique, the backside S4 technique is to come out of his weave and get up as fast as possible to fill the alley. His angle will likely make him ahead of the interior pursuit, so he generally fills the outer three-fourths of the alley. The S4 technique may check for a vertical down the middle as he weaves on the "no-level" flow away. If he picks up a vertical, the S4 technique will cover him, as the likelihood of a play action is high. The playside S4 technique would have weaved to the outside one third of his zone and would be out of position to cover the middle vertical. The backside S4 technique always seeks out a middle threat on his weave before breaking into his alley-filling role.

For the S4 technique, the most important thing to remember is that he is a deep zone player, responsible for one half of the field. We want to err on the side of caution at this position. The cornerback will eventually gain the confidence and skills to become a quicker run-support player. First, he must learn how to recognize the dangers to the deep zone and be there when these dangers present themselves.

THE S4 TECHNIQUE AGAINST LEVEL TWO

The S4 technique weaves on level two with the flow of the ball. The weave will place the S4 technique in the position of deep one-third zone players. The S4-playside technique will weave to a S3 technique on level two toward him. The backside S4 technique will weave to a S6 technique on level two away from him. The backside S2 technique will sink to the outside one third as the ball goes level two away from him. This rolling response allows the secondary to slide and compress with the ball movement, providing better coverage.

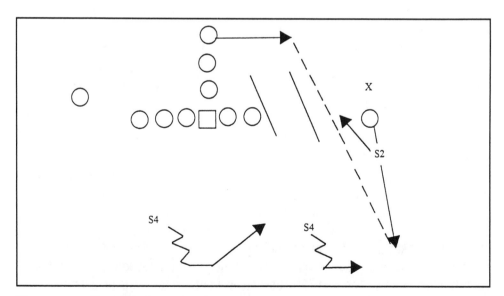

Diagram 7-4: The right S4 technique reads level one toward him and weaves while sneaking a peek at number one, the "X." Failing to confirm the commitment of the "X" to blocking the S2, the S4 plays the halfback pass.

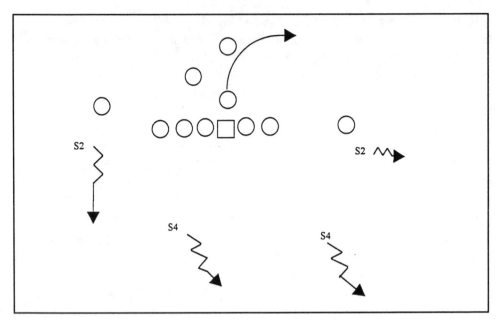

Diagram 7-5: Level two to the defensive right, the S4 techniques weave to the thirds.

LEVEL THREE AND THE S4 TECHNIQUE

The S4 technique continues his backpedal on level three and immediately peeks for the number one receiver. The S4 cornerback may get a jump on the three-step fade route by reading the quarterback mechanics. However, the availability of the jump is limited to a single-receiver side of the formation in the Cover 20 series. Two receivers set weakside against Cover 2 would also cancel the opportunity to jump the number one on the three-step mechanics. As mentioned, the S4 technique peeks to find the action of the number-one receiver. The receiver will give clues to the combination of routes. Against four verticals, the S4 technique should have underneath help on the outside from the S2 technique. Both S2 techniques will be sinking under the number one receiver given no threat to the flat. The help can be guaranteed by the defensive coordinator by adding a "sink" call to the coverage.

The S4 technique should backpedal closest to the inside receiver on the four vertical routes. Even if the S2 technique is not sinking under the outside vertical, the S4 technique should favor the inside receiver vertical as he covers his deep one-half of the field. The S4 technique favors the inside vertical because the ball has to travel farther in the air if thrown to the outside receiver. The easier pass to complete on a vertical is the inside vertical. Also, by favoring the inside vertical, the S4 technique takes away the option of hitting either receiver. The quarterback is forced to go to the outside receiver. Another principle of the foundation of the Forty Nickel defense is seen. The Forty Nickel scheme wants to force the offense to attempt the only option offered. If we are successful, we know where they are going and we specifically practice on attacking their only option. Few things are more disheartening for the athlete at the S4 technique than to backpedal between two vertical receivers and be able to cover neither. Ask any offensive coordinator who is successful at this route; the S4 technique cannot defend both receivers against a good quarterback.

Ideally, the defensive coach wants four-deep coverage versus four verticals. Forty Nickel S4 technique reads should generally support this reaction. If the reads do not allow for four deep defenders, the quarterback can be discouraged from throwing to the inside vertical by the defensive back favoring the inside receiver. In favoring the inside receiver, the defensive back hopes to force the ball to be thrown to the outside receiver. The Forty Nickel S4 technique drills are usually tailored to simulate the four-vertical situation.

A key coaching point is that the S4 technique does not cover the inside vertical. He only favors the inside vertical. If the quarterback were to go for the inside vertical, the S4 technique could easily break on the ball and defend the route. The S4 technique must keep some distance from the inside vertical in order to successfully cover the outside vertical also. The 5-quarters technique keys the movement of the ball along with the triangle. Keying the triangle and the S2 technique pre-snap and triangle keys are detailed elsewhere in the text.

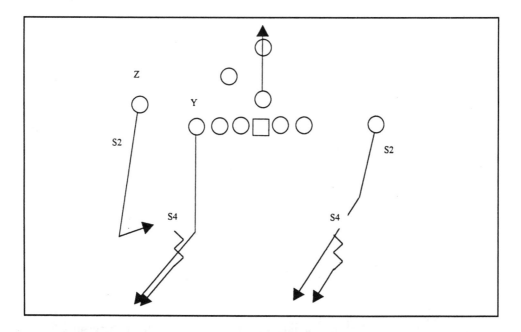

Diagram 7-6: The "Z" and "Y" are running a smash. The S4 technique gets a double peek. The first peek at the inbreak of the "Z," the second peek to the "Y." The "Y" vertical tells the S4 technique to lay off the "Z."

READING THE DROP

One theory of play at the S3-technique position, as well as other deep-zone techniques such as the S4 technique, is reading the number of steps in the quarterback drop. Since the defensive back cannot see the feet of the quarterback, he looks for certain visual cues to alert him to the short drop. A quarterback taking the three-step drop will seat the ball at the chest, holding the ball near the shoulders. When on a deeper drop, the ball tends to drop from the shoulder area. The three-step drop will usually translate into one of the shorter routes by the receiver. The one exception to this connection would be the fade route. When playing the steps of the quarterback the cornerback may align five yards off the line of scrimmage—a "tight" call alignment. The cornerback may have difficulty step-reading the quarterback when focusing on the feet of the receiver prior to the snap. Therefore, the coach may want to allow the S3 technique to focus on the quarterback as a primary pre-snap key, particularly when in the tight-call alignment at five yards.

If the S3 technique picks up the visual cues of the three-step quarterback drop—the ball high on the chest grasped in both hands and the quarterback looking off to the other side—the S3 technique drops his hips and sits on the receiver. The out-and-up move is a good route against this technique, so the S3 technique "tight" player will naturally drill on the out-and-up move daily. If the S3 technique sees the quarterback go to five steps, he backpedals, ready to settle on the intermediate route—the ten- to twelve-yard route of the shallow curl and five-step out route, to name two. If the S3 technique reads seven steps he knows the post corner is a threat. This knowledge enables him to squeeze the post, but on recognition of the drop's depth the cornerback may back off the post move and sink for the post corner.

Reading the steps of the quarterback is especially useful in playing the combination routes. One combination route designed to burn the S3 technique deep is the smash route combination. The S3 technique who does not read the quarterback properly may settle on his backpedal on the outside receiver's curl. Meanwhile, the number two receiver breaks a corner route behind the cornerback. If another receiver is splitting the middle, the free safety will be occupied and will not be able to help the cornerback cover his error. Reading steps will not necessarily help the cornerback stop the smash route. The corner route can still be run off a five-step drop. However, two other factors present in this scenario could allow the cornerback to recognize the danger of settling for the curl.

The first factor is the tilt of the shoulders of the quarterback. If a quarterback takes a five-step drop and shows a shoulder tilt with the front shoulder higher than the throwing shoulder upon presentation of the ball, the quarterback is about to put some air under the ball. He is trying to hit the corner route of the combination.

Seeing a curl in front of him while focusing on the quarterback with a high front shoulder should sound an alarm in the S3 technique's head: deep, deep, deep. If the cornerback did not see the corner route, he should have. The quarterback's shoulder is a dead key to the deep route and one way for the cornerback to stop the transcontinental route with a deep curl as bait. If the cornerback *feels* no threat deeper than the curling receiver *and* he sees that the quarterback's shoulders are level, the cornerback can be assured that no deeper receiver threat exists. The cornerback may settle and play the curl route over the top. Reading the shoulders is especially helpful for the S4 technique, the deep-halves zone player. The Forty Nickel cornerbacks also play the S4 technique. The S4 technique may read the steps of the quarterback and concentrate on the level of the quarterback's shoulders.

The S4 technique can also weave in the direction which the quarterback is facing. The S4 technique backpedals after reading through the uncovered lineman to the ball. The uncovered lineman will give the S4 technique, like the S6 technique, a quicker run-pass diagnosis. If the ball continues at level three, the S4 technique will backpedal, surveying the route of the number two receiver by sneaking a peek. If the number-two receiver to his side is not a vertical threat, the S4 technique may widen two to four yards to the widest receiver.

The S5 technique is responsible for the number two vertical strongside on Cover 2. A linebacker will be responsible for the number two vertical weakside. Consequently, the weakside S4 technique is more of a true halves technique. The weakside S4 technique cornerback in Cover 2 must be acutely aware of number two going vertical, particularly from a balanced ace-set formation. If the weakside S4 were to widen too much, the number two weakside vertical would be isolated on the weakside inside linebacker. The S4 technique should be mindful of the technique response of the S2 technique in Cover 2 and the Cover 20 twin coverages. The S2 technique will read through number one to the inside. The ball proceeds back on level three, the S2 technique sinks to a cushion under the outside receiver. The S2 continues to sink as long as the inside receiver does not threaten the flat. This sinking gives the S4 technique knowledge that he has underneath sinking help to the outer one-third underneath the outside receiver. The consequence of this knowledge should help the S4 technique understand why he should never overexpand to the outside receiver, particularly on a number two vertical against an inside linebacker.

Even more beneficial for the S4 technique is the "sink" call. The word "sink" can be added to the two-deep coverages. "Sink" tells ten S2 techniques to align at four yards off the line of scrimmage instead of the one-yard alignment. The width is kept at one yard outside, but the four-yard cushion belies the objective of the call. The S2 technique will not jump the flat threatening bench route on a "sink" call. The S2 technique will sink with the number-one receiver route and break up on the flat route only after the quarterback opens his front shoulder with the ball in motion backward to pass to the flat route receiver. In other words, the S2 technique will break up on the flat as the ball is thrown, not as the route is shown. The "sink" call allows the corner to sink into the curl if number one is curling. It also allows the post-corner route to be double covered with over the top and underneath double coverage, as the S2 technique will ignore the bait bench route with a deep quarterback drop.

Terry Siddall, a successful Indiana high school coach, practices an excellent coaching point that allows the S2 technique the luxury of being able to cover the curl while double covering the corner route. Again, the defensive back reads the quarterback drop, an easier task for the S2 technique. He need not worry about losing cushion and may visually lock in on the quarterback. If the quarterback shows a three-step drop, the S2 technique sinks his hips and gets ready to play slant and jam the fade. If the quarterback drops deep, the S2 breaks deep into the deep-one-third cushion, giving help to the S4 technique cornerback. The cornerback realizes that he has significant underneath help and outside sinking help on a "sink" call.

In reference to the S2 technique (all techniques are integral in a coverage, so it is impossible to intelligently discuss one technique in a coverage without reference to other techniques) another veteran high school coach, Eric Parmley of Alexandria, Louisiana, plays the "sink" call as the base S2 technique response to level-three action. The fact that these two very successful coaches from different areas of the country are both successful while using opposite philosophies of coaching the hard corner position demonstrates that the S2 technique can be done a number of acceptable ways. The Forty Nickel philosophy is multiplicity in the coverage families. To that end, the base technique of the Forty Nickel is the use of the "sink" call with the plan to play the flat threat first. These two options give the Forty Nickel scheme, as the old saying goes, more than one way to skin a bobcat—with twin safeties.

S3 TECHNIQUE PLAYING THE CRACKBACK BLOCK

An important job of the S3 cornerback is to correctly respond to the wide receiver crackback block on the S8 technique or inside linebacker. Through the years, this response has seemed to be one skill the cornerbacks have been reluctant to learn. The most common incorrect response to the crackback block path of the receiver with level-one action is for the cornerback to continue in his backpedal, making sure he doesn't get beat deep.

The S3 technique cornerback must correctly respond to the crackback block with level-one action. He does this by weaving with the crack path and sinking his hips to stop the backpedal. At the moment of recognition of the path of the receiver, the cornerback begins screaming "crack, crack, crack"—not that an outside linebacker has ever been known to actually hear the call. However, again it is a conditioning response mechanism for the cornerback. Yelling crack helps reinforce the correct physical movement in response to the crack. Yelling crack helps the cornerback realize he should get out of his backpedal and come up to provide secondary force on the perimeter. What happens if the crack is a fake? The key to not being burned versus a fake crackback is properly diagnosing the ball level. The cornerback is seven yards off and reading *level one*. Level one means that the ball is outside the tackle box or near the tackle box. The cornerback should see the receiver in his peripheral vision and measure his intensity in executing the block. There is a significant difference in the manner of a receiver going in to crack a rattlesnake outside linebacker and a receiver wanting to plant and go deep behind the fooled cornerback. Film study and repetition help the cornerback see these things as his second nature. The manner in which the ball is moving also is a key in diagnosis. Is the ball still in the quarterback's hands. If so, is the quarterback looking at the defensive end for an option read or is he looking through all that to the cornerback? If he is looking at the cornerback, then something is fishy, the crack is a decoy. Has the ball been pitched or handed off? These are the things for the cornerback to recognize.

The S6 technique free safety should be sneaking a peek at the number one receiver on level-one action. As the S6 technique free safety begins to overlap to fill the alley, he should pick up the fake crack. The Forty Nickel free safety is expected to see these things and cover for the corner's misread. The free safety can flatten his path to cover the fake crack.

CHAPTER 8

Free Safety

The Forty Nickel free safety is the fulcrum of the secondary. It is upon his talent and play that the success of the secondary, if not the entire scheme, hinges. In the Forty Nickel package, the free safety is trained to play seven different techniques. The base free safety technique is the 6 technique. The S1, S2, S3, S4, and S7 techniques are covered in detail in other chapters throughout this text. The S1, S3, S4, and S7 techniques are basic cornerback techniques. The S2 is a basic outside linebacker technique. Only the S5 and the S6 are principal free safety techniques.

FREE SAFETY CHARACTERISTICS

If the defensive end is the T-Rex of the defense, then the free safety is the Doberman. The free safety candidate is selected for his speed, aggressive nature, and tackling ability. A candidate lacking any of those three qualities would be suspect in being able to carry out the duties required of the Forty Nickel free safety. He may not be the fastest defensive back —the cornerbacks may be faster—he must be the surest tackler in the secondary. His mobility must be such that he is able to cover sideline to sideline versus the run, but without the ability to consistently make tackles, the free safety will have a long year. And if the free safety has a long year, it is guaranteed that the Forty Nickel defense will have an even longer year. Ideally, the free safety candidate is a linebacker type of hitter with the speed of a cornerback.

FREE SAFETY STANCE

The free safety aligns with his feet even or slightly staggered with his torso pitched forward and his arms hanging at his sides. His hips are flexed with a slight bend in the knees.

FREE SAFETY ALIGNMENT

The free safety (FS) aligns in various secondary techniques, including a 4 technique, 5 technique, and 6 technique. On squat coverages and zone blitzes, the FS may align in a 2 technique, or he may cheat to the 2 receiver side to discourage the hot route.

FREE SAFETY TECHNIQUE

The free safety will shuffle on the snap of the ball. This will give him the opportunity to be a factor in stopping the running game. He will often read through the uncovered lineman (center) to the ball. This technique will counter the advantage of play-action schemes. His responsibilities are outlined further in the secondary coverage portion of this text. The free safety will call the coverage to the cornerbacks after the huddle break.

Chart 8a: Free safety alignment techniques.

S1 Technique	Man-to-man on the number-two receiver from the outside, seven yards off the line of scrimmage and one yard inside.
S2 Technique	One yard off the line of scrimmage and one yard outside the number-one receiver, only with cornerback adjustment to 5-quarter technique.
S3 Technique	Seven yards off the line of scrimmage and one yard outside the receiver, only with cornerback adjustment to 5-quarter technique.
S4 Technique	Eight to ten yards off the line of scrimmage; four yards outside the hash, over the tackle when aligned on a nub, only in special situations.
S5 Technique	Seven yards off the line of scrimmage, two yards outside the tight end.
S6 Technique	Base technique, ten yards off the line of scrimmage, in the middle of the formation.
S7 Technique	Man-to-man, one yard off line of scrimmage and one yard inside receiver, only played to the left on goal line.

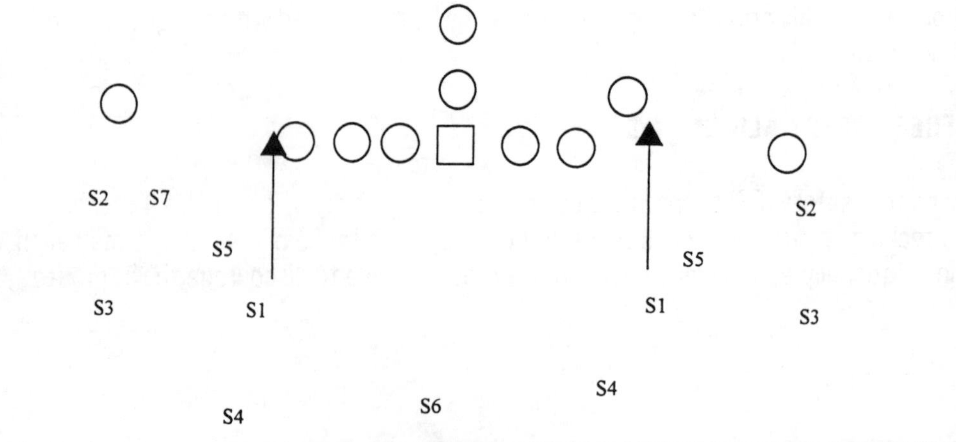

FREE SAFETY STUNTS

FIRE   Rush from 3 man side (TE side).
                Gap will be designated.

SMOKE   Rush from open end side.
                Gap will be designated.

THE S6-TECHNIQUE STANCE

The S6-technique stance is a squared stance. The toes are even and pointed toward the line of scrimmage. The S6 technique has a slight forward lean and stands light on his feet. His heels are slightly off the ground and his arms hang loosely about his waist.

S6-TECHNIQUE ALIGNMENT

The S6 technique aligns at the middle of the offensive formation. This rule of alignment usually places him over the guard or, at most, the guard-tackle gap. For a point of reference for alignment, the S6 technique uses the widest receivers on either side of the formation.

The S6 technique usually does not cheat to the multiple-receiver side. For instance, the free safety does not cheat to a three-receiver (trips) side. We use our linebackers to balance the defensive strength to an unbalanced formation such as trips. Our objective in not cheating the S6 technique is to keep him in the middle of the formation. Our philosophy is that we do not want an offensive formation taking our free safety out of the middle, unless we choose to roll the coverage to a squat coverage, as with Cover 3 Squat. The S6 technique depth is usually ten yards; however, we will adjust this depth according to the style of attack we are facing and our aims for that game week.

THE INITIAL MOVEMENT

The initial movement of the S6 technique is a shuffle. A shuffle is a compromise between the bounce and the backpedal. In the past, we have used both the bounce and the backpedal. We felt the bounce sometimes caught us flat-footed on level three while the backpedal caused us to drift or rock the shoulders keeping us from getting up in the alley on level one. We felt the shuffle would give us the backward movement needed for pass coverage while providing us the good low base to drive for the alley against level one.

S6 TECHNIQUE KEYS

The S6 technique keys through the uncovered lineman. The bright lights are on the quarterback. The focus of the free safety has more of a "clear, cloudy" description. In the free safety's line of sight is the uncovered offensive lineman. His focus is clear. In the background is the quarterback. His focus is cloudy. The free safety has a clear focus of the offensive lineman with a cloudy background focus of the quarterback. Thus, the key is described as the "clear, cloudy" key.

Against some offensive attacks the roles of the clear and cloudy objects are reversed. We may view the quarterback as clear and see the offensive lineman as cloudy. We would use this principle against teams that were principally passing teams. In this case, the key is "cloudy, clear."

The base method of recognition is to use the "clear, cloudy" key. Focusing clearly on the uncovered lineman is harder for the defensive back. In consideration of this belief, it is easier to adjust to a "cloudy, clear" technique from the "clear, cloudy" read than vice versa.

S6-TECHNIQUE PLAY AGAINST LEVEL ONE

The free safety will weave his shuffle with the "no-level" flow. Upon recognition of the level-one flow, the free safety will fill the alley. We not only want the S6 technique to fill the alley, we want him to fill the alley with bad intentions. Should the free safety shuffle, weave, and move to fill the alley—only to find it sealed by the interior front pursuit. The free safety will keep inside-out leverage on the ballcarrier. If the ballcarrier were to bounce outside the alley the free safety would overlap the alley, pursuing the ballcarrier in the manner of a heat-seeking missile.

The Forty Nickel S6 technique is expected to make tackles from sideline to sideline on level-one action. He is also expected to be wide-eyed on any no-level flow. Should the ball break into the secondary on a "no-level" play such as a quick trap, the free safety will come out of his shuffle and attack the ballcarrier.

The S6 technique is not to wait until the ballcarrier reaches him. The S6 technique attacks the ballcarrier, breaking down on the ballcarrier in the same way the headhunter of the punt coverage team breaks down on the punt returner. Like the player who covers the punt, the S6 technique closes the distance on the broken field runner. Then, as he approaches the four-yard cushion, the S6 technique gathers to hit the ballcarrier high. A player who ducks his head when he tackles cannot play free safety. For that matter, a player who ducks his head should not be allowed to play at all. A severe injury can result. We do not just talk about it, we support this belief with their actions. We can best help athletes play the game safely by not allowing them to play with unsafe techniques. This action is the quickest cure to the player's exhibition of dangerous tackling technique. We just plainly telling the athlete, when you learn to tackle with his neck bowed and his head tucked backward, he will be allowed to play. The athlete's progress in exhibiting proper and safe tackling form is usually amazing.

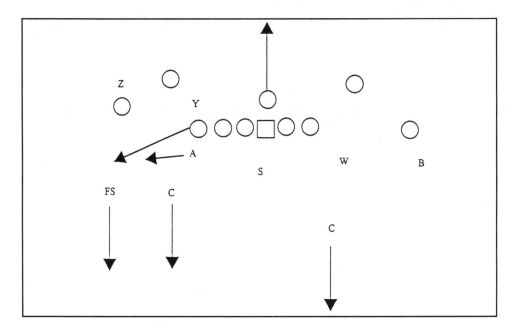

Diagram 8-1: Cover 20 with a Squeeze or Hold call—an adjustment is made to empty set formation. Right cornerback moves from S4 to 5-quarter technique. Free safety moves from S2 to S3 technique.

S6-TECHNIQUE PLAY AGAINST LEVEL TWO

The S6 technique weaves his shuffle in response to level two. Once the quarterback sets up at the tackle box, the S6 technique stops the weave and begins to backpedal vertically. His head is on a swivel, looking for a skinny post throwback.

If the S6 technique sees the quarterback continue outside the tackle box, the S6 technique may compress the coverage into the sideline, breaking into a backpedal and weaving to a point four yards outside the hashmark. From that point the free safety backpedals until he is as deep as the deepest receiver while reading the eyes and throwing mechanics of the quarterback.

S6 TECHNIQUE PLAY AGAINST LEVEL THREE

When the combination "clear-cloudy" key shows level three, the S6 technique begins the backpedal with his head on the swivel. The S6 technique backpedals to the deep middle as he looks from side to side.

Upon reading the depth of the drop, the S6 technique may sneak a peek at the number one receiver. If the number one receiver is on the skinny post route, the S6 technique will angle to meet the receiver as the ball is released. If the number one receiver is curling, the S6 technique checks for the number two receiver running the corner route and notes the position of the cornerback. In checking the receivers the free safety makes a sweeping evaluation of the receiver routes from number one on the left to the number one on the right. The crossing route and the curl routes from the number one indicate that another receiver is probably on a skinny post.

One of the most important factors for the S6 technique to consider is the formation. A balanced ace set should cue the free safety to issue a "deuce" alert. A deuce alert refers to a formation with two receivers to each side of the ball. This formation means a couple of things to the free safety. The formation is a good formation for running four verticals. If the number two to each side is flexed or split, the chance of a four-vertical pattern is extremely high. A deuce alert also makes the corner aware that the smash combination is a possibility, which alerts the cornerback to not bite on a deep curl. The deuce alert tells the cornerback to also look for the wheel.

Another situation of which the free safety should be aware is the trips formation. We do not cheat the free safety to trips, unless the backside receiver is set close. However, we will weave the free safety toward the trips on the trips-split formation. We feel putting the free safety S6 technique to the trips gives the single split receiver too much operating room against our coverage. Granted, the 8-technique outside linebacker can help sink underneath the backside route, but we feel the 8 technique is not effective in helping the backside S3 technique with the skinny post. The trips formation without a "Y" split receiver allows us cheat the free safety toward the trips side. When cheating to one side of the formation, the free safety takes a S5 alignment one yard outside the offensive tackle.

THE CHEAT CALL

The "cheat" call is made to tell the free safety to align as a S5 technique in a position one yard outside the offensive tackle. The normal S5 technique alignment is seven yards off the line of scrimmage and two yards outside the number two receiver. The free safety may keep his ten yard depth on a "cheat" call. The plan may call for the free safety to move back to the middle as the ball is snapped. The "cheat" call is used to discourage the tight end dump and disguise Cover 3 as Cover 1.

PLAYING THE OPTION

Depending on the game plan, the free safety may overlap the alley to the pitch on option. This approach would be taken if the option is fast-played. If the option is slow-played by an outside linebacker favoring the quarterback, the free safety will also overlap the alley as he goes to the pitch.

If the option is slow-played with the outside linebacker favoring the pitch, the free safety will fill the alley. The free safety will also fill the alley on lead option and speed option. Remember, even if the free safety does go to fill the alley, he will continue to overlap should an inside pursuit player get there first. In other words, if the free safety is moving to take the quarterback on the speed option and he sees a teammate come off a block and take the quarterback, the free safety will continue to overlap the alley in his pursuit. This adjustment is standard level-one pursuit for the free safety.

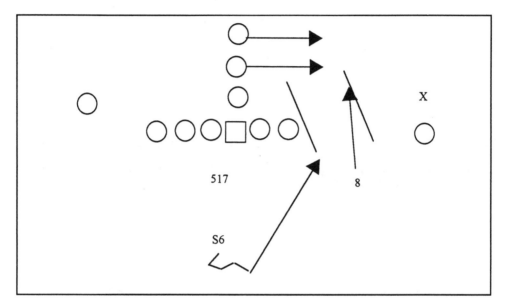

Diagram 8-2: Level-one lead option—free safety fills the alley.

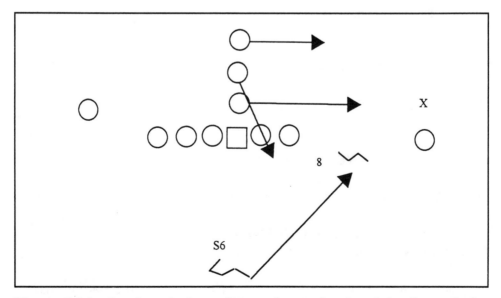

Diagram 8-3: Load option—the free safety overlaps to the edge of the alley as the 8 technique slowplays the quarterback.

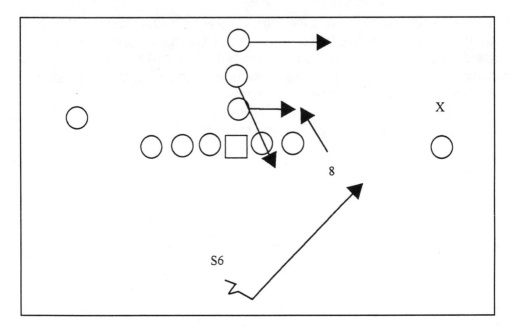

Diagram 8-4: Load option—the game plan calls for the fast play for the load option. The free safety overlaps to the pitch.

THE S5-TECHNIQUE STANCE

Since the free safety is the player who plays the S5 technique, the S5 technique stance uses the same square stance as the S6 technique.

THE S5-TECHNIQUE ALIGNMENT

The S5-technique alignment is seven yards off the line of scrimmage and two yards outside the number two receiver.

THE S5-TECHNIQUE SPLIT RULE

The S5 technique should not align wider than five yards outside the offensive tackle.

THE S5 TECHNIQUE KEYS

The S5 technique keys the ball movement through the number two receiver and the triangle (see keying the triangle in the section on the 8 technique). Since the S5 technique force responsibility resembles the mechanics of the 8 technique, the key of the S5 technique is the ball through the tight end.

This cloudy-clear keying of the triangle of the tight end, the nearback and the ball is similar to the discipline in keying from the S6 technique. The tight end or number two is in the cloudy focus, while the ball is in the clear focus of the S5 technique.

The main responsibility of the S5 technique is to defend the number-two vertical. If number two blocks, the S5 technique comes out of his shuffle and reacts to the level-one triangle. On sweep, the S5 technique attacks the alley and forms the edge. His alley-forming technique is identical to the technique of the 8 technique outside linebacker. If the triangle shows option, the S5 technique plays the option as previously discussed.

S5-TECHNIQUE PLAY AGAINST LEVEL ONE

The S5 technique is the primary force against level one to the defensive back. Against load option, the S5 technique will squat and take the quarterback. Against lead option, the S5 technique will dump the pitch. Against speed option, the S5 technique will squat and take the quarterback. A S5 technique squats by coming out of his shuffle and moving to a depth of three yards from the line of scrimmage. A S5 technique squeezes the alley by attacking in the same manner as the 8 technique who is facing a sweep or another level-one run toward the defender. The coaching points of attacking and squeezing the alley are identical to the 8-technique alley coaching points. Like the 8 technique, the S5 technique drops the anchor and wheels to check for the split flow and cutback on level-one flow away (see the 8 technique coaching points on dropping the anchor and wheeling). Also, the S5 technique uses the 8-technique mechanics of pursuit from the wheel maneuver.

S5 TECHNIQUE AGAINST LEVEL TWO

The S5 technique sinks in the strong curl on level-two flow toward the S5 technique. On level-two flow away, the S5 technique reacts as a S1 technique reacts on level two away. If the number two receiver is split or if the tight end releases, the S5 technique will cover him man-to-man on level two away. If the tight end or other close-set number two receiver blocks, the S5 technique will drop the anchor and sink, watching for the bootleg and screen back to his side.

S5 TECHNIQUE AGAINST LEVEL THREE

Upon shuffling backward, the S5 technique becomes aware of the tight end or other number two receiver's action as the ball obtains level-three status. If the tight end runs an immediate out-breaking route, the S5 technique robs the curl as he sneaks a peek at number one. If facing a pro formation, the tight end is seen on an immediate bench route and the "Z" on a curl, the S5 technique should intercept the curl pass. If given the same pro formation and the "Y" bench with a "Z" out route, the S5 will get his head to the inside and sink to find a crossing route. If a dig route is coming from across the field, the S5 technique should have adequate depth to again pick off the pass to the dig route.

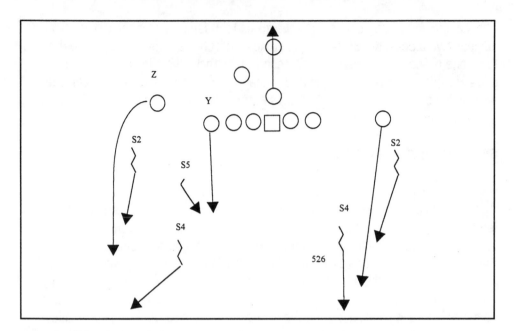

Diagram 8-5: S5 technique and Cover 2—tight end goes vertical and S5 technique jumps the "Y" receiver.

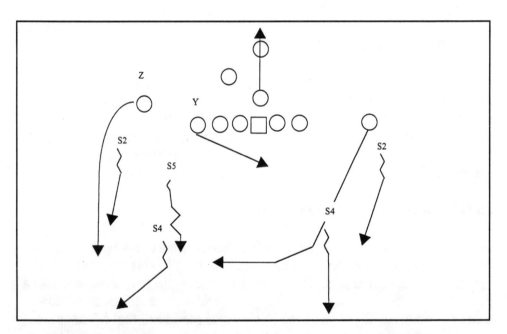

Diagram 8-6: S5 technique reads the "Y" dragging on level three and robs the curl.

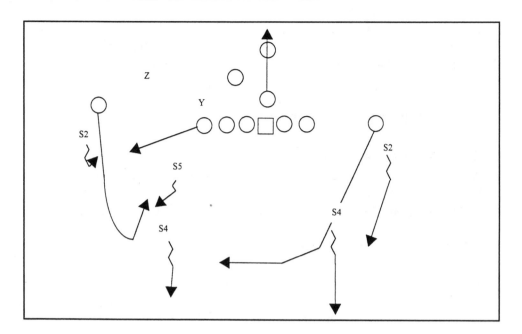

Diagram 8-7: S5 technique against "Y" bench, S5 technique robs the curl.

The S5 technique allows the coverage to be squatted to the strength of the pro formation with a three-on-two advantage. If while the ball is moving at level three, the pro formation tight end runs a vertical route, the S5 technique will cover him man-to-man on the vertical route. If the tight end were to run a drag at a shallow depth or extremely flat angle, the S5 technique would sink and rob the second layer combination drag or dig.

THE 5-QUARTER TECHNIQUE

The 5-quarter technique is identical in alignment, keys, and initial movement. The 5-quarter technique is a S5 technique with the responsibility of the deep one-fourth of the field, rather than robbing the curl or manning the number two on a vertical.

The denotement "S" is not used with the 5-quarter technique because it cannot be confused with a defensive-line 5 technique, as no 5-quarter defensive line technique exists.

WHY THE 5-QUARTER?

The 5-quarter technique is usually played by a cornerback and is an adjustment from a S4 technique against certain formations in special situations. As the need for the S4 technique to adjust to a 5-quarter technique arrives, the cornerback will make a signal to the companion S2 technique to back off to a S3 technique. The result will be the quarter-quarter look with a S3 technique and a S5 technique alignment to that side.

However, instead of the S4 technique's one-half of the field being divided into two equal portions of fourths, the S2 will align and play as a S3 technique, with one-third of the field as his responsibility. This approach will give us an overlap of zones as well as provide consistency of technique for the players.

5-QUARTER TECHNIQUE AGAINST LEVEL TWO

The 5-quarter technique will leave the strong flat open on levels two and three. He will weave with the level-two flow toward him but he will not weave more than three yards before backpedaling on a vertical. On level two away, the 5-quarter technique will weave and backpedal to the middle of the field, the middle one-third.

5-QUARTER TECHNIQUE AGAINST LEVEL THREE

On level three, the 5-quarter technique will backpedal to the near one-fourth of the field as he picks up the route of the inside receiver. The 5-quarter technique will cover the near one-fourth of the field on level three.

CHAPTER 9

Secondary Scheme

The Forty Nickel secondary scheme has eleven base coverages. Additional looks can be created by tweaking the base coverages. Changing one technique of a player of a paired position can create a completely new look to a base coverage. Of the eleven coverages, eight are zone-coverage schemes. Of the three remaining man-to-man coverages, one is a bump-and-run pressure coverage with no help—that may be tweaked to allow for a free safety help. The other two are backpedaling corner technique coverages. One of the remaining two backpedaling coverages allows for free safety help and the other is a man-to-man coverage with no free safety help.

The zone coverages provide the Forty Nickel package with:

- A two-deep coverage with a free-safety robber.

- A true two-deep coverage with a free outside linebacker on the two receiver side.

- A true two-deep coverage with a free outside linebacker on the weakside of the front.

- A three-deep coverage with double invert support from the outside linebackers.

- A three-deep coverage with hard corner support from the outside linebackers.

- A three-deep coverage with man-to-man coverage on the number-two receiver from the outside linebacker.

- A three-deep coverage rolled to a squat coverage versus the end-over formation.

- A three-deep coverage disguised as a man-to-man coverage with no free safety help.

- A four-deep victory coverage with a fifth middle safety hawking the ball.

- A two-minute three-deep coverage with two hard corners and a robber free safety.

The man coverages provide the Forty Nickel package with:

- Bump and run on the edge by the cornerbacks.

- Cushion coverage on the edge by the cornerback with free safety help.

- Cushion coverage on the edge by the cornerback with no free safety help

Included in the package are secondary calls that add features to the base coverages.

- The sink call—a call to the S2 technique telling him to cushion on level three and ignore any threat to the flat until the ball is thrown to the receiver in the flat. Allows the S2 technique to play the deeper route when the offense floods his area.

- The Mango call—a call to the 8 technique telling him to play man-to-man on the number-two wide receiver in a bump-and-run technique. The 8 technique disguises the bump and run until the last moment (see Diagram 9-1). If he has no wide receiver is to his side on the mango call, the outside linebacker reverts to an 8 technique (see Diagram 9-2). If he has a second receiver to his side, but the receiver is not split wide, the outside linebacker reverts to an 8 technique (see Diagram 9-3).

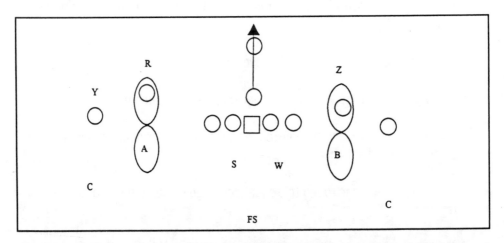

Diagram 9-1: Cover 3 Mango is similar to Cover 3 Out and Cover 3 Bum in principle. Cover 3 Mango is a combination man and zone coverage. The outside linebackers will play man-to-man on the number-two receiver if the number-two receiver is split. If the number-two receiver is not split, the outside linebacker plays the zone eight technique. Zone adjustment squirm rules apply to the linebackers.

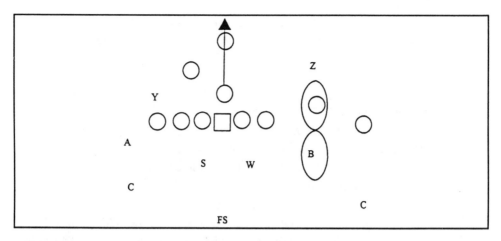

Diagram 9-2: Cover 3 Mango—Antler has no number-two receiver, so he plays the zone 8 technique.

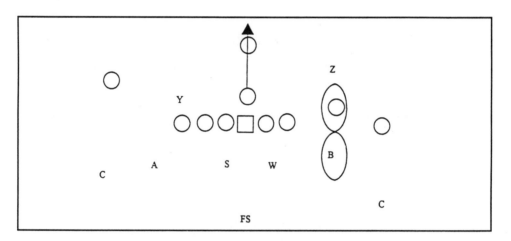

Diagram 9-3: Cover 3 Mango versus twins—Brave is man-to-man on the split number two and Antler is an 8 technique because the number-two receiver on his side is not split.

- The tight call—a common call to the S3 technique telling him to tighten his alignment to five yards off the receiver (from his normal seven-yard depth). A call used against receivers who are not a deep threat. Also used in game situations where man-to-man is too risky, but the coach wishes to challenge the routes normally open against Cover 3.

- The cheat call—a call to the S6 technique directing him to cheat his alignment toward the number-two receiver aligned to the strongside. The cheat call is used in disguising Cover 3 as Cover 1. The cheat call is often used in combination with the tight call.

- The clutch call—not really a secondary call; nonetheless, an integral call to the secondary coverage. A clutch tells the defensive end to cover the tight end or tight slot man-to-man.

- The quarters call—a rarely-used field adjustment call made by the weakside cornerback in Cover 2. The S4 technique cornerback makes the call to the S2-technique outside linebacker when the offense motions to an empty set to the weakside versus Cover 2. The S4-technique cornerback changes his technique to that of a S5 technique. The S2-technique outside linebacker loosens his alignment and changes his technique to a S3 technique.

- The out call—a call to the 8-technique outside linebackers telling them to play a 2 technique on the outside receiver. The outside linebacker cannot execute the out call to a side with more than one wide receiver. If he has more than one receiver to his side, the outside linebacker reverts back to his 8 technique.

- The bump call—a call used with the out call. The bump call tells the outside linebacker to play a bump and run S7 technique, provided he has only a single wide receiver to his side. If the has multiple receivers to his side, the outside linebacker reverts back to his 8 technique (see Diagram 9-4).

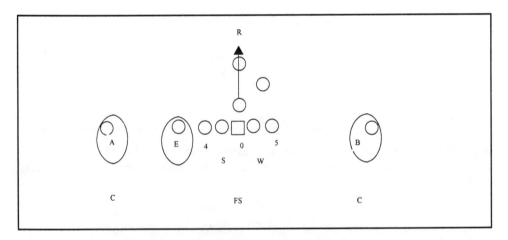

Diagram 9-4: Cover 3 Out-Bump call is shortened to Cover 3 Bump once the players understand the relationship between Cover 3 Out and Cover 3 Bump. The free safety has number two weak and number three strong. This particular Cover 3 Bump is with the 40 Clutch call. May be made with 50 Clutch call.

- The squat call—a call used with Cover 3 against an unbalanced set. The squat call tells the free safety to roll to a S5 technique to the unbalanced side. The freesafety or the weakside cornerback recognizes the unbalanced set and signals for the squat adjustment. The cornerback on the weakside rolls to the middle of the field to replace the free safety.

The teaching of the multiple secondary system is accomplished by task-analyzing the coverage makeup. The system is based upon the principle that every possible secondary coverage known to the game is composed of various independent position techniques. In the Forty Nickel system, there are ten possible techniques. The techniques are structured with such detail that one could accurately state that these ten techniques account for every standard defensive back technique that is used in football. Chart 9a shows the various secondary techniques, any combination of which form the different zone and man-to-man coverages known to the game. Chart 9b details the individual responsibilities of each technique according to their primary keys, (e.g., ball level and movement).

The multiplicity of the coverages is easily accomplished by targeting the techniques played by each position of the secondary. For example, the outside linebacker position is taught the techniques that he plays within the package.

Antler and Brave learn to play the fundamental techniques—the 8 and the S2 techniques. After they have mastered these two techniques, the outside linebackers are instructed in the S1 technique. As Chart 9c illustrates, the Antler and Brave need only to learn three techniques for their participation in eleven base coverages. Should the defensive coach wish to include the Mango call in the package, the Antler and Brave would need to also master the S7 technique. Chart 9c shows the positions and the coverage techniques demanded of each position for the installation of the complete eleven coverage package. These matchups include:

- Cornerback—plays the S1 technique, the S3 technique, the S4 technique, and the S7 technique. The base techniques for the cornerback are the S3 technique and the S4 technique. The cornerback should receive additional instruction in the S5 technique for unusual situations (e.g., no backs, unbalanced sets, etc.), as well as the S6 technique on the Cover 3 squat call.

- Free safety—plays the S1 technique, the S2 technique, the S5 technique, and the S6 technique. The base techniques for the free safety are the S6 technique, the S1 technique, and the S5 technique.

- Outside linebackers—plays the S1 technique, the S2 technique, and the 8 technique. Included in the outside linebacker instruction is the nine technique—a defensive front technique. The base technique of the outside linebacker is the 8 technique with the S2 technique ranking next in importance.

Chart 9a: Composite of secondary techniques.

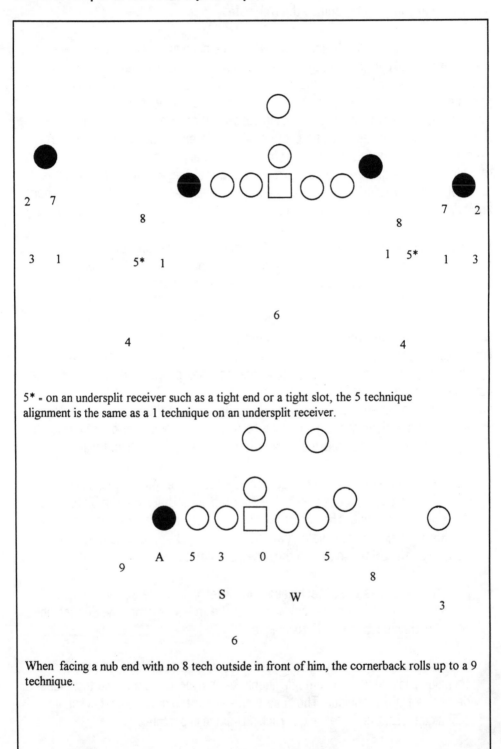

5* = on an undersplit receiver such as a tight end or a tight slot, the 5 technique alignment is the same as a 1 technique on an undersplit receiver.

When facing a nub end with no 8 tech outside in front of him, the cornerback rolls up to a 9 technique.

Chart 9b: Secondary responsibilities.

TECH	LEVEL 1	LEVEL 2	LEVEL 3
1	To: Man Away: Man	Man Man	Man
2	To: Force Away: Wheel	Flat Throwback	Jam #1 read #2 route
3	To: Outside $^1/_3$ Away: Weave to $^1/_2$	Outside $^1/_3$ Weave to $^1/_2$	Outside $^1/_3$
4	To: Weave to Outside $^1/_3$	Weave to Outside $^1/_3$	Deep $^1/_3$
5	To: 1st Threat Away: Weave to middle $^1/_3$	#2 vertical or squat in curl man on #2 crossing, #2 vertical, weave to middle $^1/_3$ if #2 blocks	#2 vertical or squat in curl
5 Quarter	To: 1st threat Away: 1/4 of field	$^1/_4$ of field $^1/_4$ of field	$^1/_4$ of field
6	To: Alley Away: Alley	Middle $^1/_3$ Middle $^1/_3$	Middle $^1/_3$
7	To: Bump and run Away: Bump and run	Bump and run Bump and run	Bump and run
8	To: Force Away: Wheel	Flat Throwback/man	Jam #2 and go to flat
9	To: Force Away: Man on nub end	Outside $^1/_3$ Weave to $^1/_2$	Deep $^1/_3$

Chart 9c: Technique assignments by coverage.

	LEFT CORNER	FREE SAFETY	RIGHT CORNER	ANTLER	BRAVE BACK	VICTORY
Cover 1	1	1	1	8	8	
Cover 1 Free	1	6	1	1	1	
Cover 2	4	5	4	2	2	
Cover 3	3	6	3	8	8	
Cover 3 Out	3	6	3	2	2	
Cover 3 Squat	3 stg—4 wk	5 qtr stg	3 stg—4 wk	8	2	
Cover 4	3	5	3	8	2	Victory
Cover 7	7	1	7	8	8	
Cover 20	4	2	4	8	2	
Cover 20 Weak	4	2	4	2	8	
Cover 23	3	5	3	2	2	Victory

Chart 9d shows the secondary technique specifications. Techniques are specified according to:

- Stance—each technique has particular stance requirements. In the lower levels of the program, younger athletes are checked for their understanding of the technique assignment. The exhibition of the correct stance is a factor in checking for their understanding.

- Alignment—each technique has definitive alignment specifications. These alignments may vary according to the split rule.

- Split rule—each technique has a split rule. This is a guideline to which the defensive player adheres when he is aligning in his technique. The split rule overrules the standard alignment rule and puts the defensive back in the best position to overcome an offensive advantage caused by unusual alignment of the offensive player.

- Initial movement—each technique is characterized by a specific initial movement on the snap of the football. This movement facilitates the defensive player's execution of his primary responsibility.

Chart 9d: Secondary techniques.

TECH	STANCE	ALIGNMENT	SPILT RULE	INITIAL MOVEMENT
1	Heel to toe	7 yds off rec 1 yd inside rec	Move outside if rec splits > 8 yds	Backpedal
2	Feet even Cocked in	1 yd off rec 1 yd outside rec	Never closer than 5 yds to sideline	Bounce
3	Heel to toe	7 yds off rec 1 yd outside Rec	Never closer than 8 yds to sideline	Bounce
4	Heel to toe	8-10 yds off LOS 4 yds outside hash; over OT on nub	Deep as widest rec is wide	Backpedal
5	Feet even Cocked in	7 yds off LOS 2 yds outside of #2	Deep as widest rec from near lineman	Backpedal
5 quarter	Heel to toe	Same as 5 technique	No wider than 5 yds from nub	Backpedal
6	Feet even Shoulders parallel to LOS	10 yds off LOS middle of formation	Never wider than OT	Shuffle
7	Feet even Cocked to rec	1 yd off rec 1 yd inside rec	Change to 1 tech if rec splits < 8 yds from formation	bump and run
8	Feet even Cocked in	4 yds off LOS 3 yds outside TE	Never wider than 8 yds from nearest linemen	Bounce
9	Feet even Cocked in	5 yds off LOS 3 yds outside TE	Not applicable	Bounce

The following coverage descriptions show the alignment of the coverage versus a pro right offensive formation. The secondary declaration versus this formation is "Left." The corresponding front declaration is "Lou." Included in the coverage breakdown are the major coaching points and adjustments of each position, as well as the strength and weakness of each coverage.

COVER 1

Cover 1 is a man-to-man coverage with no free safety help. The coverage is further characterized by the cushioning technique of the cornerback.

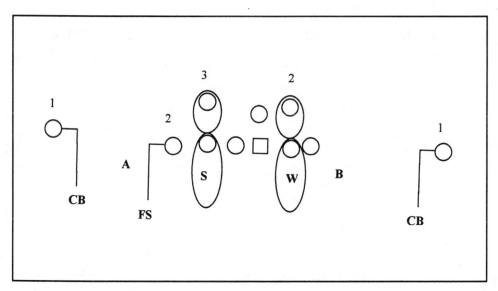

Diagram 9-5: Cover 1.

Left Corner	Plays a S1 technique on #1 receiver to his side.
Antler	8 technique or stack/stunt (go to 00 tech. LB on empty set).
Free Safety	Plays a S1 technique on #2 receiver strongside.
Brave	Free 8 technique—may stack or stunt.
Right Corner	Plays a S1 technique on # 1 receiver to his side.
Sam	Covers #3 strong or #2 weak man-to-man according to secondary strength. May check 50 clutch vs. trips to tight-end side.
Will	Covers #3 strong or #2 weak man-to-man according to secondary strength. May have to adjust by squirming.

Strengths

1. Allows for pressure.
2. Can be disguised as Cover 3.

Weaknesses

1. High Risk.
2. Linebackers have to think.
3. Free Safety is out of the middle.

COVER 1 FREE

Cover 1 Free is a man-to-man coverage with free safety help. The coverage is further characterized by the cushioning technique of the cornerback, as well as a man-to-man coverage responsibility of the outside linebackers.

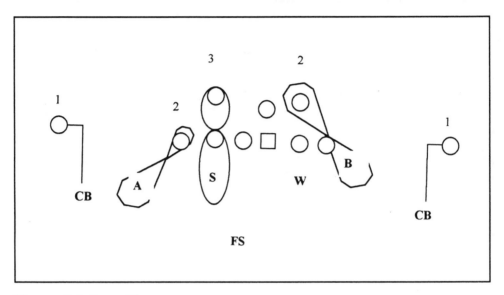

Diagram 9-6: Cover 1 Free.

Left Corner	S1 technique on #1 receiver to his side.
Antler	S1 technique on #2 receiver to his side.
Free Safety	S6 technique.
Brave	S1 technique on #2 receiver to his side.
Right Corner	S1 technique on #1 receiver to his side.
Sam	Man on #3 receiver out to his side #2 receiver if vertical from backfield and Antler stunt is called. Tight end side trips—clutch or check off out of the called Sam stunt.
Will	Man on #3 receiver out to his side #2 receiver if vertical from backfield and Brave stunts. Trips = check off the Brave and Will stunt.

Strengths

1. Man-to-man with a free safety.
2. OLB to side of single receiver can run a Lightning.

Weaknesses

1. Weak run support.
2. Soft man coverage.

COVER 2

Cover 2 is a two-deep zone coverage with a free safety available to rob the strongside vertical and curl routes.

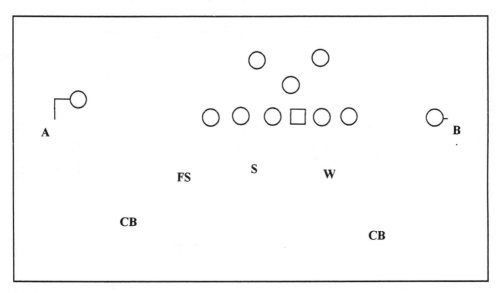

Diagram 9-7: Cover 2.

Antler	Plays S2 technique to tight-end side.
Brave	Plays S2 technique to the side opposite the Antler.
Free Safety	Plays a S5 technique to the two-receiver side.
Left Corner	Plays a S4 technique (favoring outside receiver if on the strongside).
Right Corner	Plays a S4 technique (a more disciplined half field than strongside S4 technique).
Sam	#3* receiver strong if he goes vertical—#2* weak if he goes vertical—may call 50 clutch vs. trips to tight-end side.
Will	#3* strong if he goes vertical, #2* weak if he goes vertical—he may have to squirm.

* Linebackers are concerned with 3 strong, 2 weak as the strength is called by secondary.

Strengths	Weaknesses
1. Strongside option and sweep.	1. Weakside run.
2. Takes away flats.	2. Vulnerable to verticals on weak side.
3. Strong to 2-receiver side.	3. Requires linebacker to think.

COVER 3

Cover 3 is the basic three-deep zone coverage with an invert safety to each side.

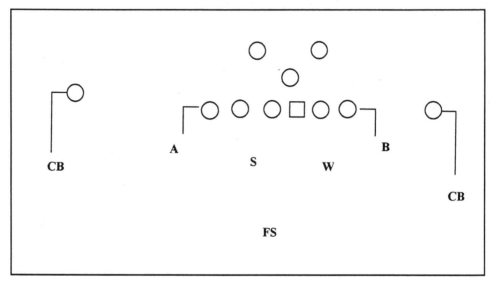

Diagram 9-8: Cover 3.

Left Corner	S3 technique.
Antler	8 technique to the tight end side.
Free Safety	S6 technique.
Brave	8 technique.
Right Corner	S3 technique.
Sam and **Will**	Normal pass drop technique.

Strengths
1. Ease of adjustments.
2. Covers deep outside routes.
3. Free safety in the middle helps stop the run.
4. Man-to-man principle of coverage within the zone.
5. Can call Cover 3 Mango—outside linebackers play S1 techniques on number two or free 8 tech motion adjustment to mango is bump linebackers.

Weaknesses
1. The out route is open.
2. The four vertical route is open.

COVER 3 OUT

Cover 3 is the basic three-deep zone coverage with an invert safety to each side. The out call tells the outside linebacker to apply his out call coaching points. Shown is Cover 3 Out versus an offensive pro right formation.

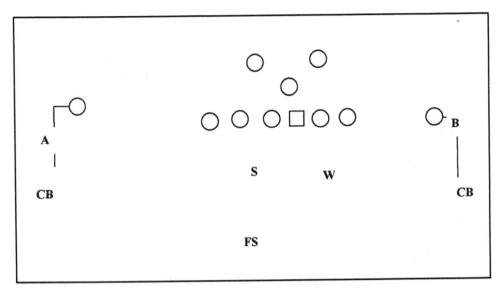

Diagram 9-9: Cover 3 Out.

Antler	S2 technique.
Left Corner	S3 technique.
Free Safety	S6 technique with a cheat call.
Brave	S2 technique.
Right Corner	S3 technique.
Sam and Will	Normal drop techniques.

Strengths

1. Stops the out route with deep 1/3 coverage.
2. Ability to double cover on the perimeter.
3. Good against 2 minute offense.
4. Can call "bump" to press wide receiver with S7 technique outside linebackers.

Weaknesses

1. Removes OLB from 8 technique.
2. Inflexible, have to check to 8 tech vs. twins.

COVER 3 SQUAT

Cover 3 is the basic three-deep zone coverage. Squat is a field call made by the weakside cornerback or free safety and results in an inside roll to the strength of the formation.

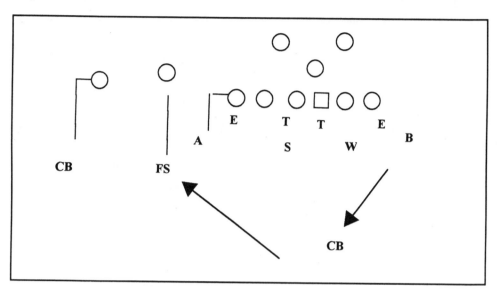

Diagram 9-9: Cover 3 Squat.

Left Corner	S3 technique (if the free safety were to go to right side, then left corner would move to a 4 tech).
Free Safety	Moves from S6 technique to squat at S5 technique versus formation.
Right Corner	Recognizes free safety squatting at S5 tech on opposite side and changes from S3 tech to S4 tech.
Antler	Remains at 8 tech.
Brave	Technically changes from 8 tech to S2 tech, but in reality no differences exists between techniques in this scenario.
Sam and Will	Normal drop rules for Cover 3, but Will covers the #2 weakside receiver on a vertical route.

Strengths

1. Gives an answer to end-over formations.
2. Gives a new look to tight end trips formations.

Weaknesses

1. Recognition of when to use it.
2. Motion adjustment from flanker is Check 3.

COVER 3 TIGHT CHEAT

Cover 3 is the basic three-deep zone coverage. Tight tell the S3 techniques to move to five yards off the receiver. Cheat tells the free safety to align over the number-two receiver strongside.

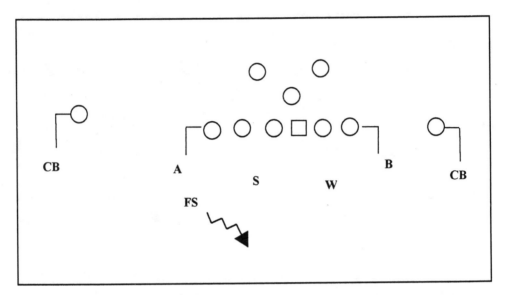

Diagram 9-10: Cover 3 Tight Cheat.

Left Corner	S3 technique 5 yards off receiver (tight) .
Antler	8 technique to the tight-end side.
Free Safety	S6 technique cheats to S5 technique alignment and sneaks back to middle as ball is snapped.
Brave	8 technique.
Right Corner	S3 technique 5 yards off receiver (tight call).
Sam and Will	Normal pass-drop technique.

Strengths

1. Ease of adjustments.
2. Squeezes outside routes.
3. Free safety disguises coverage.
4. Good with pressure.

Weaknesses

1. Riskier against out-and-up pattern.
2. Four-vertical pattern is open.
3. Tight end can run a flag behind an out.

COVER 4 VICTORY

Cover 4 Victory is the deep prevent coverage. It is used when expecting a desperation touchdown pass attempt.

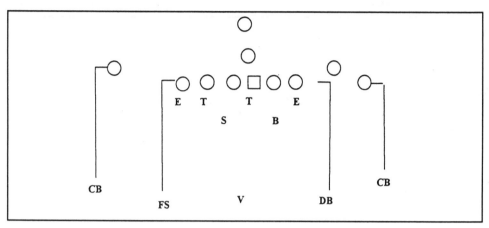

Diagram 9-11: Cover 4 Victory.

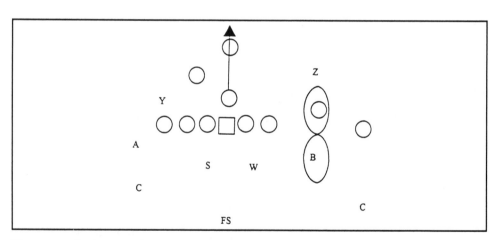

Diagram 9-12: Cover 4 Victory versus Trips.

Left Corner	S3 technique 15 yards deep.
Free Safety	5-quarters technique 15 yards deep.
Dime Back	5-quarters technique 15 yards deep.
Right Cornerback	S3 technique 15 yards deep.
Victory Back	S6 technique 25 yards deep, play the quarterback, cheat to the side of trips.
Sam	Stop the screen and draw, key the back.
Brave	S1 technique on #2 in trips formation strong or weak, play inside linebacker when set is balanced.

COVER 7

Cover 7 is the bump and run press coverage. It is best when used with a double outside linebacker blitz.

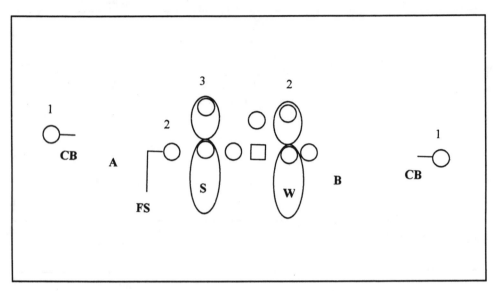

Diagram 9-13: Cover 7.

Left Corner	S7 technique on the #1 receiver.
Antler	8 technique or stack/stunt (go to 00 tech linebacker on empty set).
Free Safety	S1 technique on the #2 receiver to the strongside.
Brave	8 technique or stack/stunt.
Right Corner	S7 technique on the #1 receiver
Sam	Man on the #3 receiver strong or the #2 receiver weak according to secondary strength—may call 50 clutch on trips to the tight end.
Will	Man on the #3 receiver to the strongside or the #2 to the weakside according to secondary strength—may have to squirm.

Strengths

1. Presses receiver.
2. Allows for pressure.

Weaknesses

1. Isolates the cornerback.
2. Takes the free safety from the middle.

COVER 20

Cover 20 is a strongside overload two-deep coverage. The coverage frees the Antler for any assignment (e.g., stack, squeeze, lightning, etc.).

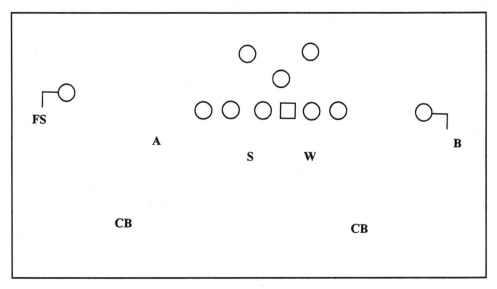

Diagram 9-14: Cover 20.

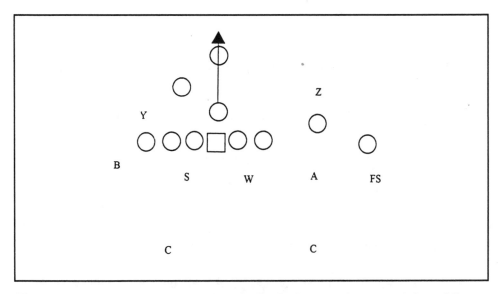

Diagram 9-15: Cover 20—against twins, Antler declares to the two-receiver side.

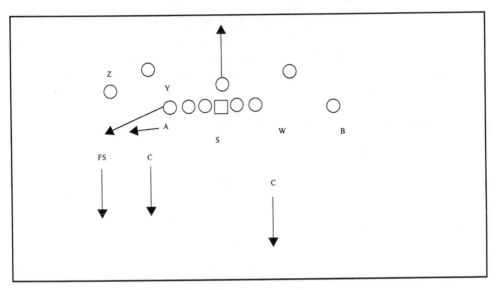

Diagram 9-16: Cover 20 with a Squeeze or Hold call—an adjustment is made to empty set formation. Right cornerback moves from S4 to 5-quarter technique. Free safety moves from S2 to S3 technique.

Antler	Free 8 technique—align to two receiver side—if stacked, unwind versus twins or trips.
Left Corner	S4 technique (true half technique)—disguise alignment as S5 tech if #2 is uncovered.
Free Safety	S2 technique to side of Antler—automatic sink call.
Right Corner	S4 technique (true half technique)—disguise alignment as S5 tech if #2 is uncovered.
Brave	S2 technique—align opposite the Antler (i.e., the single-receiver side).
Sam	Squirm or clutch #3 strongside or #2 weakside.
Will	Squirm on #2 receiver strongside on twins.

Strengths

1. Allows for 5 man pass rush without sending ILB.
2. Good against strong side option/sweep.
3. Frees Antler for specific assignments.

Weaknesses

1. Cornerbacks must play true half.
2. Linebackers must think.
3. Adjustments needed for twins, etc.

COVER 20 WEAK

Cover 20 is a weakside front overload supported by two-deep coverage. The coverage frees the Brave for any assignment (e.g., stack, squeeze, lightning, etc.).

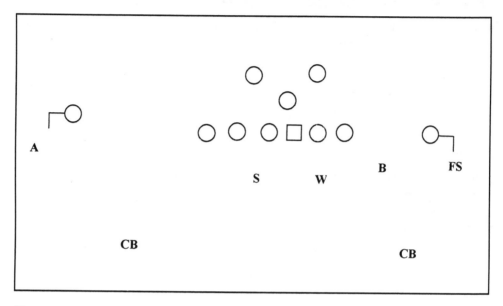

Diagram 9-17: Cover 20 Weak.

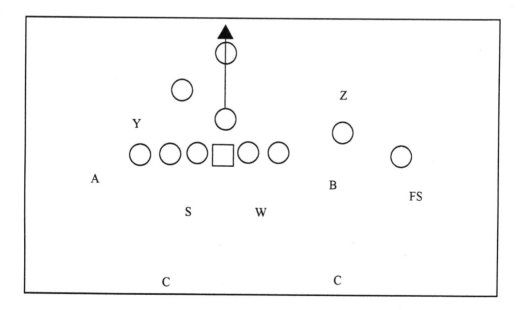

Diagram 9-18: Cover 20 Weak against twins—no adjustment needed unless Weak Stack is called. Brave unwinds to an 8 technique on Weak Stack.

Antler	S2 technique to tight end side.
Left Corner	S4 technique (true 1/2 technique).
Free Safety	Replaces Brave at S2 technique in Cover 20 Weak.
Right Corner	S4 technique (true 1/2 technique).
Brave	8 technique to normal declaration—if stacked or stunting, will have to unwind for trips/twins.
Sam	Squirm out to #2 receiver strongside on tight end trips. Sam may call clutch vs. tight end trips.
Will	Squirm on #3 receiver to the strongside on open trips.

Strengths

1. Allows for 5 man pass rush without sending ILB.
2. Good against weakside option/sweep.
3. Trees Brave for specific assignment.

Weaknesses

1. Cornerbacks must play 1/2.
2. Linebackers must think.
3. Tight end dump is open

COVER 23

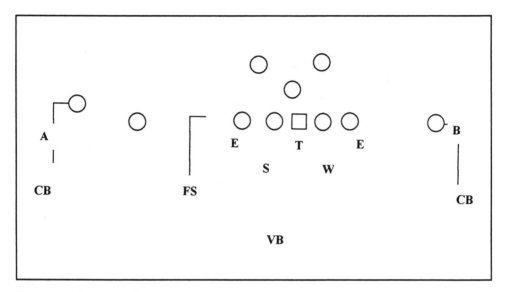

Diagram 9-20: Cover 23.

Antler	S2 technique on the #1 receiver (no adjustment to twins).
Left Corner	S3 technique.
Free Safety	S5 technique on the #2 receiver to the strongside.
Victory Back	S6 technique.
Brave	S2 technique on #1 (no adjustment to twins).
Sam	# 3 receiver strongside or the #2 receiver weakside on a vertical route see the Cover 2 rules).
Will	# 3 receiver strongside or the #2 receiver weakside on a vertical route (see the Cover 2 rules).

Strengths

1. Doesn't give up the out route on 2-minute offense.
2. Provides a 3-on-2 or a 2-on-1 ratio.

Weaknesses

1. Very weak against the run.
2. A basic 3-deep coverage.
3. Subs for defensive tackle lessens the pass rush.

CHAPTER 10

Inside Linebackers

INSIDE LINEBACKER CHARACTERISTICS

Athletes chosen to play linebacker should demonstrate average to above average speed, a higher level of upper- and lower-body strength, agility, and an aggressive nature of play. Of these factors, speed may be the most significant. Athletes with exceptional speed usually make excellent linebackers, regardless of the strength factor. Almost all athletes who desire to play linebacker will demonstrate an aggressive style of play and a love for contact, so this characteristic is usually not a determining factor in the difference between an average linebacker and a great one. Speed, concentration, and agility are the principal skills that the linebacker must demonstrate.

In the Forty Nickel package, the weakside linebacker (Will) is usually the more physical of the two players. He should also be the faster linebacker if the major offensive style of the league is a passing attack. In the standard two-deep coverage, the Will linebacker is responsible for covering the inside receiver aligned to the weakside. The strongside linebacker (Sam) may be less physical and more of a scatback type of linebacker—an excellent scraping linebacker. Due to the 50 defense resemblance on the defensive weakside in the base fronts, the Will is the plugging linebacker. The Sam is usually stacked or shaded on a defensive lineman and thus somewhat protected from the lead blocker from the backfield or offensive line.

INSIDE LINEBACKER STANCE

The inside linebacker will have an unusually close stance, with the feet four to six inches apart, and will stand in the hip flexed position so that the back is nearly parallel to the ground. The taller the linebacker, the more pronounced the forward lean. The hands will be outside the knees and relaxed.

INSIDE LINEBACKER ASSIGNMENT

The inside linebacker will step to stance as he gets his primary key read from a back. The name given to the primary key is "bright light." The primary key will move through one of four movements to which the linebacker will respond. The four movements are called "in," "at," "out," and "other." The Nickel Forty inside linebackers are downhill-playing linebackers. This description refers to the sharp angles the linebackers attack once the ball flow is diagnosed. "In," "at" and "out" are playside attack angles as well as descriptive terms used in identifying the angle and path of the ballcarrier. "Other" describes the key movement away from the backside linebacker. If the primary key flows to the other side, the backside linebacker refers to the key movement as an "other."

Considered in these four movements of the primary key are secondary keys, factors such as "flashing colors," "open doors" and "closed doors." The inside linebacker's run-stopping duties are task-specific to the four movements. The composite of linebacker play against the run is taught around the concept of labeling inside linebacker key movements as "in," "at," "out" and "other." The Forty Nickel's inside linebackers are responsible for stopping the trap and draw. Sam and Will are to blame if the trap or draw play breaks through to our secondary.

The inside linebackers have zone and man-to-man coverage pass drop responsibilities. Cover 2 and Cover 20 and the man-to-man responsibilities loom large in the defensive scheme.

Basic zone responsibilities include the concepts of "walling out" the middle; reacting to the route of the number-two receiver on straight dropback, level-three action; intersecting the line of sight between the quarterback and receiver; junctioning the crossing route; and not biting the bait. Game planning will designate secondary containment on level-two action; the plan being for the backside backer to be secondary containment versus a passing quarterback and the playside to be secondary containment against a running quarterback.

HUDDLE RESPONSIBILITY

Sam is the captain of the defensive front. Sam also helps the free safety recognize formation adjustments and backfield sets. Sam will immediately look for the defensive call following the completion of a play. Sam will step toward the sideline, find the signal-caller and receive the call. Upon receipt of the call, Sam will enter the huddle and give the front call and stunts. The free safety will give the secondary call.

Will, having set the huddle, will observe the down and distance and communicate this information to the front and secondary. If it is third or fourth down, Will should remind the defense that it is a possession down. A possession down is a down which will result in the offense giving up the opportunity for a possession should a first down not be obtained. A third down is a possession down because the offense will generally punt if a first down is not obtained.

LINEBACKER PLAY AGAINST THE RUN—KEYING IN, AT, OUT AND OTHER

Linebackers must quickly diagnose the direction and flow of an offensive play. To that end, we have utilized a system that breaks down play direction and flow into a series of keys that may be practiced daily. By practicing recognition of this series, a linebacker is practicing daily against not just the current week's opposing offense, but against the season's opponents as well.

Direction refers to the key movement toward one of three landmarks. Flow includes the action of the play along with direction, being closely tied to the speed of the play. The linebacker must quickly determine if the play is a slowly developing counter action or a quick-hitting isolation or toss sweep. After direction, the recognition of flow will allow the linebacker to stop the running play for limited gain. The linebackers are taught to recognize direction on the first day of drills by assigning the linebacker primary keys that will remain consistent throughout the season. The initial movement of the assigned key will give the linebacker a clue in diagnosing direction. Forty Nickel linebackers focus their eyes on an assigned running back as a primary key.

Keys secondary to the running back key are also included within the linebacker's field of vision. These keys will include the quarterback's actions, other backs, or possibly an uncovered offensive lineman (a lineman with no defensive lineman aligned on his nose). This field of vision, sometimes called the triangle, is what the linebacker sees with his "dim lights." An effective linebacker is able to focus his bright lights on the primary key, while is constantly processing what is occurring in his dim lights. Bright lights will illuminate direction, but the flow of the play will be determined by what is happening in the dim lights. With bright lights focused on the running back key, the linebacker recognizes movement and "steps to stance," widening a presnap stance in which he had his feet only inches apart. The eyes widen as the lead foot steps sideways to the same direction that the key stepped. The eyes should become as large as saucers "saucer eyes." We also say the eyes should go "Singletary," in honor of former Baylor University and Chicago Bear great Mike Singletary.

The linebacker gets big eyes to widen his field of focus. Direction is diagnosed and it is now a matter of confirming the flow as "in," "at," "out," or "other." In widening his field of focus, the linebacker now shifts his bright lights from the primary key to the triangle. Thus, the linebacker's attention goes from the small focus of the primary key to the big picture of where the ball is going. Diagram 10-1 shows the relative locations of the attack areas of in-at-other.

The step to stance buys time for the primary key to show directional intent. Additionally, this step allows the linebacker to shift his focus of bright lights to the mentioned triangle.

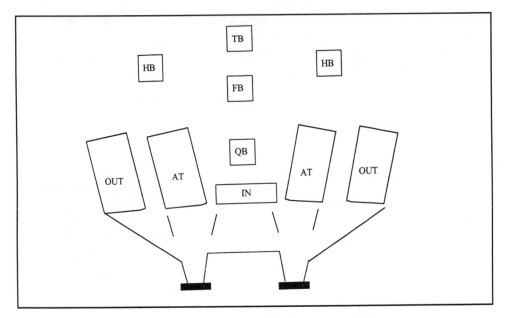

Diagram 10-1: The linebacker teaching grid with dropstep shields.

The concept is related to a player as a small stage spotlight being widened to the size of a prison floodlight. The intensity of the light increases along with the area of illumination. The linebacker's attention goes from the small, yet intense focus of the primary key to a brighter, bigger picture of where the ball is going, the flow. To teach direction and flow, a teaching grid is painted on the practice area to provide the athlete with a concrete visual cue.

As shown in Diagram 10-1 and 10-2, lines and areas marking "in," "at," "out," a starting gate for linebackers, and attack angles are drawn. On the offensive side of the ball, locations are marked so that the scout squad personnel may know where to align. Additionally, offensive lines of attack are painted to signify each of the three areas, "in," "at," and " out." These lines enable the offensive scout personnel to give a consistent picture of the angle of attack. Teaching linebacker direction and flow begins with the proper reaction to an "in" read. The "in" area as shown in the teaching grid diagram is approximately five feet in width.

The football is snapped from the center of the "in" area. To give the athlete a concrete perception of the approximate location of the "in," a rectangle with the dimensions five feet by two feet is painted in the practice area. See Diagram 10-2.

Linebackers must respond with the quickness of a mongoose when presented with an "in." The Forty Nickel philosophy appreciates the fact that traps are highly effective but opportunistic plays. Forty Nickel linebackers develop the mindset that no offense will be successful attempting to inside trap them. The linebackers are taught to expect to see traps early in the game in standard situations. "In" repetitions are numerous in the linebacker read drills. The linebacker corps knows that if the defensive front is vulnerable to the trap, the success of the defensive mission is questionable.

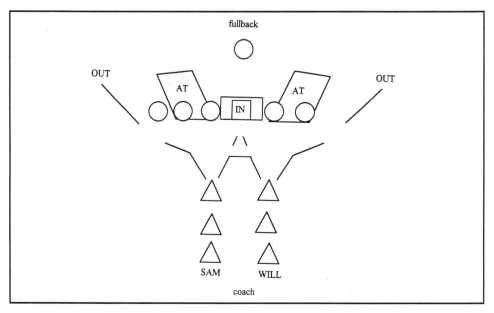

Diagram 10-2: The linebacker teaching grid.

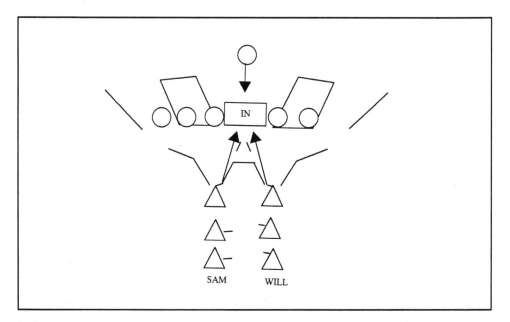

Diagram 10-3: In.

If the primary key steps straight ahead and the bright light-dim light transition confirms the direction and flow, the key is said to be attacking the "in" box. In diagnosing this example of direction and flow, the linebacker steps to stance with his inside foot, goes "singletary," and reads the "in." Recklessness is important to defeating an "in" flow due to the fact that on an "in," the offensive tackle will try to pin the linebacker. Upon making the "in" read, the linebacker attacks the painted "in" box with abandon. Most "ins" are inside trap plays, plays in which the linebacker must tackle the running back near the line of scrimmage. Failure to immediately strike at the "in" leaves the linebacker vulnerable to a devastating blindside for the outside leveraged lineman. Before extensive practicing of the linebacker reactions to "at" direction and flow, "in" reactions are honed to game readiness.

As shown in Diagram 10-4, two parallel lines angling from the backfield denote the "at" attack angle. The lines are drawn approximately 36 inches apart in pairs on both sides of the ball. The inner line which is near perpendicular to the line of scrimmage is approximately 18 inches from the edge of the "in" box. The lines are about four feet long.

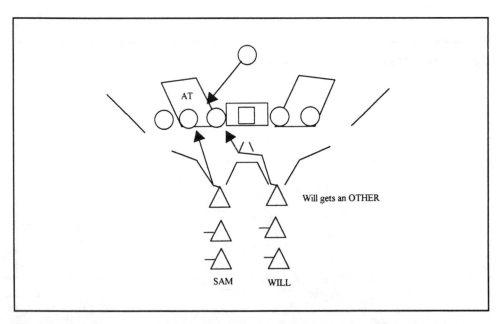

Diagram 10-4: At.

If the key attacks the "at," as shown in Diagram 10-4, the eyes of the linebacker go wide and search for a flashing color. If no flashing color is seen, the linebacker drives out of the stance to which he stepped and attacks the key. The area between the quadrilateral shape made by the angular lines is called the "at" box. The "at" and the "in" boxes are filled in with paint during the preseason drills so that these areas are more visible to the linebacker. The "at" box is angled to give the scout team back the clear perception of his path, as well as to help the linebacker understand his angle in relationship to a running back sprinting to the off-tackle hole.

A line or box marking the "out" boundary is also drawn on each side of the ball. This line is an angular line which is a horizontal image of the "at" boundary lines. This line helps the linebacker understand the angle to which he must adhere to make the play on an "out" read—as shown in Diagram 10-5.

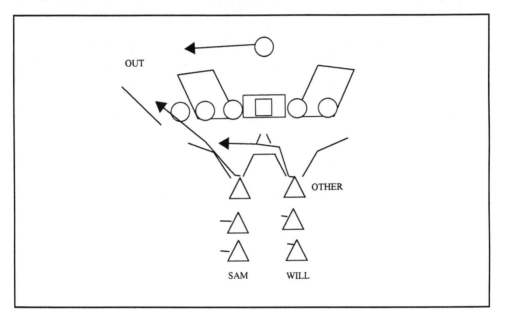

Diagram 10-5: Out.

The "out" line is approximately 48 inches from the edge of the "at" which is nearer the line of scrimmage. The "at" line extends approximately six feet from the line of scrimmage, angling outward. The "out" boundary is the farthest boundary inside which the linebacker must attack.

The linebacker should understand that if the ball was not turned in toward his proper pursuit angle, the outside linebacker did not do his job. Inside linebackers should not be forced to overrun the alley to make the tackle. Forty Nickel inside linebackers attack in the alley from inside-out. The inner wall of the alley will usually be formed near the boundary of the "out."

Diagram 10-6 shows the "out" read by the Will. The Sam gets an "in" read while the Will gets an "other." Whenever a linebacker gets an "other" read, he shuffles to the center at a slight forward angle. This movement gets him up in the "A" gap so that he is safe from a down block from the backside tackle. He checks the "A" gap with his eyes as he shuffles under control. Once he is sure that no threat of a cutback exists, he sprints to the ballcarrier's inside shoulder. A good teaching strategy is to liken the "other" response to a rubber band popping. The rubber band stretches as the backside linebacker shuffles to check cutback, then snaps as the backside linebacker begins to pursue to the ball. The backside linebacker is taught to "drag the anchor" to check cutback, then rocket to the ball once the threat of cutback is eliminated.

The primary running back key may vary according to the backfield set presented. The Sam (i.e., the strongside linebacker) has the following key progression: fullback, nearback, crosskey. Therefore if an I set is presented, he keys the fullback. However, if no fullback is located on his side of the ball, he would key the nearback; with no fullback and no nearback, the strongside linebacker crosskeys.

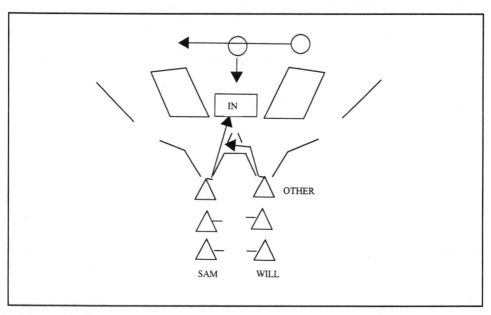

Diagram 10-6: Other.

Since the inside linebackers flip sides according to declared strength, the weakside linebacker has a different key progression. The weakside linebacker's progression is nearback, crosskey, fullback. If no nearback is on the weakside, he looks across the ball to see if a running back is set on the strongside to key. If a back is set strong, such as in a strong power I, he will key the strong back (crosskey). Finally, if no nearback or crosskey is available, he will key the fullback. During the preseason drills, considerable pre-practice time is spent teaching the key progression of the inside linebackers. The linebackers point to the keys from various sets and later take recognition steps in response to the initial direction of the individual keys. The linebackers work in pairs, using proper stance, alignment and depth during this drill. The "step to stance" coaching point helps the linebacker move on movement, yet keep his feet parallel and not wider than his armpits. This coaching point eliminates false reads and undisciplined attack angles. The singular initial step of a running back key does not provide enough information for correct defensive recognition of direction or flow. Stepping to stance trains the linebacker to be poised, and primed with his feet in the correct position, yet allows him to move on movement. The ability to move on movement is important for nurturing the aggressive nature of linebacker candidates.

INSIDE LINEBACKER STUNTS

SAM	Sam linebacker stunts through assigned playside gap.
WILD	Will linebacker stunts through assigned playside gap.
NOSE SAM LOOP	Sam stunts through weakside "A" gap.
NOW WILL LOOP	Will stunts through strongside A gap.
SAM KICK	Sam aligns on LOS and runs a lightning (see outside linebacker stunts).
WILL KICK	Will aligns on LOS and runs a lightning (see outside linebacker stunts).
SAM LINE	Sam aligns on the line of scrimmage to execute assignment.
WILD LINE	Will aligns on the line of scrimmage to execute assignment.
DOG	Both linebackers go through assigned gaps.
DOG LINE	Both linebackers align on the line of scrimmage to run the dog stunt.

OTHER INSIDE LINEBACKER ALIGNMENTS

WIDE	Linebacker on 3 technique side aligns in 40 technique.
STACK	Antler aligns at a gap 50 technique, Sam aligns at a 00 technique, Will aligns at a 50 gap technique.
WEAK STACK	Sam aligns at a gap 50 technique, Will aligns at a 00 technique, Brave aligns at a gap 50 technique.
DOUBLE STACK	Sam aligns at a 20 technique, Will aligns at a 20 technique, Brave and Antler align at a gap 50 technique.

INSIDE LINEBACKER ADJUSTMENTS

GREEN
Tells weakside defensive end and defensive tackle to adjust to blitz and 1 tech charge.
a. Used by WILL when facing two tight ends or tight end and tight slot (tight formation).
b. Must be used versus two tight end deuce formation and Cover 2 called.
c. May be used versus two tight ends with any coverage.

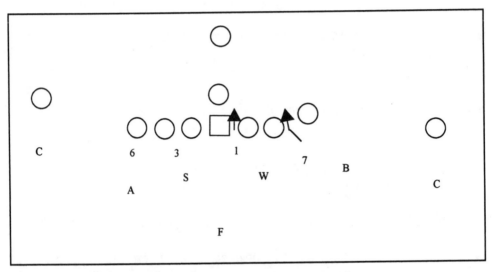

Diagram 10-7: 30 (Green adjustment to Tight Weakside Flank).

ME
a. Tells defensive end that the inside linebacker will contain, defensive end to open end must run a blitz stunt.
b. Will linebacker uses call when squirming on open end side.

CLUTCH
Tells strongside defensive end aligned on tight end to cover tight end if the tight end releases.
a. May be used against tight-end side trips formation (strong trips).
b. Must check 40 or 50 to run clutch.

SQUIRM
a. Used with "me" call or "green" adjustment so the inside linebacker can move out to cover a receiver.
b. If Will squirms out, Sam must squirm inside over the center.
c. If Sam moves out, Will must squirm inside over the center.
d. If the backside linebacker is already squirmed outside when called to replace companion linebacker, the second squirming linebacker calls the free outside linebacker to the middle (occurs only against empty set formation).

TRAP RESPONSIBILITY

Foremost in the responsibilities of the linebacker is the trap responsibility. A trap will be cued with an "in" angle by the key. The "in" is usually accompanied by the quarterback turning his back to the line, as he opens to give the running back the right of way.

Both Sam and Will are trap responsible. If the trap breaks, it is their responsibility. By giving the trap to our inside linebackers we allow our defensive linemen to be extremely aggressive in their attack of the offensive linemen in front of them.

STOPPING THE TREY

Stopping the trey is primarily the responsibility of the backside linebacker. The playside linebacker will usually be captured by a down-blocking tight end or other player. Of course, this event is the worst-case scenario. It is not acceptable for the playside linebacker to be blocked, but the possibility is acknowledged and a plan is in place to deal with that scenario. This contingency plan for the possibility of the playside linebacker being captured puts the responsibility of making the tackle on the trey totally on the shoulders of the backside linebacker.

The backside linebacker has the luxury of seeing one and two flashing colors move across his line of sight as he read steps. The backside linebacker is taught to move through the trash in a controlled manner. After reading the flashing colors of the trey, the backside linebacker drags the anchor to arrive at the hole behind the pulling lineman whose job is to seal the backside or lead the running back. The linebacker's goal is to stop the counter-trey for a two-yard gain. A two-yard gain on a trey is significant, considering that offenses who run the trey usually have a great tailback. Stopping the trey is practiced daily on the linebacker field grid. With practice, the backside linebacker will eliminate the threat of the trey.

ELIMINATING THE BUCKET STEP

Although this text does not address specific drills at the defensive positions, we feel the need to address the issue of the bucket step. Linebackers sometimes bucket step upon recognition of the primary read. Many athletes will successfully read step from the six-inch stance, but upon recognition of the direction of the key, they will step into the bucket. This step is a common technique error in a playside linebacker's reaction to an "out." Even more common is the tendency of the athlete to bucket step at the backside linebacker position.

The bucket step is a compensatory move. The athlete bucket steps either because he is not secure in his ability to either get to the ballcarrier at the proper angle or because he has been cut by a center in his backside pursuit and wants to avoid the center. The bucket step is easily cured through a task analysis of the linebacker's initial movements. Since the bucket step is made from the stance, we provide the athlete feedback at that point, instead of waiting for the completion of a practice play during the drill and approaching the athlete with the admonishment, "You bucket-stepped." A light blocking dummy is placed on the ground inches behind the heels of the linebacker (see Diagram 10-1).

The blocking dummy is kicked by the heel as the linebacker bucket steps on his next repetition. This drill allows the athlete to get feedback at the moment of the step, helping him self-correct his flaw. The coach may concentrate on praise of the athlete's effort instead of continually harping about the bucket step. Two to three days of using the dummy behind the heels generally cures the bucket step. Occasionally, you need to incorporate the dummy in front of the linebackers at the second location shown below.

The Will linebacker will also sometimes revert to bucket-stepping, particularly when the nose tackle is not doing a good job flattening the center in the 20, 30 and 40 fronts. The dummy reminds the backside linebacker to get up in the mix as he pursues. If the backside linebacker "bellys" his pursuit, the cutback is open.

The linebackers are constantly reminded that a tackle for a four-yard gain is nothing to whoop and holler about. A bucket-stepping and backside "belly" pursuing linebacker will still make lots of tackles, but the minimum gain against these technique is usually four yards. The defensive front works to allow the angles of the linebacker pursuit to remain sharp. Without this cohesion of the front and inside linebackers, the defense will be the consistency of papier mâché. Preventing the bucket step is one key element in developing a good high school linebacker.

FLASHING COLOR

Another vital coaching point which the linebacker should master is the "flashing color." A flashing color refers to any movement which overrides the primary key angle. If the key dives at an "at" and the guard pulls across the face of the linebacker, the guard is a flashing color. If a fullback dives at an "at" and a tailback counters behind the fullback, the tailback is a flashing color. If full flow shows and the quarterback bootlegs opposite, the quarterback is a flashing color.

Linebackers play flashing colors off of the read step. The read step, the step to stance step with the foot corresponding to the key direction, and a habit of going "saucer-eyed" allow the linebacker to see the flashing color and drive off the read foot. The linebacker could use the "T-step" of the defensive backs, but we usually don't overcoach the recovery. Once the linebacker recognizes the flashing color, he identifies the path of the flashing color. If the standard flashing color in front of the key has a flat path, the play is a type of trap, either long or short. If the flashing color is off the line, the play is likely a bootleg or a trey.

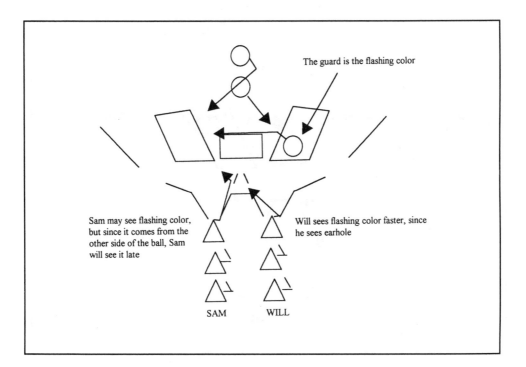

The guard is the flashing color

Sam may see flashing color, but since it comes from the other side of the ball, Sam will see it late

Will sees flashing color faster, since he sees earhole

SAM   WILL

Diagram 10-8: The guard is a flashing color.

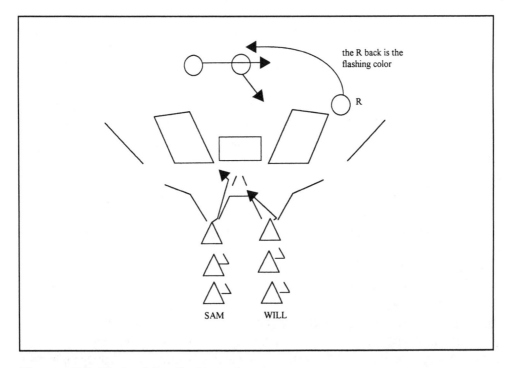

the R back is the flashing color

R

SAM   WILL

Diagram 10-9: The back is a flashing color.

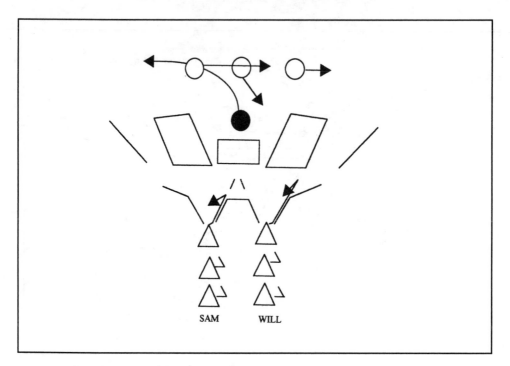

Diagram 10-10: The quarterback is a flashing color.

The path of the flashing color is easily read if the specific path of the color is that of the play being simulated from the weekly scouting report. The path of the flashing color doesn't always mean the same thing for all teams. In general though, the linebackers are familiarized with the depth and angle of the flashing color as being an indicator in the aforementioned plays.

Each linebacker will have different moments of recognition for the same flashing color. For example, if the key dives to the defensive right on an "at," and the left offensive guard pulls across the ball, the linebacker on the defensive right will see the flashing color before the linebacker on the left. The pulling guard takes a few seconds to appear to the backside linebacker.

To help with the recognition, we teach our linebackers to yell "pull-pull-pull" as they see the earhole of the flashing color. The flashing color will usually "show the earhole" as he opens to pull. The sight of the earhole is the specific indicator of a flashing color. Screaming "pull-pull-pull" does two things. First, it *does* help the backside linebacker in recognizing the offside flashing color. Without the yelling, our backside linebacker sometimes gets to the center on his check for cutback. This movement gets him caught up in the trash and sometimes cuts off the backside linebacker who recognized the flashing color. Upon hearing the "pull" alarm, the backside linebacker brakes and moves to gain outside leverage on the deep pulling color or smash the flat pulling color. This reaction allows the backside linebacker to clean up and make the big hit on the unsuspecting ballcarrier.

Second, yelling helps condition the playside linebacker to consciously react to what he knows is a flashing color. Early in the preseason, a coach can ask the athlete, "Didn't you see the flashing color?" The athlete will usually say that he saw it, but for some reason, his body didn't respond to his visual recognition. The verbal affirmation of yelling "pull, pull, pull" helps the athlete make the connection from recognition to reaction. Your linebackers should be trained to yell "pull, pull, pull" on every drill and on every snap where a flashing color is seen.

Training the athlete on recognizing the flashing color starts with the bag shuffle drills. First, let me interject one fact in regard to the bag drills. When shuffling through the bags, linebackers should work forward over the bags as shown in Diagram 10-11.

The linebackers should never shuffle over the middle of a line of bags (blocking dummies). Linebackers should be continually reminded on moving forward, gaining ground in attacking a ballcarrier. Having the athlete shuffle over the middle of the bags undermines this objective.

In a typical bag drill, the linebackers are shuffling uphill. The coach faces the players. The linebacker coach usually will allow several repetitions straight through and so forth before incorporating the flashing-color drill.

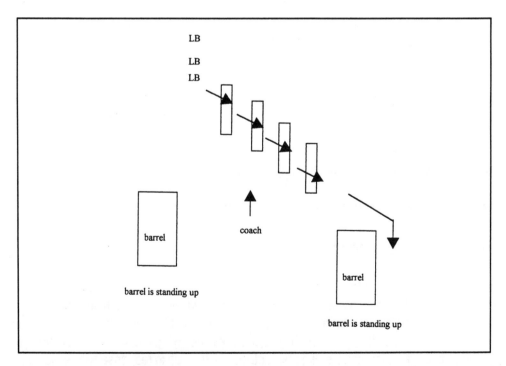

Diagram 10-11: Linebackers run through the bags at an uphill pursuit angle.

During the initial phases of teaching the flashing color, the coach takes a three-point stance to face the shuffling linebacker. The coach will allow the linebacker to shuffle. As the linebacker shuffles, the coach shows him an earhole. The linebacker then immediately redirects his path. The linebacker should not shuffle back over the dummies upon recognition of the flashing color. Instead, he attempts to gain ground and leverage on the flashing color. In this drill, the linebacker is asked to come out of the bags, simulating an uphill attack of the flashing color. The placement of two barrels at either end of the drill allows a linebacker a reference point to which he should redirect. If the coach does not give the earhole key, the linebacker continues his upfield shuffle through the bags and attacks the barrel with outside leverage. The barrel actually simulates a quarterback, either running on the edge or on a bootleg.

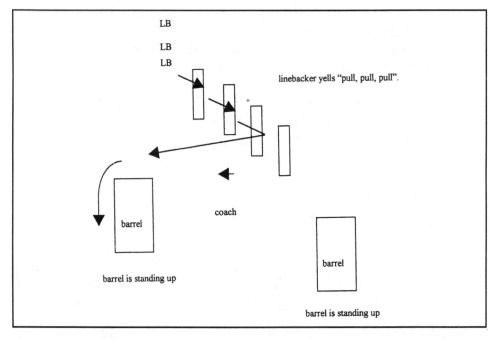

Diagram 10-12: Linebackers run through the bags at an uphill pursuit angle and coach shows the shuffling linebacker his right earhole from a three-point or crouched position. Linebacker redirects and sprints to obtain leverage on the barrel.

OPEN AND CLOSED DOORS

The linebacker to the side of the 0, 1, or 2 technique must know how to play the open and closed door. The door is open when the defensive end 5 technique is blocked out. The door is closed if the offensive tackle blocks inside on the linebacker and the defensive 5 technique squeezes the "B" gap and closes off the running lane. If the defensive end doesn't close off the gap in response to the inside block of the offensive tackle, then the door is not closed. The defensive end must close with the down block for the door to correctly read as closed.

It is usually the Will linebacker who has to read the open and closed door, because the Will is generally on the side of the tackle who is playing a 0, 1, or 2 technique. The Sam is usually on the side of the 3 technique or 4 technique tackle. Regardless of the technique of the tackle, the linebacker must read the open and closed door whenever he is on the side of both a 5-technique defensive lineman and a 0-, 1-, or 2-technique defensive lineman.

A linebacker only reads open and closed door in the specified circumstances of an "A" gap defensive lineman and a "C" gap defensive lineman because the door is automatically closed when the tackle is a "B" gap defender (e.g., 3 technique or 4 technique). You should also note that the 50 front requires both linebackers to read open and closed door.

Linebackers who have difficulty reading open and closed doors may be brought along slowly in the instruction of the technique. Until they master the open and closed door reads, the linebackers should be limited to playing in the 32 and 33 fronts. A Will linebacker who is unsure of reading the open and closed door may be helped out by making weakside blitz calls. The door is automatically closed when the weakside defensive end slides inside on a blitz stunt. Just as the door can be automatically closed with the blitz call, the door may be automatically left open by the linebacker making a "you" call to the defensive end. The "you" call tells the defensive end or tackle 5 technique to ignore an inside block and not close with the blocker, should he block inside.

Open and closed door recognition reads are practiced daily with live defensive ends and the defensive end coach. This technique is not mastered in one week. Waiting to teach the concept on the week of the big game versus the veer team will result in a breakdown on the weakside. Also, without the linebacker's ability to make proper reactions to the open and closed door keys, the multiplicity of the defensive front is greatly inhibited.

PASS COVERAGE RESPONSIBILITIES

The linebackers have coverage responsibilities specific to the coverage called. The basic zone responsibility for the linebacker is to squirm against trips or more to his side. This squirm is to prevent the hot route being thrown to the uncovered receiver. The linebacker squirms so he may be able to discourage this route, but still be able to provide some run support.

A squirm is when the linebacker moves. A linebacker who squirms outside the tackle box always makes a "me" call to the defensive end. The "me" call tells the defensive end that the linebacker is now responsible for the outside containment on the bootleg play. More important, the "me" calls tell the 5-technique defensive end to run a "blitz."

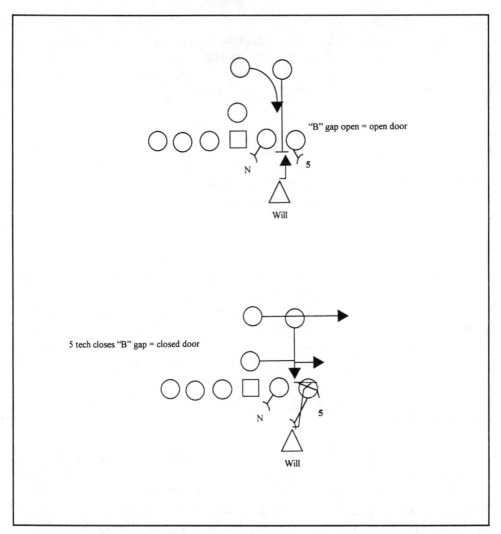

Diagram 10-13: Open—closed door reads.

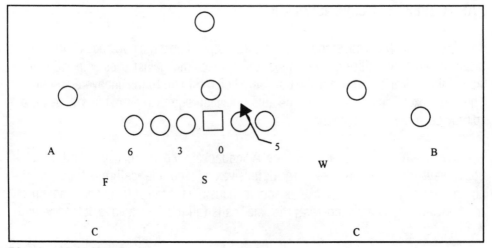

Diagram 10-14: Will Squirm.

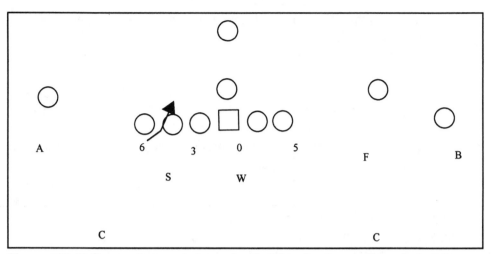

Diagram 10-15: Sam squirms and gives a "me" call to the strongside end who blitzes.

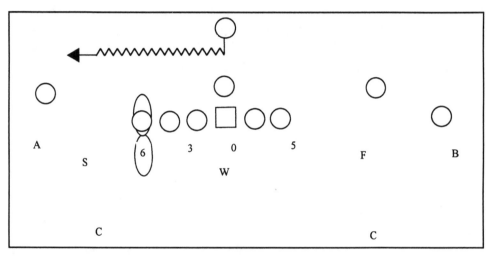

Diagram 10-16: Sam Squirm and Strong End Clutch.

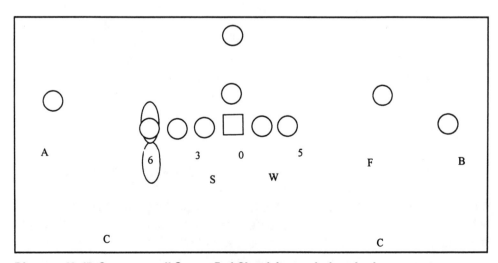

Diagram 10-17: Sam may call Strong End Clutch instead of squirming.

The "blitz" shores up the "B" gap and replaces the squirmed linebacker. Another important coaching point is that whenever a linebacker squirms outward, his companion linebacker must squirm to the 00 technique over the center.

A squirm is a movement of a linebacker accompanied by an adjustment by the other linebacker. In rare circumstances, such as goal line and in defending the empty set, the squirm will involve one of the outside linebackers. The foundation for the goal line is the squirming of the second level of players. Through this foundation, the goal line will always have some form of run support on the edge with linebackers mirroring the strength of the running backs. Linebackers usually apply their squirm rules according to the secondary strength call, not the front. If the free safety calls out, "Strong Right," the secondary strength call is to the defensive right. "Strong Left" means the secondary strength is to the defensive left. On Cover 2, for example, the inside linebackers will have the rule of 3 strong, 2 weak—verticals.

If the free safety calls strong left and the front is "Lou," the Sam is on the strong side. He will have number-three strong should three strong go vertical. If the free safety calls strong left and the front is "Ray," the Will is on the strong side. He will have number-two weak should two weak go vertical. Thus arises the question of front-secondary strength congruence. If the calls are congruent (e.g., Ray and Strong Right, Lou and Strong Left), Sam will have number three on the vertical and Will has number two on the vertical. If the calls are incongruent (Ray and Strong Left, Lou and Strong Right), Will has number three and Sam has number two on the vertical. Sometimes the inside linebacker coverage is not linked to the secondary strength.

The linebacker coach must teach the linebackers the coverages and help them understand which call is the reference call for a particular coverage. The linebacker coverage rules are included in the coverage descriptions within this text. Linebackers will also squirm on man-to-man coverages. When squirming on man-to-man coverages, the linebacker will lock on the man. However, should the man motion across the formation, the linebacker will squirm back to the linebacker position as the responsible party for that number man on the other side picks up the motion. In other words, the basic motion adjustment of man-to-man coverage is to bump. Man-to-man coverages are bumped except for goal-line coverage. Goal-line coverage rules call for the defender to run with the man.

LINEBACKER BAIT

Many one-back passing teams will use "bait" to get an inside linebacker to sit on a shallow crossing route. The tight end's route below in Diagram 10-18 is about four yards deep. This route is a bait route. The Sam will check for draw and collision the tight end. Sam should realize that the route is shallow and therefore is bait. Sam should come off the wall of the tight end and sink off the line of scrimmage into coverage. In doing so, he looks through the receiver in the direction of the tight end's route. This look allows him to see the crossing route from the opposite side. He moves backward to junction this route and screams "cross, cross" to his teammate.

Will must get his head back around and look inside as he squares up under the crossing route of the R back, as shown in the diagram. Will must be in position to break up on the pass to the tight end and tackle the tight end for a short gain. Linebackers should never take the bait.

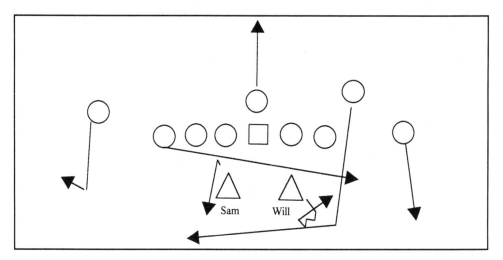

Diagram 10-18: Will jumps the shallow receiver through his zone once the deep receiver clears.

INSIDE LINEBACKER PLAY AGAINST THE DRAW

The inside linebackers pivot upon level-three pass recognition. They will open their hips and drop their outside foot, but they will leave their inside foot planted until they are positive the threat of a draw is no longer present. Draw is no longer to be considered a threat once the ball has moved past the deepest back in the backfield. The inside linebacker must play run first and pass second. A linebacker may compensate for the lack of getting a jump into his drop by adjusting the depth of his alignment before the snap and aligning deeper than normal, but the technique of draw first and pass second does not change.

Ironically, sitting on the draw can be an advantage in the pass defense. Sitting on the draw before flying out to their zones accomplishes several things.

- Checking draw baits the quarterback into thinking the linebacker is not going to his zone drop—a quarterback may think the inbreaking route is open and throw the ball, only to see the linebacker intersect the line of sight at the last second and pick off the pass.

- Checking draw baits the receivers into thinking the coverage is man-to-man—whenever there is a combination coverage called, the receiver may have some difficult in reading whether it is a man-to-man coverage or a zone. Receivers are taught to read the linebacker drop to make this determination and adjust their route accordingly. If the linebacker is sitting on the draw, the receiver will initially read this action as a cue to man-to-man coverage. If the coverage is a zone, the receiver will run across the field on a crossing route and not settle in the hole. A crossing route misread of the zone drop will result in a big play for the defense as the receiver continues across the field into a waiting zone defender's area.

- Checking for draw allows the linebacker to make a definitive evaluation of the inside receiver's break. By getting a better read of the route of the number-two receiver, the linebacker often gets a better opportunity to junction the number-two vertical or hook route.

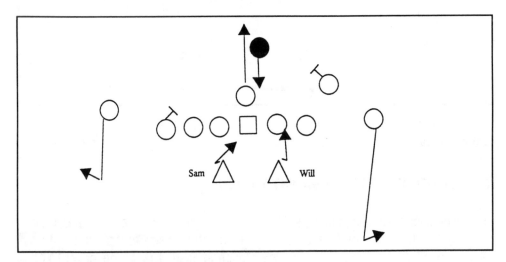

Diagram 10-19: Linebackers should play run first.

FUNDAMENTAL INSIDE LINEBACKER PASS DROPS

Sam and Will step up and check draw. Once the threat of draw has passed, they continue into their drop off of their outside pivot. They read the route of the number-two receiver and peek inside to the number-three receiver or outside to the number-one receiver. To whom they peek depends upon the route of the number-two receiver. If the number-two receiver runs an outbreak, the linebacker peeks to the number-one receiver. If the number-one receiver is running an inbreak, the linebacker will then move to junction this route in the curl zone. If the number-two receiver runs a vertical route or an inbreak, then the linebacker peeks at the number-three receiver. If the number-three receiver is running a seam route with the number-two receiver route vertical or inbreak, then the linebacker applies the overflow rule.

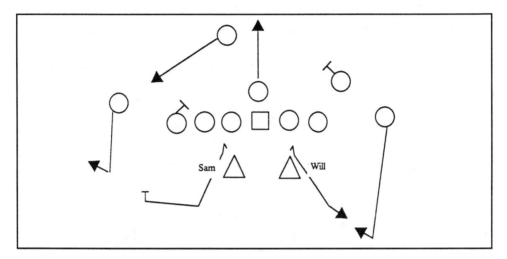

Diagram 10-20: Linebackers should read number two on level three.

INSIDE LINEBACKER DROPS VERSUS LEVEL TWO
WITH A PASSING QUARTERBACK

Against a passing quarterback, the backside linebacker will provide secondary containment against level two. The playside linebacker will cover the curl. This determination of responsibilities is made in the game planning from week to week.

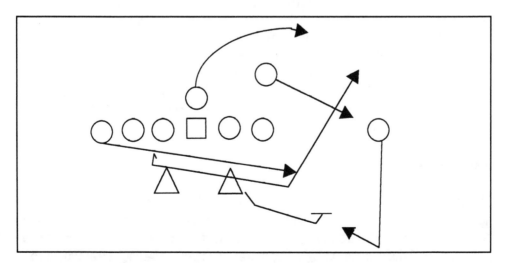

Diagram 10-21: Level two drops and secondary containment versus a passing quarterback.

INSIDE LINEBACKER DROPS VERSUS LEVEL TWO
WITH A RUNNING QUARTERBACK

Against a running quarterback, the frontside linebacker will provide secondary containment against level two. The backside linebacker will cover the curl. This determination of responsibilities is made in the game-planning from week to week.

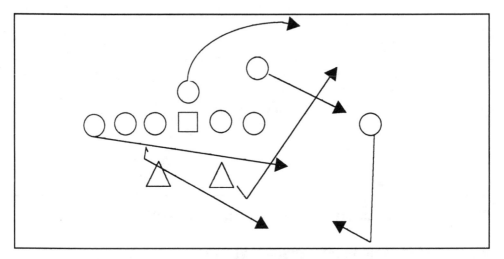

Diagram 10-22: Level two drops and secondary containment versus a passing quarterback.

INSIDE LINEBACKER DROPS AGAINST THE NUMBER-TWO VERTICAL

If the number-two receiver runs a vertical route, the linebacker will move to junction the route of the receiver. He will attempt to wall the receiver out of the middle. Keeping inside leverage, the linebacker will look back to the quarterback as he walls the vertical route out of the middle hook zone. When looking back to the quarterback, the linebacker takes notice of whether a third receiver is slipping out of the backfield and into the seam zone. If a third receiver is running a seam route outside of the vertical route of the number-two receiver, the linebacker runs through the junction point and covers the seam. The backside linebacker will slide to the middle upon recognition of the overflow.

SNEAKING A PEEK

Should the number-two receiver block with the level-three action, the linebacker goes to the curl but sneaks a peek at the number-one receiver's route. If the number-one receiver makes an outbreak, the linebacker settles in the seam zone, looking for a split route. If the number-one receiver makes an inbreak, the linebacker works to the curl to get into the line of sight between the receiver and the quarterback. He should keep his head on a swivel and slide to the hook if he feels the receiver continuing on a crossing route.

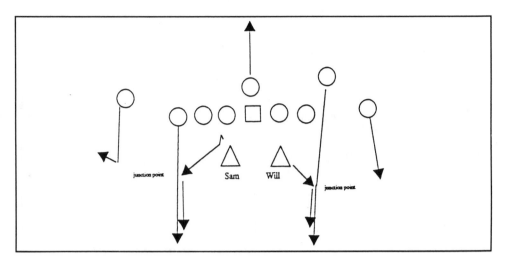

Diagram 10-23: Linebackers junction number two on a vertical against level-three flow.

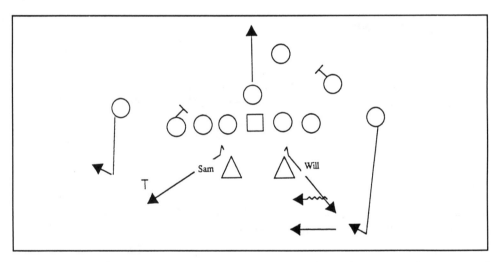

Diagram 10-24: Linebackers react to the action of number two versus level-three flow.

DEFENDING THE SPLIT ROUTE

Described in the section on inside linebacker drops against the number-two vertical, the split route is a route run to the seam zone. Whenever he reads both backs flow to one side, the linebacker must overrun the number-two vertical and settle in the seam zone. This type of pattern is called an overflow. The backside linebacker will reverse his pivot to the inside and settle in the hook.

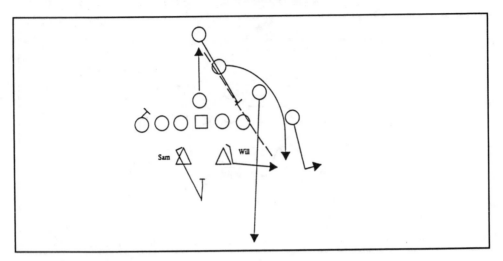

Diagram 10-25: Will overruns the wall of number two if a third receiver threatens the seam.

STUNT DESCRIPTIONS

There are eight principal inside linebacker stunts. Inside linebacker stunts are usually run with man-to-man coverage. They may be run as a predetermined stunt on the snap of the ball or as a read stunt. A read stunt is run only when the flow comes to the side of the linebacker, on an "in," "at" or "out." Even so, an inside linebacker stunt such as a 30 Sam might only be executed on the "in" and "at" reads.

The gap through which the linebacker stunts is identified by the front numbers. In each front, the linebacker has a specific gap for which he is responsible. These gaps are identified in the chapter on defensive fronts in the section illustrating the fronts and the responsibilities of each front defender.

- Sam—the Sam stunts through his responsible gap when SAM is called in the huddle. The tackle to the side of the stunt is alerted that Sam is stunting to his side when the strength call is made. A "Ray" call means that the Sam is stunting on the right side; a "Lou" call means that the Sam is stunting on the left side. The tackle on the side of the call will loosen his alignment and run an upfield charge through his gap.

- Wild—the Will stunts through his responsible gap when WILD is called in the huddle. The tackle to the side of the stunt is alerted that Will is stunting to his side when the strength call is made. A "Ray" call means that the Will is stunting on the left side; a "Lou" call means that the Will is stunting on the right side. The tackle on the side opposite of the call will loosen his alignment and run an upfield charge through his gap.

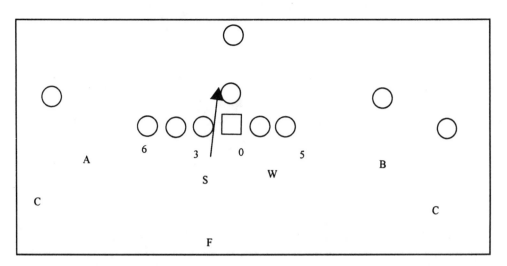

Diagram 10-26: 30 Sam.

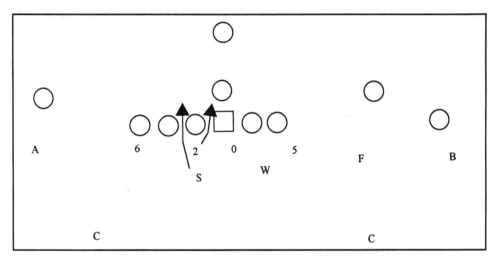

Diagram 10-27: 20 Sam.

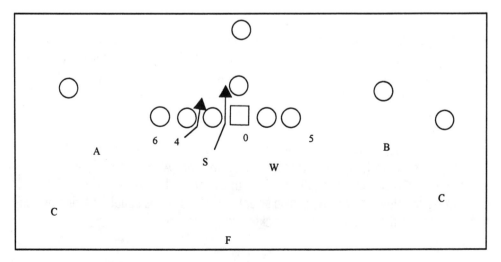

Diagram 10-28: 40 Sam.

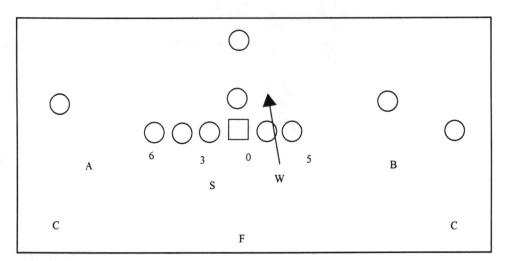

Diagram 10-29: Wild.

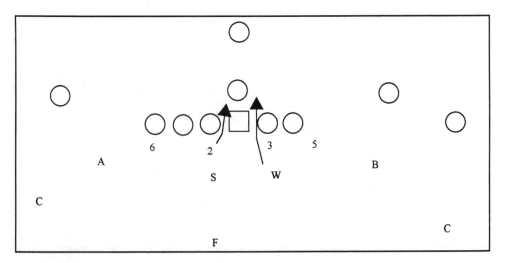

Diagram 10-30: 23 Wild.

- Nose Sam Loop—the nose runs a nose stunt (i.e., a strong slide) and the Sam linebacker loops behind him through the weakside "A" gap. In running situations, the stunt is usually carried out by the linebacker only if the weakside flow shows. In passing situations, the stunt is usually carried out on the snap of the ball by both the tackle and the linebacker.

- Now Will Loop—the nose runs a now stunt (i.e., a weak slide) and the Will linebacker loops behind him through the strongside "A" gap. In running situations, the stunt is usually carried out by the linebacker only if the strongside flow shows. In passing situations, the stunt is usually carried out on the snap of the ball by both the tackle and the linebacker.

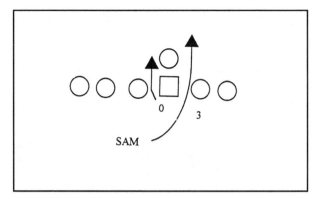

Diagram 10-31: Nose Sam Loop.

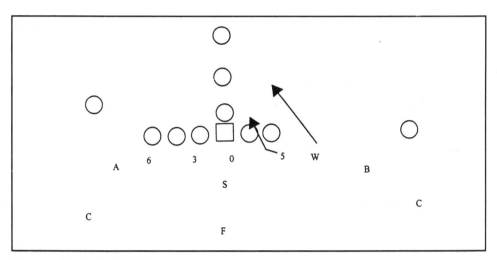

Diagram 10-32: 30 Will Kick.

- Sam Kick—the Sam moves outside of the strongside end and makes a "me" call. He runs a lightning stunt path. (see the outside linebacker lightning).

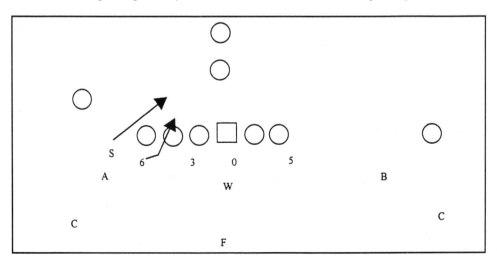

Diagram 10-33: 30 Sam Kick.

- Sam Line—the Sam executes a SAM stunt from the line of scrimmage. The Sam aligns on the line of scrimmage in his assigned gap and runs the stunt.

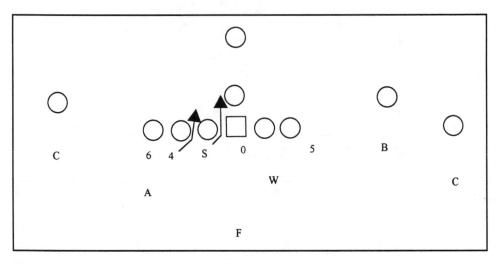

Diagram 10-34: 40 Sam Line.

- Wild Line—the Will executes a Wild stunt from the line of scrimmage. The Will aligns on the line of scrimmage in his assigned gap and runs the stunt.

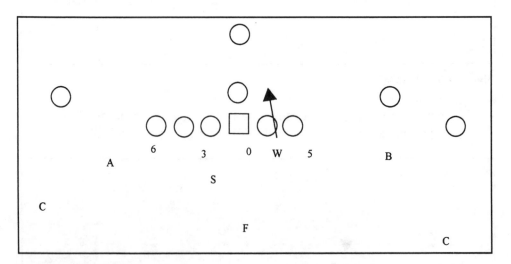

Diagram 10-35: 30 Wild Line.

- Dog—both linebackers stunt through their assigned gaps. The Dog is a SAM and WILD stunt.

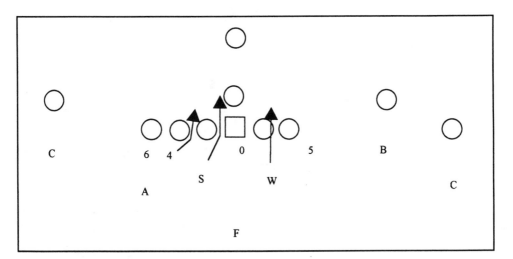

Diagram 10-36: 40 Dog.

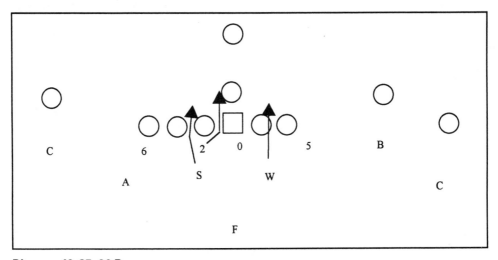

Diagram 10-37: 20 Dog.

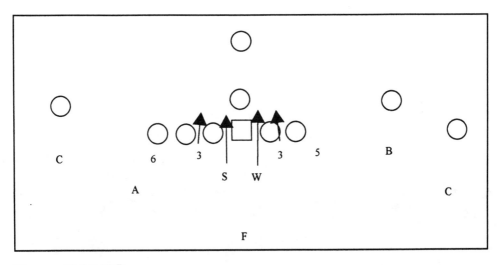

Diagram 10-38: 33 Dog.

Pass Zone Coverages

A. Flat Zone—The area including behind the LOS that extends from OT outward to the sideline and reaches a depth of about seven yards.

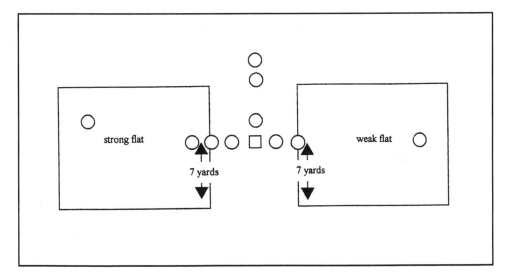

B. Curl Zone—1. The area approximately five yards inside of the widest receiver extending to a depth of about 16 yards. 2. Against multiple receivers, the Curl may be directly in front of the vertical midline of the relative spacing between the widest and the nub of the formation.

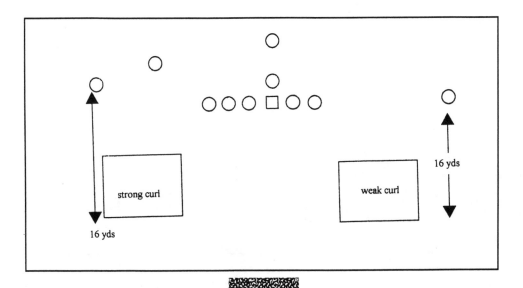

C. Hook Zone—The area extending from the TE to TE which reaches a depth of about 20 yards.

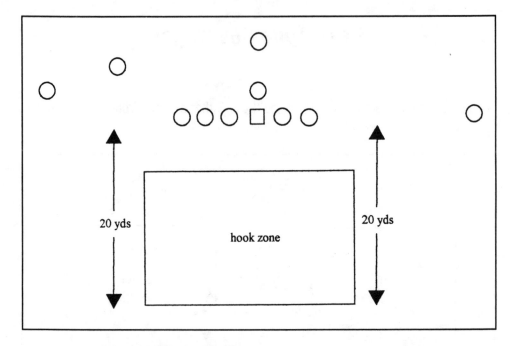

D. Seam—1. The Seam, not really considered to be a zone but an area of which the pass defenders are to be aware, is a narrow alley between the curl and hook. 2. Usually exploited by third receivers from the backfield on a level 3 (dropback) pass.

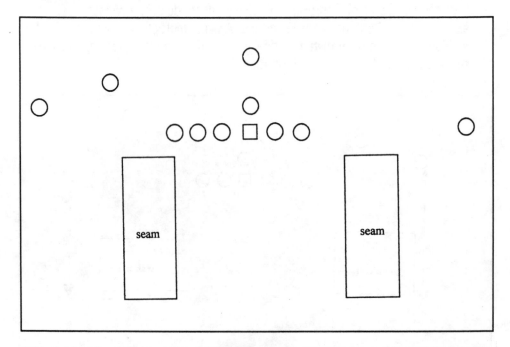

E. Void—1. Another area similar to the seam, not really considered a zone but an area of which 4 technique defensive backs are to be acutely aware. 2. 2 techniques are also practiced on sinking into the seam area should the ball go level 3 and number 2 (counting from inside) does not threaten the flat.

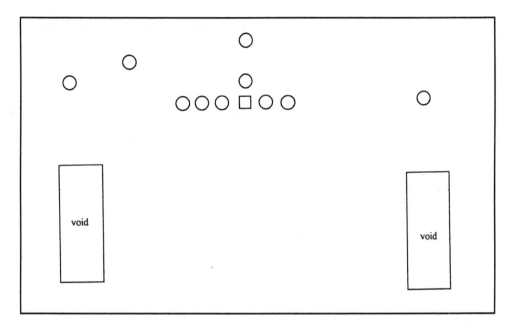

F. Outside Third (O ⅓)—1. A zone measured from the sideline to a point 16 yards inbounds, just outside the hashmarks. 2. Usually the top of the numbers is the midline of the O ⅓. 3. Begins at the deepest boundary of the curl and hook zones 16-20 yards deep respectively. 4. Extends to the end line of the end zone. 5. A 3 and a 9 technique play the O ⅓.

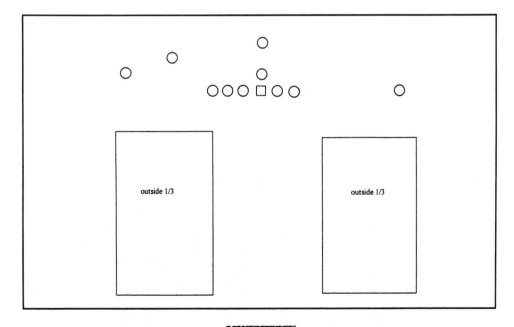

G. Middle Third (M ⅓)—1. A cone in the middle third of the field, from just outside the left hashmark to just outside the right hashmark. 2. Begins at the deepest boundary of the hook zone, about 20 yards from LOS. 3. Extends to the end line of the endzone. 4. A 6 technique plays the M ⅓.

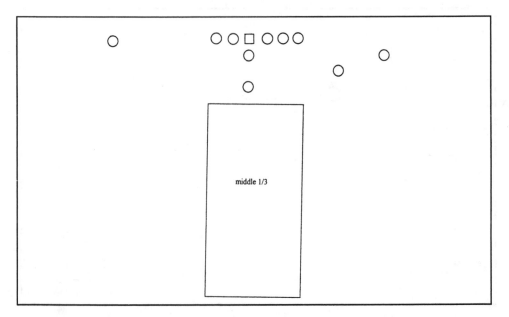

H. Quarter (1/4)—1. One of four deep-coverage zones which divide the field into 4 parts. 2. Each ¼ begins at the deepest boundary of the hook and curl zones, 16 to 20 yards deep. 3. Each ¼ extends to the end line of the endzone. 4. Most used in the coverage scheme is the Middle ¼ zone. 5. 5-quarters technique plays the Middle Quarter on level 3 pass.

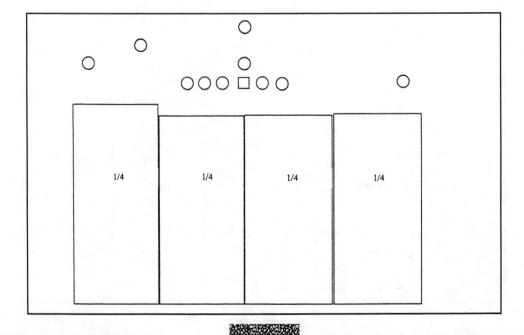

Defensive Game-Plan Worksheet

1st and 10
Front   Stunt   %( )   Cov
1.
2.
3.

Best Runs   **Best Passes**
1.   1.
2.   2.
1.   1.
2.   2.
1.   1.
2.   2.

2nd and Short   Base   Mixer   %( )   Stunt
1.   1.   1.
2.   2.   2.
3.   3.   3.

2nd and Norm   Base   Mixer   %( )   Stunt
1.   1.   1.
2.   2.   2.
3.   3.   3.

2nd and Long   Base   Mixer   %( )   Stunt
1.   1.   1.
2.   2.   2.
3.   3.   3.

3rd and Short   Base   Mixer   %( )   Stunt
1.   1.   1.
2.   2.   2.
3.   3.   3.

3rd and Norm   Base   Mixer   %( )   Stunt
1.   1.   1.
2.   2.   2.
3.   3.   3.

3rd and Long   Base   Mixer   %( )   Stunt
1.   1.   1.
2.   2.   2.
3.   3.   3.

4th   %( )
1.   1.
2.   2.
3.   3.

Extremely Long   **Prevent**

Special Defenses   **Trick Plays**

No Huddle

Unbalanced   **Goal Line**   ( )
1.
2.
3.

2 Point Play
1.
2.

Best Run Blitz   **Best Zone Blitz**

Safest Blitz   **Best Man Blitz**

Jeff Walker is a 14-year coaching veteran. His experience ranges from junior high coaching to the Division 1 college level. He has coached every position on the field in the high school ranks of Florida, Louisiana and Texas.

During his career, Walker has worked for five different head coaches who have won state championships. Two former mentors are in the Louisiana High School Athletic Association Hall of Fame. The combined record of five of the more successful head coaches under whom Walker has worked number over 1000 victories.

A former high school coordinator in Louisiana's highest classification of both offense and defense, Walker is an author of both offensive and defensive articles for *Scholastic Coach* magazine. Jeff and his wife, Paula, have one son, Gabriel Dayson-Alexander.